A WWII SOLDIER IN THE PACIFIC

A WWII SOLDIER IN THE PACIFIC

DURING AND AFTER 1943-1945

ROBERT THOBABEN

Illustrations by Virginia K. Hess
Comments to the Author by E. B. Sledge

Pen & Sword
MILITARY

AN IMPRINT OF PEN & SWORD BOOKS LTD.
YORKSHIRE - PHILADELPHIA

First published in Great Britain in 2025 by
Pen & Sword Military
An imprint of
Pen & Sword Books Ltd
Yorkshire – Philadelphia

Copyright © Robert Thobaben, 2025

ISBN 978 1 03611 428 2

Typeset by SJmagic DESIGN SERVICES, India.

Printed and bound in the UK by CPI Group (UK) Ltd.

The Publisher's authorised representative in the EU for product safety is Authorised
Rep Compliance Ltd., Ground Floor, 71 Lower Baggot Street, Dublin D02 P593,
Ireland.
www.arccompliance.com

For a complete list of Pen & Sword titles please contact

PEN & SWORD BOOKS LIMITED
George House, Units 12 & 13, Beevor Street, Off Pontefract Road,
Barnsley, South Yorkshire, S71 1HN, England
E-mail: enquiries@pen-and-sword.co.uk
Website: www.pen-and-sword.co.uk

or

PEN AND SWORD BOOKS
1950 Lawrence Rd, Havertown, PA 19083, USA
E-mail: uspen-and-sword@casematepublishers.com
Website: www.penandswordbooks.com

Contents

PART I: MY EXPERIENCES IN WWII

PART II: THE INTERVIEWS

PART III: THE ARTICLES AND ESSAYS

CONCLUSION

Acknowledgements

Four women deserve special mention for the help they so willingly gave in the preparation of this book. First is my wife, Janet Thobaben, a steadfast member of the Centerville-Washington Township Historical Society. She filmed every one of the interviews included in this book. In addition, she taught me the significance of the pre-interview discussion with the interviewee, and finally – the interview process itself. She coped with it all.

Second is Pat Aldrich, who meticulously transcribed all the interviews from videotape to paper. She then typed up the edited interviews, a necessary step prior to the final editing. Transcribing is an arduous task. Pat did all of that and more, and always in good spirit.

Third, I want to acknowledge the terrific work of Virginia Krause Hess. Virginia drew all the illustrations included in this book. These drawings dramatize the material for the reader and contribute to the level of understanding. They breathe new life into my words – something that only

Virginia K Hess

art can do. They also unify the book and add an aesthetic value. You may be interested to know that her work, both drawings and sculpture, are known worldwide; for example, her sculpture of Charles E. Taylor, who designed and built the first engine for the Wright Brothers, is in the Smithsonian Institute in Washington D.C. as well as in other places around the world.

Fourth is Susan Fox, former teacher, and author, who edited the text and gave valuable suggestions regarding organization – the introduction, text, and conclusion of the book. I am in debt to all these women.

Many people supported my effort, but I alone am responsible for any factual or interpretive errors in this book.

Information about the author

Robert G. Thobaben is a Professor Emeritus of Political Science at Wright State University in Dayton, Ohio, where he taught courses in political theory and ideology for forty-two years, from 1964 to 2006. He is the author, co-author, and editor of six books (two in their 6th Edition) and over forty essays and articles. During the 1980-81 academic year he was a Visiting Fellow at Clare Hall at Cambridge University in England, and in January of 1993 he was a Visiting Professor at the Chinese University of Hong Kong. Whilst at Clare Hall he talked and tutored a number of graduate students from all over the world as well as getting to know quite a few professors from both sides of the Atlantic and from Asia. This was an introduction to a range of different cultures and a memorable time in his life.

Also, in 1964, the Marxist-Christian Dialog (MXD) began at Charles University in Prague, Czechoslovakia. Charles West, a friend who taught at Princeton Theological Seminary, attended that proceeding event. Thobaben heard about this new attempt at cooperation and in 1968 a colleague of his, Nicholas Piediscalzi, the Chair of the Department of Religion at Wright State University, joined him to offer a course on the MXD. They continued to teach it for about twenty years – until 1988. They attended dialogues in the United States and in Western Europe – Germany, France, Yugoslavia, Sweden, and the USSR – The Soviet Union. This expanded his experiences through further travel, culture, and interesting new people.

During WWII he was a soldier in the 111th Infantry in the Pacific Theater and participated in three campaigns: the Gilbert Islands 1943, the Marshall Islands 1944, and the Palau Islands 1945, where he became a medic. He holds the Combat Medic Badge and the Bronze Star Medal.

The 111th Infantry

On November 21, 1747, the military association of the city of Philadelphia gave Benjamin Franklin permission to found the 111th Infantry Regiment (the associators) and he did so on December 17, 1747. The regiment, composed of civilian males from the citizenry of Pennsylvania, fought in the American Revolution, and is now part of the 28th Division of the National Guard. It served in the Revolution and in the War of 1812, under the command of General George Washington, and has fought in every war since then including the Civil War, World War I, and World War II.

The United States chose to field 89 Army Divisions and 6 Marine Divisions in World War II. In 1942 the US Army streamlined their infantry divisions. They changed from four to three regiments in a division. The 28th Division removed the 111th Infantry Regiment and it was named a combat regiment. The new streamlined division went to Europe and the 111th regiment went to the Pacific. During World War II the 111th Infantry participated in three campaigns in the Pacific – the Gilbert Islands in 1943, the Marshall Islands in 1944, and the Palau Islands in 1945, as Mop Up troops in America's war with Japan.

In terms of total service men and women, the army, including the Air Force, consisted of approximately 11,200,000 soldiers, the Navy had 4,200,000 sailors, and the Marine Corps had 660,000 Marines in 6 divisions.

MOP – Up Troops

So, what are Mop- up troops? Support troops, or Mop-Up troops, complete the military conquest of an island or area by capturing or killing the remaining enemy troops after the assault troops leave the area. Mop up troops bring the campaign to an end by defeating the enemy thoroughly. This is the very meaning of the word. The Army would have referred to us as support troops, but we referred to ourselves as Mop Up Troops.

We participated in the Gilbert Islands Campaign in the fall of 1943. The Marines invaded Tarawa, and the 27th infantry invaded Makin – about 100 miles north of Tarawa. When the assault was over the 111th replaced the 27th Infantry on Makin Island. Our job there was to simply endure the daily bombing and strafing by the Japanese, and to prepare our defenses in case of a counterattack. Then we moved north about 200 miles. The 7th Division captured the main island in the Marshall Atoll, Kwajalein and the 111th captured 11 islands near

the south pass of this Atoll. We were based on Ennylabegan Island. Later we went back to Hawaii for a few weeks to a rest camp.

The last campaign, which occurred in 1944-1945, was in the Palau Islands, which are 5,000 miles west of Hawaii. The assault troops were the First Marine Division. Within 6 weeks they ceased to exist as a fighting unit and were replaced by the 81st Infantry Division that had been fighting on Angaur Island. Then the whole regiment, the 111th Infantry, from Philadelphia, Pennsylvania, went into The Palau Islands at Peleliu after the island was declared secure.

Why did we do this? Because it saved the surviving assault troops who would become the cadre for the new recruits in the assault divisions. We did this by daily patrols, machine gun outposts, island sweeps, and ambushes. Later you will read about my participation in an ambush on the day the Japanese surrendered. We also created water supplies for ships at sea.

Tech Duty

Tech Duty – what did the people on tech duty do in World War II? Medics were divided into litter bearers, aid men and tech sergeants. If surgery or dentistry was required, an officer trained in those skills would be brought in. In the Pacific, hygiene and the handling of infection was a serious problem, as was boil drainage and the treatment of wounds from shrapnel. YAWS (a venereal disease) and the hygiene of genitals were an ongoing problem, and there were many cases of this. Gentian Violet was used for hygiene issues, and bismuth and mafarison were used for Yaws. Shots in the arm and buttocks were administered for yellow fever, scarlet fever, tetanus, etc. Bathing in the ocean was critical; it was better than the showers and important to hygiene.

On patrols, medics, and I was a medic, carried a Carbine and a water tech kit with medical supplies. Island security in the Marshall Islands was a concern for all of us. The concern increased in the Gilbert Islands due to the buildup of defenses and also from bombing and strafing, and a fear of reinvasion by the Japanese.

It should be noted that anyone who needed medical help received it, including injured Japanese soldiers. Also, on Koror in the Palau Islands, we treated Korean women, a number of them, who had been captured, trafficked, and kept by the Japanese as "comfort women." Nearly 200,000 such women were controlled by the Japanese in the Asian theater of war in WWII.

Those Who Served

Looking back at their personal histories, millions of Americans who entered the armed forces during World War II recall their service as the central event of their lives. Then and later they knew that they were caught up in a great maelstrom, a great struggle somehow affecting the destiny of their generation and many generations to come.

For those who had to meet the enemy in direct combat, the war, no matter its elemental meaning for freedom, was brutal and terrible. The infantrymen who fought in the hedgerows of Normandy, the Marines who clung to the bloody beaches of Iwo Jima, the pilots who flew a gauntlet of fire over Germany, the sailors who exchanged gunfire with the Japanese fleet all suffered the psychological and physical wounds of battle. If any men wanted to embellish their days in uniform, to "remember with advantages" what feats they did, they had that right.

The vast majority of soldiers and sailors, though, engaged the enemy at a far remove and seldom were participants in the fighting for blood and ground. Rather, they were support troops driving trucks laden with food and ammunition, securing a captured area, servicing the machines of war, and manning desks on the home front. Though theirs was not the blood of battle, they believed, or at least hoped, that they were instruments of success, that they had something to do with victory.

Whatever the role they played in the war, these men and women knew that they all shared, to a lesser or greater degree, in a frustrating crusade. For they could not escape the ironies, the incongruities, the absurdities inherent in the massing of men and women for gigantic ventures. Inevitably they developed some irreverence for the system that seemingly held them in the embrace of useless routine and jaded ritual. In retrospect, as the years passed and they searched for meaning in their lives, they might invest their experience in war with the sheen of nostalgia or excitement. But they might also place it in a realistic perspective, tinting it with the gentle cynicism

of age and reducing it to its proper proportions, even though, in its proper proportions, it was important at the time.

In Part I of the book, My Experiences in WWII, as well as in Part II, The Interviews, that follow, and even in Part III, The Essays, you will find a variety of military service personnel. Some met the enemy in direct combat, while most lived at the fringe of battle, almost a century ago; and probably, like thousands of their comrades-in-arms, they have abiding recollections of the days of their youth when they stood ready to drill and die for our nation. Measured by any one of several adjectives – ordinary, typical, common, conventional – their millions of interests and abilities seem to be those of Everyman in uniform. Yet they transcended from individuals into a complete organism, everyone contributing to the whole. Their memories spring out of the ordinary routines and relationships of a military made up of citizens at war, not out of extraordinary exploits, and not out of the habit of command assumed by men wearing stripes on sleeves or bars and stars on shoulder straps. Their recollections strike no grand chord of decision-making by generals and admirals reviewing the numbers and strategic dispositions of soldiers and sailors. But there seems to be some worth in setting forth the short and simple annals of the military common man/ woman, depicting along the way the quirkiness of life among ordinary men and women at war.

Robert G. Thobaben

A Name to Remember:
Eugene B. Sledge

Anyone who is familiar with WWII, especially with the war in the Pacific, will already know the name of E.B. Sledge and his book, *With the Old Breed: At Peleliu and Okinawa*. In my opinion it is the finest memoir of World War II.

I discovered that Sledge and I had something in common; we both served on the same island in WWII – Peleliu in the Palau Islands. Sledge was in the 1st Marine Division which made the assault on the island. The Division actually ceased to exist as a fighting unit because of the high casualties. The 81st Division then stepped in and finished securing the island. I, on the other hand, served in the 111th Infantry that did the "mop up" of the island after the island was secured.

About 30 years ago I wrote to Sledge and told him about the 111th Infantry experience on Peleliu. I also shared with him that I was a professor, as was he, and that I had used his book with my students, with whom it had been a big hit. Lastly, I sent him my copy of his book and asked him if he would sign it. He did; and he wrote a kind and generous comment, which you will see on the following pages.

There is an important quotation from the book. It was a turning point for Sledge. "Everything my life had

Eugene B. Sledge

been before, and has been after, pales in the light of that awesome moment when my amtrac started in amid a thunderous bombardment toward the flaming, smoke-shrouded beach for the assault on Peleliu." Coming under enemy fire is one thing. An assault on an enemy's major base is quite another. The 111th Infantry Regiment did the former. The 1st Marine Division – Sledge's division – with help from the 81st Division did the latter. Indeed, a turning point.

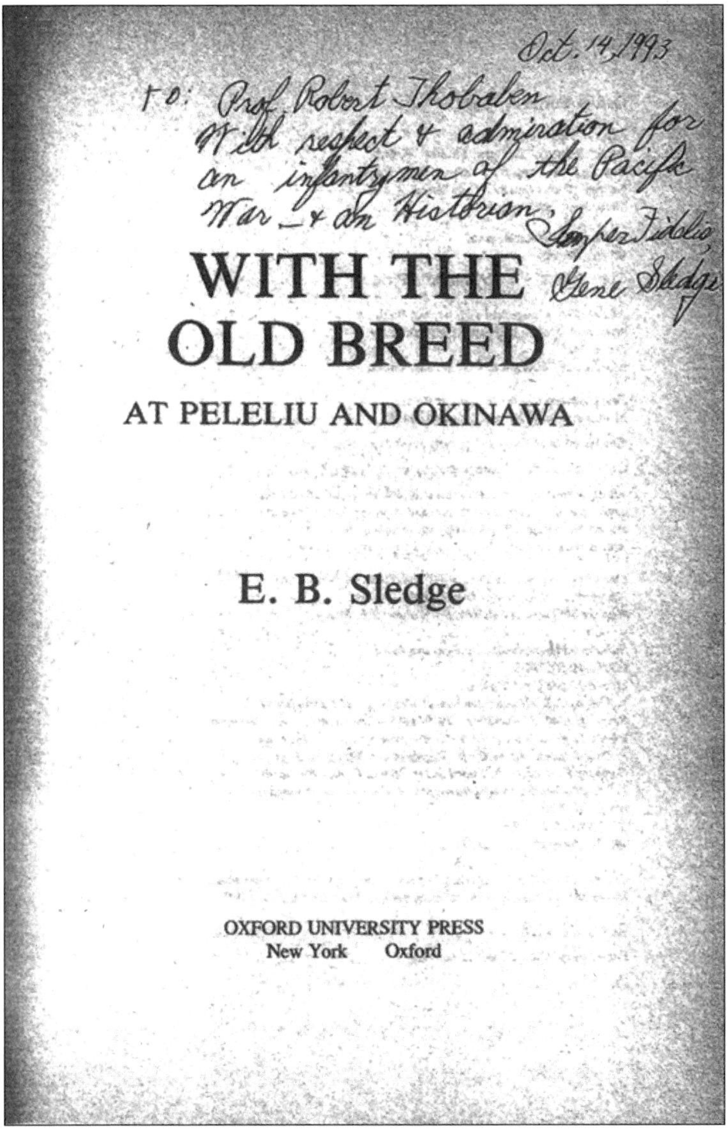

Oct. 14, 1993

To: Prof. Robert Thobaken
With respect & admiration for an infantryman of the Pacific War — & an Historian. Semper Fidelis

WITH THE
Gene Sledge

OLD BREED

AT PELELIU AND OKINAWA

E. B. Sledge

OXFORD UNIVERSITY PRESS
New York   Oxford

THE UNIVERSITY OF
MONTEVALLO

E B Sledge
299 Cardinal Crest Rd.
Montevallo, AL 35115-3947

Sept. 29, 1993

Dear Prof. Thobaben,

Thank you for your nice letter of Sept. 15. I appreciate your kind remarks re W.T.O.B. & am flattered that you & Prof. Becker will be using it in your course. I hope the students respond positively. Several Faculty members from about 15 other campuses have written & have said they have, or are, using W.T.O.B. c̄ good results & positive responses.

Prof. Becker wrote me once that Millett said in some of his writings that W.T.O.B. has reached "cult" status in the U.S.M.C. (I hope that is good.) I looked over Semper Fidelis in a book store but didn't see the statement.

Would be delighted to inscribe your copy of W.T.O.B. Please send along a self addressed book mailer. Would like to look up your book.

Montevallo, Alabama 35115   Telephone: 205/665-6460   Semper Fidelis
The University of Montevallo is an affirmative action-equal opportunity institution.   Gene Sledge

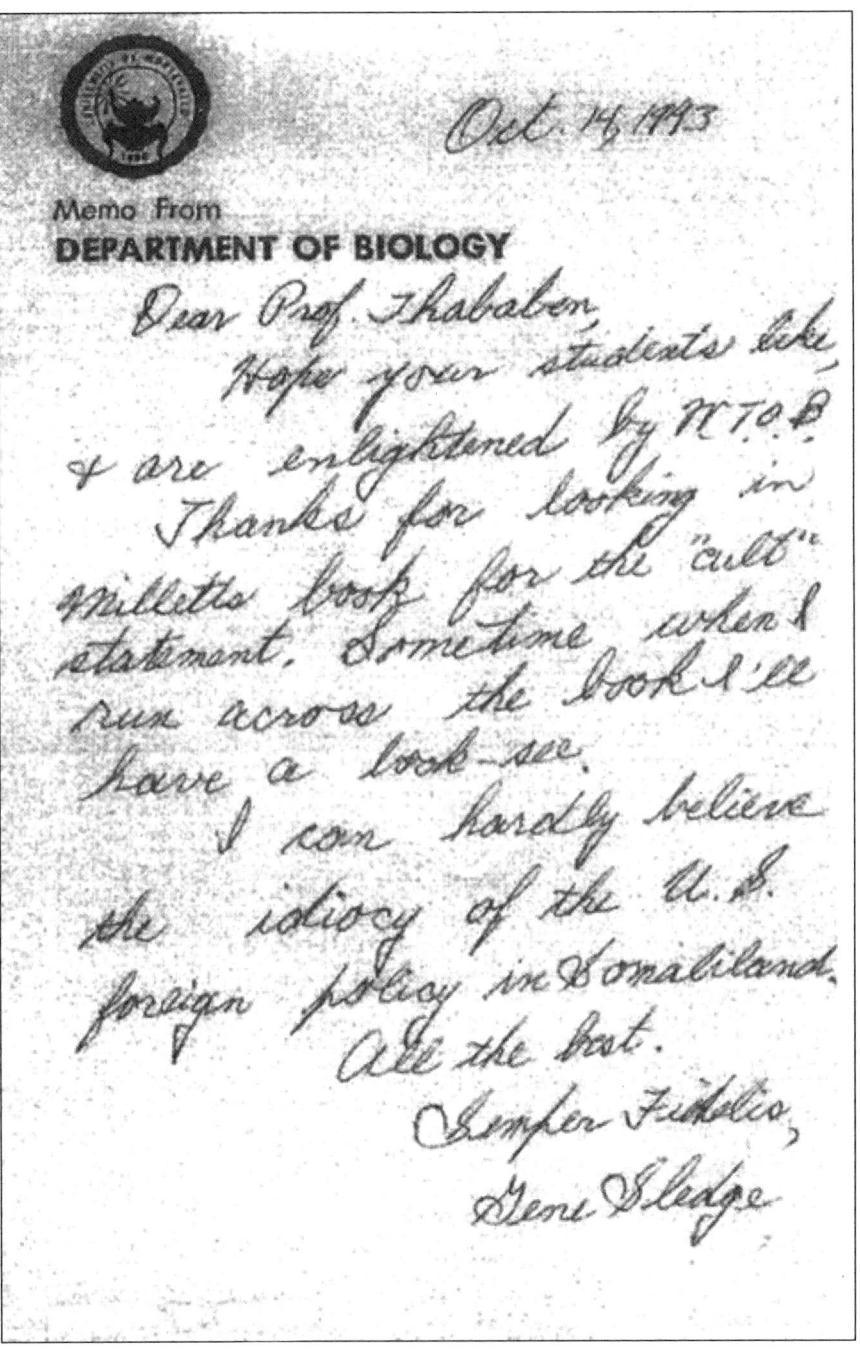

Oct. 14, 1993

Memo From
DEPARTMENT OF BIOLOGY

Dear Prof. Thababen,
Hope your students like,
& are enlightened by W.T.O.P.
Thanks for looking in
milletts book for the "cult"
statement. Sometime when I
run across the book I'll
have a look-see.
I can hardly believe
the idiocy of the U.S.
foreign policy in Somaliland.
All the best.
Semper Fidelis,
Gene Sledge

A Little Background

World War II began due to unresolved issues following the end of World War I. The most horrendous event in history, WWII is directly responsible for 50 million deaths or more, at least 25 million more from disease and an additional 50 million civilian deaths. These are of course estimates with the total dead ranging from 50 million to more than 80 million. This is not even a consideration of famine and starvation, the general suffering, the overall destruction, and the experiences of the prisoners of war.

The war began with Germany's dissatisfaction with the terms and reparations at the end of WWI. The Germans saw the armistice as an agreement upon certain principles whereas the western powers saw it as a defeat. In retaliation the Germans began to rebuild their state, its economy, and its military power, none of which was agreed upon by the western allies. In 1938 Germany reclaimed the Sudetenland, followed by Austria. International tension and expansion by both Nazi Germany and Fascist Italy led to the German invasion of Poland on September 1, 1939. Two days later Britain and France declared war. The United States remained neutral, at least in theory, until Japan attacked Pearl Harbor in 1941.

Italy had aligned itself with Germany, not only to protect itself but also because it's an advantage to be on the winning side. The Tripartite Pact agreement was concluded by Germany and Italy on June 10, 1940. On September 27, 1940, one year after the start of World War II, Japan, after hesitating, finally joined them. This created a defense alliance between the countries, the Axis Powers, and was intended to deter the US from entering the conflict.

On July 26, 1941, in response to the Japanese occupation of key airfields in Indochina – which followed an agreement between Japan and Vichy, France – the US froze Japanese assets; and on August 1, 1941, the US established an embargo on oil and gasoline exports to Japan as well. This eventually pushed Japan into attempting to destroy the US Pacific Fleet as

well as its aircraft carriers as a way of preventing the US from interfering with Japan's Pacific operations.

As the war spread globally, from Europe, to Africa, to Asia, to the sea and beyond, it created many different scenarios for those involved. My focus in the book is primarily on the Pacific, and the war with Japan, because that was my experience – as you will see in Part I of the book. Those in Europe, on the home front, or elsewhere, had much different experiences, whether on the front line or as a support. The interviews in Part II of the book will give you a glimpse into this. Perhaps these experiences will broaden your understanding of WWII. And even more importantly, a broader understanding, by today's generation, may help generate efforts for peaceful solutions and discourage such conflicts in the future.

The Giant Awakens

Yamamoto Isoroku was the Japanese Admiral who planned the surprise attack on the US Naval Base at Pearl Harbor. The purpose of the attack was to destroy the US Pacific Fleet and the aircraft carriers in order to keep them from interfering with Japanese plans in the Pacific. Having lost 94% of its oil supply, Japan was intending to resupply with sources there. What Japan didn't know, but should have, was that the aircraft carriers were out at sea and were not at Pearl Harbor at the time of the planned attack.

Prior to this, Japan and the USA had each made moves, taken steps, that had had huge consequences. Japan had made far reaching advances in China and Indochina that had infuriated the United States, and the United States had countered with racist decisions, property ownership regulations, and immigration policies that were degrading to Japan. In July of 1941 the United States froze Japanese assets and then in August cancelled Japanese contracts for oil, gas, and steel. Japan needed all of these materials, but especially oil, and if the United States refused to supply it, then Japan had no choice but to get it somewhere else, in the Pacific.

Back to Yamamoto, who was an exceptional person. He had studied at Harvard University (1919 – 1921) and had served two terms as a naval attaché in Washington D.C. He spoke fluent English, had travelled extensively in the US, and understood US customs and business practices. His experiences and knowledge made him wary of provoking the United States into entering the war.

And he was right. Pearl Harbor was attacked on December 7, 1941. It was a devastating blow. On the following day, December 8, 1941, President Franklin Roosevelt delivered his "Day of Infamy" speech, Congress declared war, and the United States entered WWII.

Supposedly, after the attack, Yamamoto wrote in his diary: "I fear that all we have done is to awaken a sleeping giant and fill him with terrible resolve." How right he was.

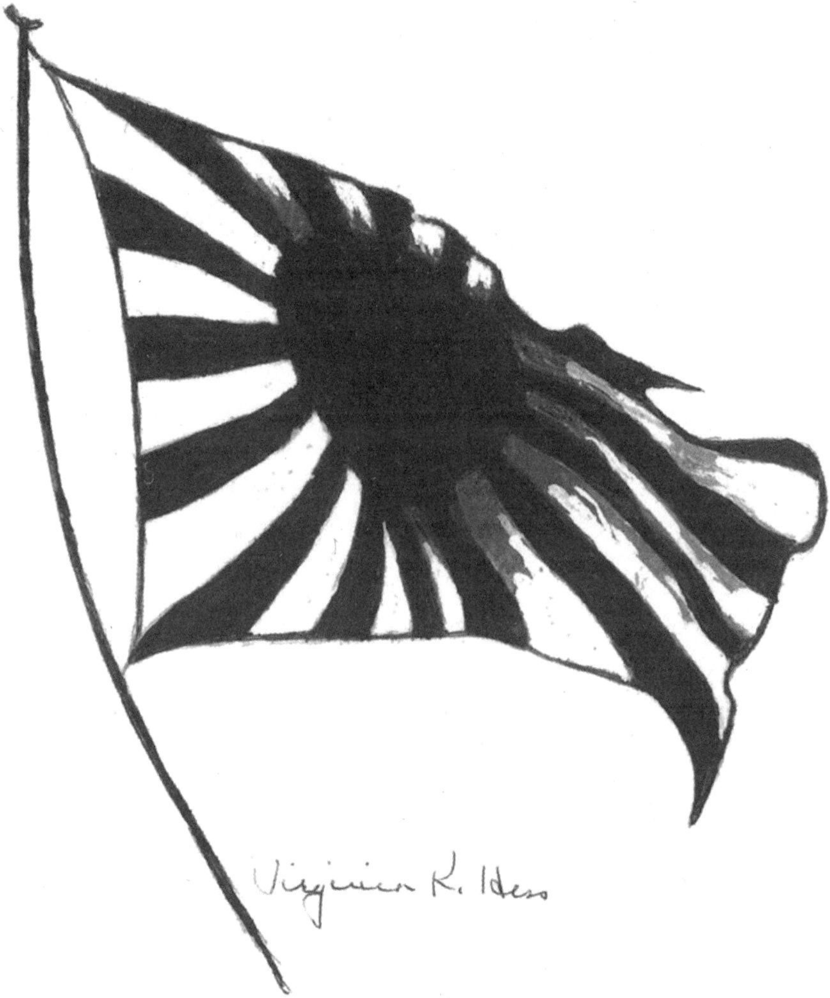
Virginia K. Hess

Japan's Next Moves

Japan didn't waste any time. Immediately after the attack on Pearl Harbor the Japanese launched attacks on the US territories of Guam, Wake Island, and the Philippines, as well as British controlled Hong Kong, Malaya, and Burma.

Within a month, Japan had captured Manila, the capital of the Philippines, and the US and Filipino defenders of Luzon were forced to retreat to the Bataan peninsula. There they held out for three months. Finally, as many troops as possible were moved to Corregidor in Manila Bay, but about 75,000 Allied troops remained trapped and eventually were forced to surrender. The following day, April 9, 1941, the Bataan Death March began.

About 75,000 Allied troops were forced to walk approximately 65 miles, under unbearable conditions, to board a train to a POW camp. Deprived of food, water, and medical attention, the soldiers, many of whom were ill and exhausted, suffered physical abuse, mental trauma, and death. At least 500 Americans and 2,500 Filipinos died before even reaching a camp, where they faced yet more hardships and brutality. At Camp O'Donnell, for example, some 26,000 Filipinos and 1,500 Americans died of starvation, disease, and abuse. Of the approximate 22,000 Americans captured on Bataan, only about 15,000 finally returned to the US.

Every year, both Filipinos and Americans participate in marches to remember and honor those brave soldiers who marched their way across the Bataan Peninsula.

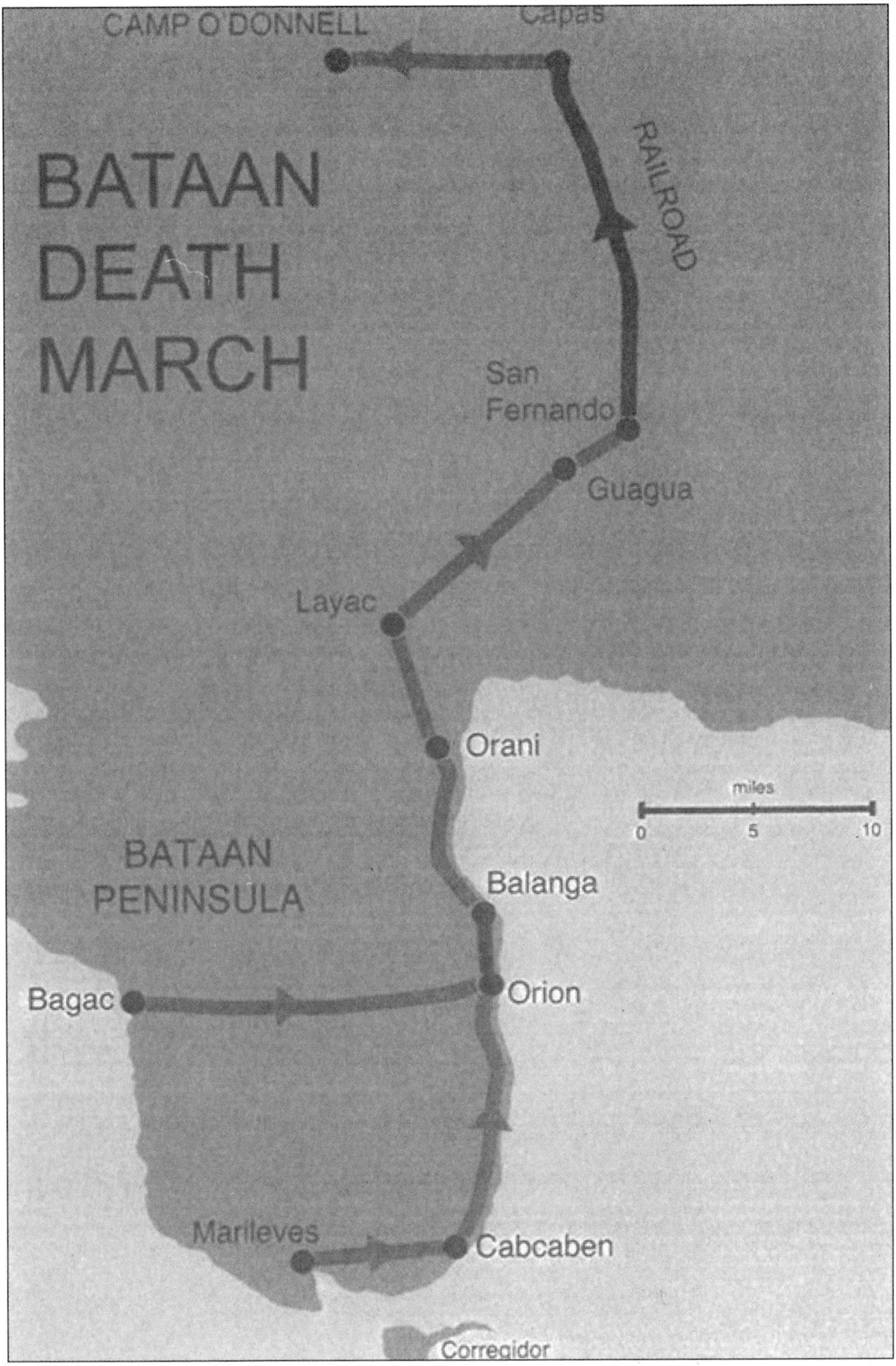

CAMP O'DONNELL

Capas

BATAAN
DEATH
MARCH

RAILROAD

San
Fernando

Guagua

Layac

Orani

miles

0   5   .10

BATAAN
PENINSULA

Balanga

Bagac

Orion

Marileves

Cabcaben

Corregidor

Pacific Timeline

1941	
Dec. 7	Japan launches a surprise attack on Pearl Harbor
Dec. 8	United States declares war on Japan
Dec. 11	The U.S. declares war on Germany and Italy
Dec. 25	Hong Kong falls to the Japanese
1942	
Jan. 2	Japanese forces occupy Manila
Feb. 15	Singapore falls to Japan
Apr. 9	American forces on Bataan surrender
Apr.18	U.S. B-25 Airplanes bomb Tokyo (led by Col. Doolittle)
May 4-8	Battle of the Coral Sea
May 6	Gen Wainwright surrenders U.S. forces on Corregidor to Japan
June 3-6	Battle of Midway-U.S. Navy wins a major victory over Japan
Aug. 7	U.S. Marines land on Guadalcanal and a six month battle begins
1943	
Feb. 7	Japanese troops evacuate Guadalcanal
Mar. 2-4	Japanese naval forces lose the Battle of the Bismarck Sea
May 11	U.S. forces land on the Aleutian Island of Attu
Nov. 20	U.S. Marines invade Tarawa while Army troops invade Makin (Gilbert Islands)

1944	
Feb. 2-7	U.S. Army and Marines invade Kwajalein and Roi-Namur (Marshall Islands)
Apr. 22	Mac Arthur's troops land at Hollandia
June 15	American forces invade Saipan in the Mariana Islands
June 19	First Battle of the Philippine Sea (The Great Mariana Turkey Shoot)
July 21-23	Marines and infantry land on Guam and Tinian (Mariana Islands)
Sept. 15	Invasion of Peleliu (Marines) and Anguar (Army) in the Palau Islands
Oct. 20	U.S. forces land in Leyte in the central Philippines
Oct. 23-26	Battle of Leyte Gulf
1945	
Jan. 9	American forces land on Luzon, Philippines
Feb. 19	U.S. Marines invade Iwo Jima
Apr. 1	American forces invade Okinawa
Apr. 12	Franklin D. Roosevelt dies and Harry Truman becomes President
Aug. 6,9	U.S. drops atomic bombs on Hiroshima and Nagasaki
Aug. 14	Japan surrenders unconditionally (Hirohito remains as Emperor)
Sept. 2	Surrender signed on board the USS Missouri in Tokyo Bay

European Timeline

1941	
Dec. 11	The United States declares war on Italy and Germany
1942	
Aug. 17	First all-American bombing run in Europe
Nov. 8-29	Operation Torch: U. S. invasion of North Africa begins
1943	
Aug. 17	First USAAF bombing raid on Germany- Wilhelmshaven
Feb. 14-25	Kasserine Pass Campaign begins (a loss by Americans)
Mar.5-20	A crisis of Atlantic Battle shipping losses
Apr. 22	American First Army attacks at Bou, North Africa
July 10	Operation Husky-Allied landings in Sicily
July 22	Americans capture Palermo, Sicily
Sept. 8	Eisenhower announces Italy's surrender
Sept. 9	Salerno, Italy-landings by American troops
Oct. 1	Fifth Army captures Naples
Oct. 4	Corsica is liberated
Dec. 3	Fifth Army opens new offensive in Italy
1944	
Jan. 22	Anzio, Italy-landings by Sixth Army
Jan. 7-16	German counterattacks at Anzio almost cut lines
May 23	A breakout from Anzio begins
June 5	Fifth Army captures Rome

June 6	D-Day in Normandy for American forces and allies
Aug. 4	Eighth Army enters Florence, Italy
Aug. 15	Seventh Army invades southern France: Operation Anvil
Aug. 25	Allied forces enter Paris
Sept. 12	U. S. First Army enters Germany
Sept. 5,8,26	Fifth & Eighth armies enter Pisa, break Gothic Line, cross Rubicon River
Dec. 16-25	Battle of the Bulge in the Ardennes (Patton relieves Bastogne)
Dec. 17	The Malmedy Massacre of American trips by the SS
1945	
Jan. 16	Ardennes salient (the Bulge) eliminated
Feb. 9	Allies break through Siegfried Line
Mar. 2-3	The U. S. Army captures Trier and Cologne
Mar. 7	First Army crosses Rhine River at Remagen Bridge
Mar. 17-20	U. S. forces capture Saarbrucken and Coblenz
Apr. 1	First and Ninth armies encircle German army in Ruhr
Apr. 10	Ninth Army captures Hanover
Apr. 12-29	Belsen, Buchenwald and Dachau concentration camps are liberated
May 7	General Jodi signs unconditional surrender
May 8	The war in Europe ends

PART I

MY EXPERIENCES IN WWII

In the Beginning

Pearl Harbor was bombed by the Japanese on December 7, 1941. This brought The United States into WWII. One month later, in January of 1942, I graduated from Shaker Heights High School in Ohio at the age of 17. I worked from January until September of that year and then I attended Ohio University where I enrolled in the ERC (the Enlisted Reserve Corps). That allowed me to complete one year of university education before going into the military; otherwise, I would have been drafted in April when I turned 18. This bought me a few extra months.

In the Spring my friends and I intended to go to Cleveland to join the Navy. I was 18. At the last moment I backed out for an important reason. I had a date with a cute blonde and I didn't want to break it. That decision steered me away from the Navy and towards the Army. Anyway, later, on June 1, 1943, I went on active service. I headed for downtown Cleveland where I had a physical, took the oath, and headed for Fort Hayes in Columbus, Ohio. I received a uniform and learned to salute. I was in the Army.

In a few days I took a train to Camp Wheeler in Macon, Georgia, for basic training. While I was in my four- month basic training, I applied for the paratroopers (Why? I was a teenager and their boots were cool.) and the ASTP. I passed the tests for both, but I chose the second which allowed me to return to what was called a Star College. My entire battalion, except for the half a dozen of us who had passed one or both of the tests, headed for California. Then, unexpectedly, ASTP was cancelled, and I was given a 14-day delay en route to Fort Ord in California. I boarded a train for the four-day journey to California, and after about 5 days at Fort Ord, I was sent on to Camp Stoneman for a few days. There I was put in a medical detachment of the 111th Infantry. I was to become an aid man, about which I knew nothing. But I was told, "We're going to teach you on the boat going over."

On November 8, 1943, 1 boarded the troop ship, the West Point, left California, and headed for Hawaii. On that very day I began keeping a diary, which I kept for one year. I had always liked writing and did it just for myself; I wanted to keep a record of some of my wartime activities, even though some of the entries were brief. No one else knew I was keeping the diary.

I simply forgot about the diary – for eighty (80) years. Then three months ago, while cleaning out a closet, I discovered both the diary and a pack of 196 letters that I had written home. My mother, Unbeknown to me, had saved them all. As I read through the diary, I was somewhat disappointed. For some reason I had omitted some of the more exciting events; perhaps I didn't have time to write everything down or maybe I thought I'd remember everything. But one thing was certain, never in my wildest dreams did I think that anyone else would ever read it.

Remember, I was young then, about 19 or 20. with not too much perspective. Today, at 99, I'd like to think I have a little more. Anyway, at the time I didn't think of myself as anyone special – just a human being acting out this thing called life. I still think that. I also thought then, and I still think now, that my life has been awesome – both personally and professionally – and that includes my years in WWII.

The Diary will follow. Included with it is some commentary, material that I thought might be of interest to the reader but which I had omitted from the diary. It is inserted in approximately the time frame where it occurred, but not necessarily on an exact date. In order for you to identify it, it appears in bold face type and in parentheses. Reading the diary brought back a host of memories I failed to write after the war.

THE ARMY SONG
Music: John Philip Sousa (1917)
Lyrics: Harold W. Arberg (1956)

March along, sing our song,
with the army of the free.
Count the brave, count the true,
who have fought to victory.

We're the Army and proud of our name.
We're the Army and proudly proclaim.

First to fight for the right,
And to build the Nation's might,
And the Army goes rolling along.
Proud of all we have done,
Fighting 'till the battle's won,
And the Army Goes Rolling Along.

Then it's Hi! Hi! Hey!
The Army's on its way.
Count off the cadence loud and strong.
For where e'er we go, You will always know
That The Anny Goes Rolling Along.

After a long history, this became the Army's official song, dedicated on Veterans' Day, November 11, 1956. Only these three verses are typically sung. It is traditionally played at the conclusion of U.S. Army ceremonies and soldiers are expected to stand at attention and sing.

The Diary

(Additional commentary will appear in parentheses)
From San Francisco to Hawaii, Makin Island (Butaritari), Kwajalein, Oahu, and Kauai

Sunday, November 7, 1943
We took a ferry from Camp Stoneman for a few hours to San Francisco where we are now. We're on a good ship, the West Point, but I don't know where we're going – that'll come later.

Monday, November 8, 1943
We left Frisco at about 10 am, fooled around in the harbor till about 2 pm, then were ordered to quarters for abandon ship drill. While we were there we headed for the open sea. Played crap. Did ok!! I feel good but the sea is really calm. We sat around and sang at night and listened to some marine's jukebox.

Tuesday, November 9, 1943
This morning I didn't feel so tough. The boat started going up-down, up-down and so did my damn stomach. So I headed for my bunk. I slept and then in the afternoon I felt as good as a sailor. The ocean is as blue as blue ink. That's what it reminds me of. The water is rough.

Wednesday, November 10, 1943
The ocean is calmer today. Didn't feel sick at all. This ship is a two piper. We have about 10,000 men on board.

Thursday, November 11, 1943
The ocean is calm as hell. It's really like you read about. It is a beautiful blue. It's gorgeous. Saw flying fish today; they're funny things. I think we

5

are getting to Hawaii tomorrow. I hope. One thing for sure, I caught up on my sleep on this trip.

Friday, November 12, 1943
Well today was uneventful except we saw land about 1:30 this afternoon. It sure looked good. A destroyer convoyed us. It kept cutting back and forth in front of us. Saw a few planes. Well, we docked at Honolulu at 5:30 tonight, and my first view of Hawaii was the tower with ALOHA on it. The island so far is beautiful and all palm trees, mountains in the distance, but we didn't debark tonight. I guess we get off tomorrow.

(I learned that Hawaii is a chain of about 137 islands with 8 major ones. It is the most isolated archipelago in the world. At the time it was a US territory but not a state.)

Sat. November 13, 1943
Well I beat my feet on foreign soil today. We had debarkation at about 8:30 am. We walked through Honolulu to the train depot, got a boxcar, really half a boxcar, no top. I've read about them but never rode one. 40 men to a car. It's all small gage rails here. Well, we left Honolulu for Schofield barracks. We went past Pearl Harbor. It's a big place.

Then we went by Hickam field. Then we hit open country. It's like you see in the movies only it's better. We went along the ocean and then went inland. We saw groves of palms with coconuts on them. Then miles of pineapples, millions of them. Well, we finally got to camp. There's an airfield next to us. Bombers and pursuit planes tearing over all day. The camp is fine – a big auditorium, a movie, bowling alleys, skating rink, gym. I was put in the Med Dept attached to the 3rd Bn. of the 111th Inf, looked around the post, saw a couple of Hawaiian girls, and they were all-rite. In fact they looked god-damn good. Nice figures, tan skin, and black hair. That's about all today.

Sunday, November 14, 1943
Well we're confined till Tuesday afternoon. Damn-it, all we've been doing is getting confined. I'm sick of it. We can't even leave the Co. area. This is a bitch. Hawaii is really beautiful though. Mountains in the background and palm trees all over. And these Hawaiian girls are really stacked. I'm going to beat my butt to Honolulu the 1st chance I get.

Monday, November 15, 1943
Very exciting day. We didn't do a thing. We went out to drill and this outfit is really a sad kick when it comes to close-order drill. We are still restricted but it's being lifted at noon tomorrow. Boy I sure miss the folks at home. Well, that's about all for today. Shot a little crap.

Tuesday, November 16, 1943
Well our restriction was lifted today. We got our shot for Yellow Fever today. So far haven't felt anything. Itched a little. Went up to the Service Men's Club in camp. It's nice. Then went to the post movie. On the way back to the barracks we heard some Joe in "K" Co. had gotten scarlet fever and that we were restricted again.

Wednesday, November 17, 1943
Had a few calisthenics this morning and we were supposed to have a hike this afternoon but it was called off on account of the scarlet fever inspection. We're restricted till Sat. mom. Been bummin around with John Survill from Jersey, Earl Wingo from Richmond, and John O'Neill from Cleveland Heights, right next door. May go to movies tonite.

Thursday, November 18, 1943
Did some calisthenics today. Came back to barracks about 10:30 am. Layed around and did some bandaging all afternoon. Went to a show. Wing is transferred to Co. D as an aid man.

Friday, November 19, 1943
Didn't do anything in the morning. I heard we will be stationed here for a while and also that O'Neill will be transferred to H.W. Med. leave. Went to a show. Saw Follies Girl.

Saturday, November 20, 1943
Well today I was C.Q. (Charge of Quarters) so I loafed around the barracks all day. At nite O'Neill, Survill, and I saw The Human Comedy. A good show. When we got back we had our first mail call. I hit the jackpot – 5 letters.

Sunday, November 21, 1943
Had a clothing inspection today. I never got my B bag so I'll get all new stuff. Went to the main P.X. Saw a couple of nice Hawaiian girls there. Walked around at nite.

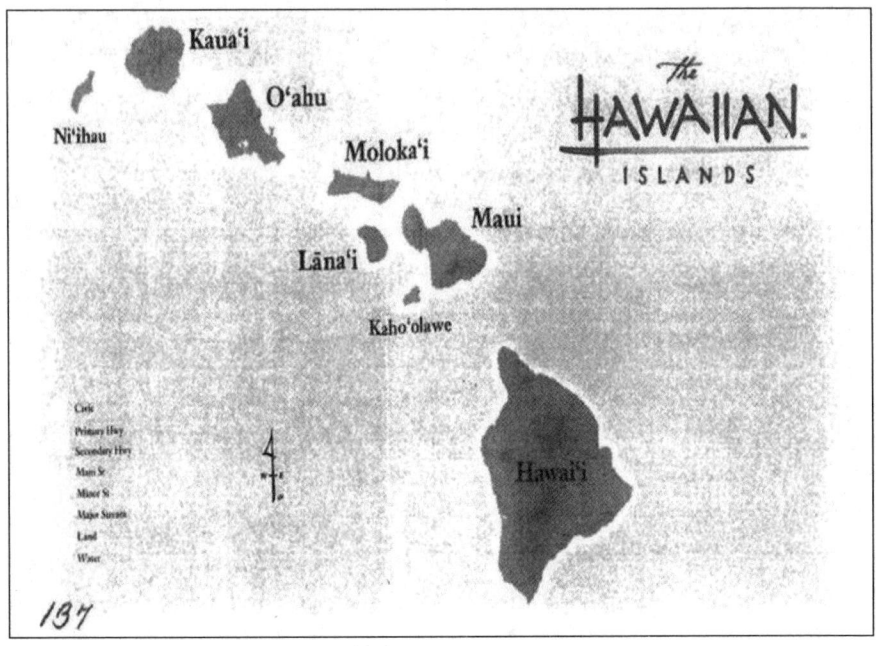

Monday, November 22, 1943
Today I really jackpotted. I got 13 letters, not bad huh! Went to the show tonite with O'Neill and Survill. We're not doin much. Played baseball.

Tuesday, November 23, 1943
Played baseball today, and had a little drill. Went to the show. Boy I'm plenty low on the old money problem. I'm glad pay day is comin up.

Wednesday, November 24, 1943
Well today we got our Medical kits. Also a new address -
Robert G. Thobaben 15311634
q. Co. 3rd Bn. 111th Inf. Regt. A.P.O. #957
c Postmaster, San Francisco, Calif. U.S.A.

Thursday, November 25, 1943
Applied for a pass for tomorrow. Borrowed 60 bucks from Klonsky. Went to a show again tonight. Played football today, 1st time in a long time.

(It was real football, with one exception – we played without shoes, because of the rain.)

Friday, November 26, 1943
Well Survill and I finally went to town. We got the bus and went to Honolulu. Walked all over. It's crowded with servicemen. We looked all over for a place to get a beer but they don't sell it till noon. The town is nice but too crowded. So we hopped on a bus for Waikiki. Boy that's beautiful. We sat on the beach and it's beautifully lined with palm trees. Not crowded at all. Had quite a few beers. Felt fine. It's very modem and beautiful. Went to the Chicken Coop and a couple other beer parlors. Went to show at nite.

Saturday, November 27, 1943
Had drill and Physical Fitness this mom. Played ball this afternoon. Got all my clothes today. I finally have something to wear. The only thing I wore to town yesterday of my own was my underwear and my hat and shoes.

Sunday, November 28, 1943
Loafed around all day today. Went to the P.C. etc. Went to service club at nite and played records. Then went to a show. There was a U.S.O. show at the Bowl – an auditorium. It's a huge bowl-shaped place.

Monday, November 29, 1943
Sent my laundry out today, played ball, and got our second set of cholera and typhus shots. Boy those are really stinkers. They really slam you. Went to a show tonite.

Tuesday, November 30, 1943
Got paid today and like a jerk I dropped some in a crap game. Had classes on medical stuff today. Found out tonite we're moving out. I think we're going to Makin Island, one of the Gilberts. We just took them but there are still plenty of Japs there. We turned in our B bags tonite.

Wednesday, December 1, 1943
Just monkeyed around today. Didn't do anything important. Went to the show and went to our farewell beer party tonight. We get the boat tomorrow.

Thursday, December 2, 1943
Went up to the P.C. this morning and bought a bunch of stuff I'll need. I'm the "four" of the battalion. I'm the last man. We rode in regular boxcars. It's a beautiful ride down to the boat. We saw loads of coconuts and I saw my

9

first bananas growing today. Well, we hit the boat. It's a small cargo ship called the "Sea Fox" [Mormacport written above]. The other boat was the "West Point." At first I was in a hole worse than the black hole of Calcutta, but I moved. We pull out tomorrow.

(Well, plenty of bananas, pineapples, coconuts – and fish! A paradise of food!)

Friday, December 3, 1943
We left Honolulu at 11:10 this morning. The seas are pretty heavy and this tub really rolls. I felt a little sick but not much. Had to abandon ship drill. There are Air Corps and Seebees with us. Only the 3rd Bn of the 111th Inf Reg. is going.

Saturday, December 4, 1943
Feel good today. Only this damn salt water won't lather so you can't wash but no one's going to see us so what the hell. The ocean is still rolling but I like it now. The chow is a hell of a lot better than on the West Point. All rumors are that we're headed for the Gilberts.

Sunday, December 5, 1943
Been reading magazines most of the time. Nothin really to do. They played a few records over the P.A. It sure makes you miss home. Didn't do anything else.

Monday, December 6, 1943
Well I sat in the sun for an hour or so and got a nice burn on my back. They had boxing exhibitions on hatch 4 of the ship tonite. They were good. We're supposed to hit Canton Island to pick up some more Air Corps guys tomorrow.

Tuesday, December 7, 1943
Well we don't hit the Island till tomorrow morning. Today is the 2nd Anniversary

of the attack on Pearl Harbor. We sailed all day. They had practice with the 3 inch guns on the boat. Saw a boat on the horizon and our destroyer went bad-assin it out to see if it was an allied ship or not. We also had the destroyer tail us. I think they thought there was a sub there.

Wednesday, December 8, 1943
Well we sighted land this morning and it's really a bleak place. There are a total of 3 trees on about 8 islands. This is Canton Island. We'll lay over and get supplies. I'm pretty sure we're going to Makin. This Canton Island is all white sand, not a thing here. The water here is very light blue, really nice and crystal clear. You can see the fish. I saw a shark (small) swimming yesterday. They have a bunch of flying boat bombers here. Oh! I forgot, yesterday evening about 6:30 pm we crossed the equator line so now we're what you call shellbacks.

Thursday, December 9, 1943
Well I sat and read a magazine all day today. Nothin else to do. Watched them fish for a while. The guys on the island put on a show for us on the boat. They had a bass and a set of drums they had made, and they were darn good. It was a novelty show.

Friday, December 10, 1943
Well, we left Canton Island in the afternoon and headed towards the Baker Islands. Boy you really get dirty and sweaty on the boat. About 3,000 on this one and it's jammed. You sleep 5 deep [drawing of 5 bunks] I'm on the bottom. Slept on deck tonite.

Saturday, December 11, 1943
Read most of the day. Tomorrow we land. I can't find out for sure what the time is. It's all SNAFU.

Sunday, December 12, 1943
Well we hit the Ellis Islands today and there are about 15 ships docked here. Rumors are that it will build up to 52 and is a task force. And also I'm not sure whether tomorrow is Monday, or Tuesday, cause I think we crossed the international date line and so we should lose a day. I got sunburned and peeled today so I'll have to start all over again.

Tuesday, December 14, 1943
We lost a day so today is Tuesday. One thing nice is they play records for a couple hours a day so that's better than nothing. We had boxing exhibitions today.

Wednesday, December 15, 1943
Well we left the Ellis group of Islands today. And the rumors were much bullshit. We left with our 1 destroyer and 1 destroyer escorted us as usual. Left at 8 and am heading for Tarawa in the Gilberts.

Thursday, December 16, 1943
It seems funny that you hear newscasts about a cold wave in the Ohio valley and it's hotter than a son of a bitch down here. That hold where we sleep is

a stinkin hole. 3000 men crammed in a ship made for 300. But I guess they can't help it. The food ain't too tough though.

Friday, December 17, 1943
Well we sighted Tarawa about 9 am. We've piloted in and dropped anchor. The Seabees, 41st bomb group, and some ordinance men got off. I saw movies of the destruction on Tarawa. I've never seen a place as beat up as that. The island isn't too large but there isn't a tree left with its palms whole. Looks like a tornado hit it. It's really wrecked.

Saturday, December 18, 1943
Left Tarawa about 2 pm. Didn't do much of anything today. But I do know we'll hit Makin tomorrow. We've been on the boat quite a while.

December 19, 1943
Well we sighted Makin about 10 am and dropped anchor. We left the ship in landing barges. Really got plenty salty on them. Landed and the 1st thing I noticed was a wrecked Jap flying boat (big plane) plus we saw some little Jap Tanks. We went to our bivouac area and stopped. It's really nice looking but we talked with the guys from the 165th (they invaded and captured Makin) and they told us stories of how the Japs don't give up. They commit hari-kari. In one instance they found 9 Japs with their big toes on the trigger of their rifles and the muzzles in their necks so when they fell asleep they shot themselves. Well we drank coconut milk and Survill and I put up our pup tent and dug a slit trench. We got our 1st taste of the enemy at about 3 am in the morning. They didn't drop too many bombs but it gave us the idea.

Monday, December 20, 1943
Well we finished our slit trenches and then the topkick decided he wanted dugouts (a big hole with logs over it) so we worked like hell making that. We got bombed again tonite and I got plenty scared for the 1st time and I guess everyone else was too. But the bombs dropped about 400 yds away. They almost hit us. Accidents happen in the army yeah they happen daily.

(When I was in the Gilbert islands on what we called Makin Island, a native father and son were in our area one day. I asked the father if he could get a coconut down from the palm tree for me – so he waved his hand, and the kid ran up the tree. Well, he climbed the tree, in about 1 minute, and he sent down a big coconut. I still have that coconut- it's sitting on the breakfront in my dining room right now as I write this. But how it got to Cleveland, Butler PA, Pittsburgh, and Dayton, Ohio – that's another story!)

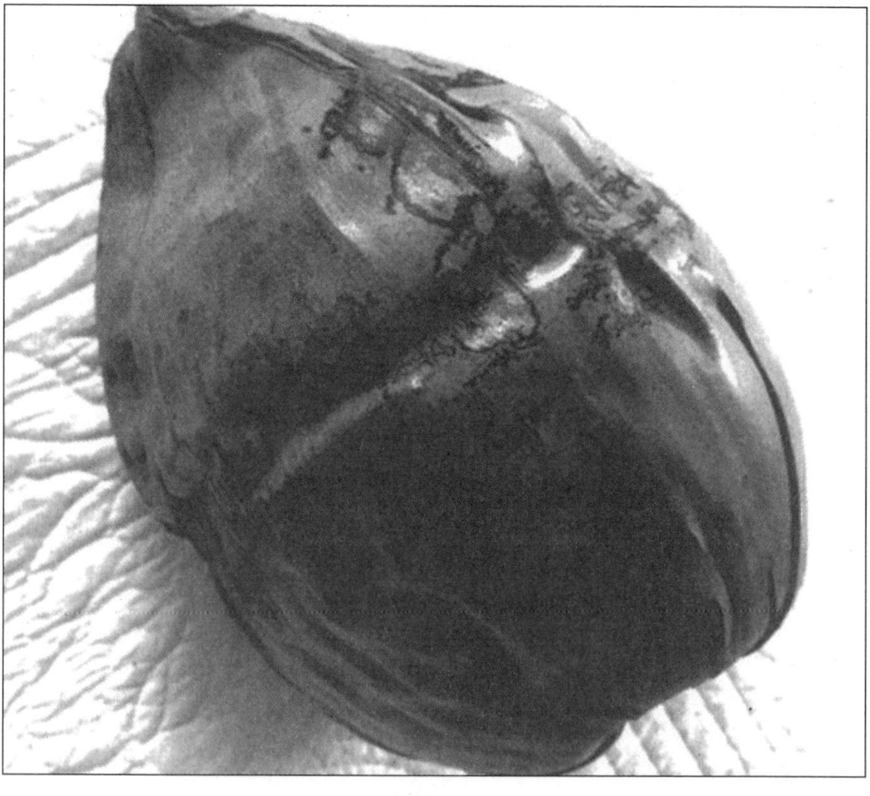

The Famous Coconut

Tuesday, December 21, 1943
Well today we went into the native village and looked around. 1 bought a grass skirt for 4 packs of cigarettes. It sure seems funny to see all these native people. The women wear only grass skirts, no tops at all. Most are not so hot but some are pretty nice. I'm getting a pretty fair suntan. Well bed-check Charley – that's the nickname for the Jap who comes at 3 am in the morning – didn't come but I was plenty miserable with dysentery.

Wednesday, December 22, 1943
Well today we moved into a new area. We're a little above the airport and we have cots and sleep 7 in a tent. I'm in with Combs, Hossler, Schaffer, Stanford, Frey, and Robuck. They have the dugouts all built. We worked in the area mostly today. No bombing.

Thursday, December 23, 1943
Well today I had K.P. We got our kitchen set up. We had just about finished the job and it was about 7:15 pm. We were carrying a GI can to empty it and we got the air- raid signal so we hit a dug-out by the ocean. We waited about 20 min. (for the Radar picked up the Jap planes that far away) and then they came. And did they come. I thought every bomb was on top of our trench. From where I was I thought I could see the bomb flashes hit about 75 yds inland in a string from the air-strip up through our area. Then a couple landed near us and I was really scared.

One especially hit close. I was shaking when it stopped. Well that was the closest they came but I saw 5 piles of dirt where they'd hit about 20 yds from us in the sand and water. They kept at it till about 10 pm. Then we got all-clear. I came back to the aid station and boy what a wreck. The C.P. tent was half down and all the stuff in the aid-station was on the ground with shrapnel all over the place. Then they brought in the casualties. And it was the most pitiful thing I've ever seen. One guy who was on a litter kept asking about his two buddies. M Co. had about 4 of their tents smashed and an ambulance got a direct hit. 7 shrapnel holes. Went to bed and at 2 am. Had no bombs. At 4 am we had another raid but no bombs. That's all but I hope and pray to God it's never like that again.

Friday, December 24, 1943
Well we were raided two more times today. Once during breakfast and once during dinner, so we screwed them and had supper at 4 O'clock instead. Played a little cards. No nite raid tonite. I was never so glad about anything in my life.

Saturday, December 25, 1943
Well today is Xmas. And I'm a pretty long way from home. Mostly out here all you talk about is "the states." We had a small meal today but Xmas or no Xmas the Japs might come so we worked like hell on our dugout. Now we have a pit covered by a layer of logs, then sandbags, then logs, then sandbags. It's a pretty good one. Played a little cards, our dive- bombers raided Mille – the Jap held island in the Marshall Islands. (There are about 5 or 6 islands in this group and altogether they are the Makin Islands. We are on the biggest with the Air Force. It is called Bu-tari-tari. The Natives all celebrated Xmas singing and dancing with nothin on, which is what everybody wears because it's too hot.

Sunday, December 26, 1943
Well it's after Christmas now. I wrote a couple letters today and filled up sandbags. Went to a church. It's funny. The roof of the church is held up by poles with Jap writing on them. At 7 pm tonite we had another raid but the Japs didn't get through. Our P-39 (aircobras) held them out at sea. We've been a little worried for the Japs sent 10 reconnaissance planes over Friday, and they took pictures which might give away our position.

Monday, December 27, 1943
We worked on our tent today. The concussion the other nite loosened it all up. We have 6 guys in it and have it fixed up pretty good. Took a shower and gave our pet pup a bath. We call him Makin. Had another raid at about 6:30. It lasted till about 8:45 pm. It got hotter than hell in the shelter. Got a few letters from home.

Tuesday, December 28, 1943
Well today we unloaded a lumber truck and then policed our area. And then I read the rest of the day. Tonite at about 7 pm we had another raid. It lasted till about 8:30. Those A.A. really shake the ground and so do the bombs. It's

getting so every time I even hear a whistle I jump for the shelter. We had one case of hysteria tonight.

(In one case I went down to the airfield and was giving some candy to the dive bomber pilots. I liked them because they were bombing the Japs, and I thought that was great. Then on the way back to the shelter there was a strafing attack and I started running like mad. I had about 1/2 mile to make the trip and as I neared the base I leaped into a hole by the airfield. Oh, no! Right next to me a 90-millimeter anti¬ aircraft gun went up! I decided, "I'm getting out of here!" So, I started running for home and as I approached the camp I saw a guy who had been taking a shower. He was covered in soap. He was running through the woods right near me – no, a little bit ahead of me – but I never mentioned it in my diary at all. So, as in a lot of the daily diary entries, I don't have all the drama that was involved – just a mere stating of facts, cold hard facts.)

Wednesday, December 29, 1943
Had K.P. today. I had it only a few days ago. Well, we just finished at nite and I thought a fuckin tornado hit the joint. The wind and rain really came but it kept tojo away anyhow. No raid tonite.

Thursday, December 30, 1943
Well this morning Frey and I washed our clothes. What a job. It's for the birds. Then we fixed up the tent. This afternoon 25 dive bombers escorted by 23 P-39 air cobras went out on a raid. All 25 dive bombers came back. Bad weather again tonite kept tojo from his nightly visit over Butaritari. Had a good nite's sleep. Tomorrow's a big day and nite at home.

Friday, December 31, 1943
Well today is the last day of 1943. Today we worked on some kind of drainage pit. Took the jeep out on the Pacific (the tide was out) and got coral to fill it up. I was tech on duty tonite. We celebrated the new year with a canteen cup of chlorinated water and G.I. issue cigarettes. No raid – bad weather I guess. Well tomorrow's the 1st day of 1944.

Saturday, January 1, 1944
Got some mail today and a Xmas package from home. It was beat up cause they left it on the deck at Tarawa for 3 days but it was wrapped up

so it didn't damage it. We dug another drainage pit again today. Got a miniature checker game. It's pretty good. Well, tonite was the 1st nite that was clear that we didn't have a raid. Our A-24 dive bombers are really givin them hell. One type dive bomber carries 3 500lb. bombs. The other carries 1 1000 lb. bomb plus 2 100 lb. bombs. So it's the beginning of a new year today.

Sunday, January 2, 1944
Worked on the tent a little today. Got it fixed up. Got another xmas package from home. It was really pretty nice. Went to church services. Had an air-raid at about 7:15 pm that lasted till 9:30 pm. I was right in the middle of opening my xmas packages when it came.

Well we got the all clear and got out. Then 10 minutes later we had another raid. It lasted till about 10:45 pm. They must have doubled back trying to get us off-guard. But the Radar can pick up anything. It's really a marvelous instrument. That's two raids tonite which is plenty.

Monday, January 3, 1944
Worked on the tent today. We have it spread out good now. We'll finish it tomorrow. Cleaned the area of some of the trash left from bombings and the invasion. Had another raid tonite that started at 7:30 pm and lasted till 9:45. Dropped 8 bombs but the A.A. was firing like hell. Those Japs seemed to be diving tonight and we were all plenty scared. Today 24 of our A-24 dive bombers escorted by 26 P-39s (aircobras) took off with full bomb loads. And they didn't bring the bombs back. I imagine they caused plenty of hell. All the A-24s got back but I didn't count the P-39s.

Tuesday, January 4, 1944
Finished work on the tent today. It's really fixed up swell. We have a native bringing us more mats for the floor. We learned to talk a little native. Just essential words. Had an air raid at about 1 1:15 am today that lasted till around 12 noon. 25 P-39s took off and turned them back. Went up to the Air Corps bivouac area and saw a movie.

(Some of the islands were uninhabited; others had small communities. They were all friendly to us and helpful. They seemed to have no formal government on any of the islands, except for Koror. On the Gilbert Islands

I noticed that they simply worked together on communal projects or issues. They also joined together to farm, fish, sing, dance, etc. – men, women, and children.)

Wednesday, January 5, 1944
Had K.P. today. It's not such a hard job but I just don't like it. We got beer tonite believe it or not. 2 cans per man. It really tasted good. No raid today. It's about time they missed one. About 7 B-25s took off from our strip here today. They are sure a sweet bomber. They're building a fake air strip out on the ocean sand.

Thursday, January 6, 1944
Went on tech duty today. Am learning a little. We were supposed to get some P.X. supplies that they just landed, but as per usual Capt. Demo just didn't seem to be able to get them. That guy gives me a pain where a pill won't reach. Played some cards tonite. Bad weather tonite stopped Bed-Check-Charley from his daily visit, which is O.K. with all of us. Heard rumors of a task force headed for the Marshall Islands 140 miles N.W. of here.

Friday, January 7, 1944
Well in the morning Schaffer and I went out and sprayed diesel oil over pools of stagnant water. I guess to prevent malaria. Had an air raid at 7pm that lasted till 8:15pm. Then we just got out and about 8:45 we had another raid lasting till about 9:15 pm. They must have doubled back. Some fellow who works steady K.P. tried to kill himself tonite with an Ml, but before he could, someone knocked his aim off. He said he was too scared by the raids. Really feel sorry for a guy like that. All our nerves are on a jagged edge.

Saturday, January 8, 1944
Cleaned out the tent. It was a mess. Got some P.X. supplies. Got 2 bars of candy and a pack of gum. We did some work the rest of the day and had a storm at nite. I thought it was a hurricane. Tojo couldn't get through I guess.

(As in Adam Smith's book, A Theory of Moral Sentiments, there is a quality in human beings called empathy. In other words, we feel we have a connection with other people. We feel sorry for them, empathetic towards them, or have some intuition that we should do the right thing towards them. Here's an example: we had a guy in our outfit who simply couldn't deal with the bombings or violence. He wasn't bucking for a Section 8; he just couldn't deal with it. Some of the guys would tease and taunt him, and it would really upset him. I told them they shouldn't do that. It was just how I felt, but they wouldn't let up on him. He would wash his hands continually-- I think he was trying to wash out the fear; he simply couldn't deal with bombing attacks and violence. No doubt he was not alone.)

Sunday, January 9, 1944
We worked some this morning but it was pretty bad weather in the afternoon so I did some reading. After dinner we listened to the recorder they had at the mess hall. Then we went over to "M" Co. to hear the natives sing. They are really good. Their tunes are weird but they use good harmony. Then a couple of our guys started jitterbugging and so then the natives start singing one of their songs and clapping their hands only on the 1,2,3 beat of 4/4 time. Then one would holler and get out and dance. They made some kind of motions and made a sound like "uhg" on the offbeat. Then one or two others would join in. We really all had a good time. They sang the Jap Marine song although at 1st they didn't want to. It was all in all a damn good show.

Monday, January 10, 1944
Well we got paid today. I got $47.25. Then we played some cards and I won about $17.50 so it ain't bad for a few hours. I think I'll send most of the money home. We pulled tree stumps out today. And filled up a taro patch to prevent malaria. We just got to bed and about 10:30 pm Tojo came so we badassed down the shelter. The raid only lasted until about 12:15 am. Played some checkers and went to bed.

Tuesday, January 11, 1944
Well this morning we finished filling the taro patch and put up the other tent. Then in the afternoon, Frey, Combs, and I went in the air raid shelter and played poker. Made out O.K. Played some more cards after supper and had 5 cans of beer, our weeks rations. Felt almost drunk but not quite. About 1:30 am we had a raid. It lasted till about 2:30 am. Went back to bed and at 4:30 am had another raid which lasted till about 5:15 am. As for sleep! We didn't get it. The Japs are pulling a new trick. Just when the Radar picks them up they unload tinfoil which the Radar picks up. Then the actual plane swoops in low so it's pretty good. I damn near had to go in the shelter with no pants during the second raid.

Wednesday, January 12, 1944
Had K.P. today so there is nothing really to write. It rained the hardest I've ever seen it. But the days are hot. But we always have a wind from the West to keep it cool. No raid I suppose due to bad weather.

Thursday, January 13, 1944
Well we worked on another Air Raid shelter because the other one filled with water and got weak. The one we're building will really be a good one. Yesterday 21 dive bombers and 23 P-39s raided Mille or other parts of the Marshalls. Today 21 dive bombers (A-24s) and 23 P-39s raided them again. Then 8 B-25s raided them. Then 2 B-24s went out. Hell of a lot of Air Activity.

Friday, January 14, 1944
Finished up the shelter. It's really a fine one. Well tonite was a perfect nite for Tojo, but for some reason he didn't come. We went up to where the Air Corps lives and saw a movie. We also were issued 4 bottles of coke. Got some mail today.

Saturday, January 15, 1944
Well we blacked out the shelter so we could have some light. Filled a slew of sandbags today. We went to a movie tonite. 1st time they got hold of a camera. About a half hour after it started – Wham! it's a raid, so we all battailed it for the shelter. It started at about 8PM.

The Japs came in over the dock. Dropped 2 bombs in our area. Started a fire in "M" Co. mess hall and hit 15 feet from an ammo dump. It set off

21

some carbine and M1 ammo but lucky that was all. We heard a bunch of bombs dropped but they were farther up. Went back and saw the rest of the movie. Then went to bed. Had another raid at about 2 am till 3 am – The first raid ended about 9:40 pm. – Then again at about 4:15 am another raid. Lasted till about 4:45 am. A new bunch of engineers landed today and because they didn't dig in for some reason, they went into their mess hall and a bomb hit and 8 were killed, approximately 12 injured. Somebody's failure to order the men to dig in caused plenty of trouble.

Sunday, January 16, 1944
I was on tech duty today. We were right in the middle of lunch and again – wham! an air raid. The P-39s went up and must have intercepted them. Today we sent up 25 A-24 dive bombers and 8 P-40s each carrying 2 500lb bombs and I suppose 20 P-39s, though I didn't count them. All came back except 1 P-39 whose pilot bailed out and was picked up by a Navy PBY flying boat. A funny or rather unusual thing happened. A B-25 was very low bombing a Jap freighter approximately 50ft above the ship. He dropped his load and the concussion pulled him down so low. He hit the mast of the ship, ripping off a cable, bamboo, and a Jap flag. The left motor was put out of commission but he flew back 500 miles with all that stuff stuck in his left motor. Went to church held in the mess hall.

Monday, January 17, 1944
Well Combs and Frey were taken sick today with some fever. So we are shorthanded. Shaffer and I were down looking at the dive bombers about 2:pm when the air raid came. I think we broke the world record for the dash back to our shelter. It was a good half mile. We sprayed some more taro patches today to cut down mosquitoes. Tonite around 11:00 pm we had another air raid. But our fighters went up like they were shot out of rockets and I guess they turned them back. I read that story about "no atheists in the air." Well I'm sure there are none on the ground either. It is our biggest help.

Tuesday, January 18, 1944
Well I had K.P. today but we worked fast and we got through pretty early. Tonite it clouded up and we didn't have an air-raid. Today 25 A-24 dive bombers and 8 P-40s took off. Each P-40 carried 2 500lb bombs and a bunch of fighters. One fighter was injured. The pilot bailed out and was picked up by a P.B.Y. flying boat. There is some Navy ship in the harbor.

It looks like a light cruiser but they said it was a mother ship to subs and destroyers, and destroyer escorts.

Wednesday, January 19, 1944
Well we didn't do much work today. Played some checkers. I had tech duty at nite. So I started to sleep in but the mosquitos got so bad I came over into our own tent. Had a raid at 6:00 am which lasted till 6:30 am. Immediately 11 P-39s and 9 P-40s took off and must have stopped them.

Thursday, January 20, 1944
We cleaned up our area a little today. We have strict blackout now at nite so we can't have a light in our tent. So we go into the Air-Raid shelter and play cards or read. The nite was pretty cloudy and Tojo didn't come around.

Friday, January 21, 1944
Well we did work around the area today trying to clean it up but that's a bunch of baloney. You can't keep it clean. We got 4 cokes apiece today so that brought up our morale. And it rained like hell tonite so the Japs couldn't get over. 23 dive bombers went up, 8 P-40s, and the usual 25 P-39s went on a raid. They all came back.

Saturday, January 22, 1944
Well today we ripped down our air raid shelter. The sides were caving in from the concussion of the bombs. And when we did get the logs off, man I don't know how it held up as long as it did. We worked all day on that. Got a R.C.A. radiogram from Barb. She's not going back to Bradford. We got 4 cans of beer tonite. Very clear nite but Tojo didn't come.

Sunday, January 23, 1944
Well I had K.P. again today. Damn it, without a doubt that's the most fucked up job there is. There has been one hell of a lot of Air Activity. At nite we are starting to hit them. A flight of B-25s went out at 6 pm and came back at 10 pm. Immediately a flight of B-24s went out as soon as they landed. Tojo didn't come tonite either. I guess we must be blasting him pretty heavy.

Monday, January 24, 1944
We rebuilt our shelter today. The damn thing was caving in. So we fixed it up pretty good. Around 4:00 pm a bunch of us went swimming in the

lagoon. The water is really fine. Had an Air Raid at 11:00 pm that lasted till 11:35 pm. Today 24 dive bombers and 8 P-40s with a P-39 escort bombed Mille in the Marshall Islands. Coombs and I went down to the Air Strip and talked to the gunners on the A-24s.

Tuesday, Jan25, 1944
Today all we did was loaf around. I didn't get up for reveille, so I had an hour's work to do after supper. We were all issued four cans of beer so I didn't care. They have a victrola at the mess-hall and those records really sound good. We used everything from safety pins to hypo needles to make it play. It rained tonite and Tojo didn't come over. 25-dive bombers went out. All came back (bombed Jaluit in the Marshalls).

Wednesday, January 26, 1944
Wrote a few letters today. The B-25s and B-24s went out bombing. A flight of B-25s (9) went over and they really kicked up a roar. For recreation we've been playing the strenuous game of checkers. Really rough huh! The Japs didn't come over today.

Thursday, January 27, 1944
Was on tech duty today. 23 A-24 dive bombers went out today. B-25s and B-24s went out to bomb also. The Japs didn't come tonite.

Friday, January 28, 1944
I got hold of the diary of a Jap Officer today and made a copy of it. It's very interesting. It tells what he did from Nov. 17 till December 13 when he was shot. Air activity was mostly B-25 and B-24 planes. Japs did not bomb tonite. I had night tech duty.

Saturday, January 29, 1944
Today we worked most of the day pulling the stumps of coconut trees out that had been shot off. Then we went out and climbed coconut trees. 18 dive bombers and 13 P- 40s went on a raid. B25 and B24 bombers kept going out all night. The air corps dropped surrender leaflets on the Marshalls. It said they would bomb them every hour of the day until they surrendered. And they seem to be doing it. A sad thing happened though, 2 6F6 Navy pursuit planes saw 2 B25s and thought they were Japs. They shot one down and crippled the other.

Sunday, January 30, 1944
Had K..P. today. Our planes were all big bombers that went out today. B- 24s mostly and some B-25s. General Hale, Commander of the 7th Air Force, flew his B-17 fortress here today. They are really bombing the hell out of the Marshalls now. No Jap raid tonite.

Monday, January 31, 1944
Well today there was plenty of Air Activity here. 20 A-24 and B-24 dive bombers, a large no. of P-39s, 9 Liberator B-24s and 9-B25s went out and hit the Marshalls today. They are really bombing the hell out of them. I heard that Allied soldiers landed on the Marshalls, but I doubt it. They have been keeping the Jap bombers away from here too. No raid again tonite. Had a lot of rain today.

Tuesday, February 1, 1944
Well today we really had some good news. The allied Infantry (Americans) hit the Marshall Islands. They hit Malelop, Wojie, Juliet, Milli, all at once. This is really good news for us and takes a hell of a lot of worry off our shoulders. Milli was only 150 miles, a mere hop for a plane. Now they will only be able to bomb us from a pretty long distance. I sure hope the boys who hit the Marshalls make out fine. I know God will help them. We had a veritable hurricane today but the B-25s and B-24s still went out and hit the Jap positions on the Marshalls. No air raid tonite.

Wednesday, February 2, 1944
Well today we worked on the tent, ditching it and so on, because I damn near floated away yesterday. The rain came up over the legs of my bunk and I had to get a can and start bailing. Air Activity was 17 dive bombers and 12 P-40s. Just a few B-24s and B-25s were used today. They are bombing the Jap positions on the Marshalls. We had our first movie tonite.

Damn good. The men who hit the Marshalls are coming along alright.

Thursday, February 3, 1944
Today I had day tech duty and was busy on that all day. Air Activity was light. P-40s and P-39s went out to strafe. I guess they are afraid to bomb because they didn't know how far the infantry has advanced on their positions in the Marshalls. We had another movie tonite. The only thing the matter with them is that the film always breaks and then you're halfway through the picture when it gets going again. But nobody cares, a movie's a movie.

Friday, February 4, 1944
Well today we had four Generals here giving out medals etc. Today we got paid. I got $47.25, paid off my debts, dropped a five in poker, and I'll send the rest home. We had a movie tonite. The boys on the Marshalls are going along o.k.

Saturday, February 5, 1944
We had mail call today and it sure was good to get some mail. Man it comes through slow, although I did get one letter postmarked Jan. 28, only 8 days ago. We heard that nurses were coming here the 16th. It'll be funny to see a white woman. No raid tonite. The news from the Marshalls is limited. Coombs and I walked up to Asron to see a movie but we'd already seen it.

Sunday, February 6, 1944
Well today we just loafed around. Went swimming in the lagoon. Dive bombers went up escorted by 12 P-40s. Today the heaviest load ever carried by a P-40 in combat. 16 P-40s each carried 2 1000lb bombs. It sounds fishy but it's true.

Monday, February 7, 1944
Well today we worked on our shower cause nurses are landing tomorrow. Went down to the village and tried to talk to the natives. We got along O.K. Went swimming. Then tonite we had a show.

Tuesday, February 8, 1944
Found a wonderful raft. I took it down to the lagoon and the damn thing sank like a rock. We took the dog swimming with us. Air Activity was strictly heavy bombers. Flight of 9 or 10 B-24s went out at 1600 today and didn't come back till 2230. Saw a movie up at the sub-depot. Nurses were supposed to land but I sure as hell didn't see any.

Wednesday, February 9, 1944
Quite a few ships in the harbor today. Went swimming. The lagoon is as clean and clear as crystal. 21 A-24 dive bombers and around 8 P-40s went out at noon today. Those boys are still hitting Milli in the Marshalls pretty hard.

Wednesday, February 16, 1944
Well this morning we decided the engineers had swiped enough stuff off of us so we grabbed a Jeep and went down and swiped a whole floor out of

their tent and got it set in ours. Saw a white nurse today, a redhead, first one I've seen in 3 months. Air Activity was 11 A-24s and 14 P-40s with 500lb bombs.

Thursday, February 17, 1944

This morning Frey and I went down to where a mess hall had been built and pried the boards off of the floor and hitch-hiked back with them. You could get a ride even if you were carrying a damn derrick around. Well we got those boards in the floor and we can finish it tomorrow. We also built a frame (wood) aid station. It sets on 48 logs driven in the ground (what a fuckin job). Tonite the officers had a party for the nurses. We waited till they were all drunk and then sneaked in and got salami sandwiches, pineapple juice, cookies, peanuts, pickles, and all in all had a good feed. Even the Major was passing us out cigarettes.

Friday, February 18, 1944

Went out and got enough wood to finish the floor this morning. Had a fight with Combs, but nothin to it. 22 A-24s went out to bomb Milli this afternoon. We also heard radio news that the Navy is shelling Truk, which is where Japan gets all her supplies. Truk is to Japan as Hawaii is to us in the South Pacific. On the Marshalls we now have superiority of the air and sea, and so the Japs left on Milli, Maleolap, Juliet, and Wojr will be starved out, which is better than sending troops in. It has rained pretty hard lately.

Saturday, February 19, 1944
Had day tech duty today. Was pretty easy all day. Tonite we played Cassino. A Navy task force hit Truk hard today. I found out today that the 106th Inf. Reg. hit Enewintok, the northernmost of the Marshalls. Harry Kramer was in that bunch.

Sunday, February 20, 1944
Coombs and I had all day off, so we went down to I Co, then ate at L Co, then went to the hospital to see what the nurses looked like. Then we went up to K Co. and had supper. Played volleyball tonite against H.P. and played some more Casino.

Monday, February 21, 1944
Today I did my washing. What a job! 1 really had a lot of it but I'm glad it's out of the way. Played volleyball tonite. Went swimming in the lagoon for an hour or so. It's really a beautiful place to swim. 43 Voight Corsairs came in today. I presume they came off of some carriers in the vicinity.

Tuesday, February 22, 1944
Well today I built myself a locker box to keep my junk in. That took most of the day. Then we went swimming. It's really a fine place to swim. Then tonite we got 4 bottles of beer, the first we've had in one hell of a long time. We also were able to write home and say we are in the Gilberts. It's about time. They've been wondering for 3 months. Had nite tech duty.

Wednesday, February 23, 1944
Today didn't do much of anything. We did get some mail through today. Then at night we saw Anthony Adverse. Good show but it was old as the hills. Shot the shit and then hit the old fart sack.

(It may sound like some days we didn't do much but remember that Tech Duty is unpredictable, sometimes stressful, and time consuming. Also, our job as Mop Up Troops was to clean up the islands that had largely been taken, secure them, kill or capture any remaining Japanese, help prevent counter attacks, and be ready to lend support wherever it was needed. Plus we had to immediately build our defenses, take care of ourselves, tents, aid station, equipment, supplies, etc.)

Thursday, February 24, 1944
Capt. Demo and I went all over the island looking over the Out Posts. There must be a good 15 of them. The island is more like this [drawing of island shape] – like a big "T". It's a pretty fair size. An officer told us there were still 4 Japs running around loose. So we were armed. They live on coconuts and hide all day I guess. Got our ration of 4 bottles of beer tonite.

Friday, February 25, 1944
Today we heard they were going to start a training program. Man that's strictly for the birds. Frey and I went out to the reefs to hunt for these pretty stones. Got 35 of them. Then tonite went to a movie at the A.A. gun area. Then to a movie at I Co. Two in one nite, not bad.

Saturday, February 26, 1944
Boy someone's nuts. We had to cut down a whole hill today to make a CO. [cut off]. Then we had to pull palm trees out by hand cause they didn't get us a 2 'A ton truck. Had more beer tonite. Not bad for this week. Regular training starts again next Monday.

Sunday, February 27, 1944
Well tomorrow starts our training. Today we had off. We went out and picked up shells to make a necklace and bracelet. I have enough to make a set now. We played volleyball. Beat A. and P. (Ammunition and Pioneer) and that leaves us with 6 wins and a few losses so far. We had a movie tonite. Fair.

Monday, February 28, 1944
Well today I had tech duty and so that was pretty easy. Then Ed and I went up to "K" Co. and played volleyball. We examined some of the shiny stones we saved to make necklaces and bracelets.

(Another thing I should mention is the lighting inside the underground shelters that we had built. We were under blackout conditions, and it was usually dark outside, so we had to actually blacken out the shelters so we could have a light on in there. We spent a lot of time in there just to play checkers or drink coffee or whatever while the bombing was going on. I think the bombing had become more of an inconvenience than anything else. Nobody could see us and if we took a direct hit, it wouldn't make any difference anyway we would all be blown up.)

Tuesday, February 29, 1944
Well today we worked outside and then Samford and I went down to hear about mosquito control. We have to cut out the Aedes mosquito which gives us dengue fever. Then at night we played volleyball and went to a show at the A.A. batteries.

Wednesday, March 1, 1944
Had some more mosquito stuff today. I guess they're really bad. Had a blue alert last nite but no actual raid. Today a hell of a thing happened. A Navy pilot in a Corsair was coming into the strip. It was raining and that made a fog, and he misjudged the field and hit in the ocean about 20 feet from shore. He must have been killed instantly. His plane burned so hot that they couldn't put it out. Played volleyball again tonite and saw a show at the Fox radar.

Thursday, March 2, 1944
Today it rained like hell most all of the day so there wasn't much work to do. Some Allied troops have landed on the Admiralty Islands. We got our 4 bottles of beer rations.

Friday, March 3, 1944
Went over my area to get the mosquitoes under control. Went up to "K" Co. Area in the afternoon. Played "M" Co. in volleyball and beat them. Went to a show tonite at the Fox radar. Tomorrow we have a ten mile hike.

Saturday, March 4, 1944
This morning we loafed around. Then this afternoon we had a road march. It wasn't long but back in the jungle it was hot and sticky. A tough thing happened. A guy dropped over today with heat exhaustion and later died. It's really too bad but there was nothing the aid man could do. Tonight we went to a show at the A.A. guns. Pretty good. Had nite tech duty.

Sunday, March 5, 1944

Today we just loafed and did plenty of it. It's our 1st day off. Reading and swimming was what we did. Got a letter from Gerratt in England. Took 3 weeks to get here. Played Bn. Hg. in volleyball. Beat them. Then went up to the Air Corps. Sub Depot and saw a movie.

Monday, March 6, 1944

Today Shaf. and I went up to the native village and fooled around. Went swimming in the afternoon. Then tonite we played volleyball. We lost. Saw a movie.

Tuesday, March 7, 1944

Shaffer and I went out to hunt mosquito breeding places to cut down dengue fever. Had lectures this afternoon. Went to the Sub. Depot to a show tonite. Had our 4 bottles of beer. There's a pretty straight rumor that we're movin out. I don't know where, maybe the Marshalls. No one really knows.

Wednesday, March 8, 1944

Well today I had day tech duty so not much else. Went up to "K." Co. and played volleyball. We lost. Came back and went for a movie at the A.A. guns.

Thursday, March 9, 1944

Today we had training in the morning. In the afternoon I tried to clean up some of my shells. I think we'll be moving out in about a week or so. Anyhow that's the rumor. Went to the sub-depot and saw a movie. Then we went up to the native village. They have a big tribal dance when the moon is full. They really put plenty into their dancing and singing. They make motions with their hands. They got all fixed up, even with flowers in their hair. It was a big time.

Friday, March 10, 1944

Today we had a little training. Then Frey and I went down to Hen Village and traded with the natives. We got 3 grass skirts, saw a picture of a native girl with a soldier, (His arm around her and elsewhere), went to play L Co. in volleyball, and got rained out. Started to see a movie – rained out. Then we had an Air Raid tonite. The 1st one in quite a while. But P-40s must have stopped them. We have a road march tomorrow.

Saturday, March 11,1944

Had a road march in the morning, got back and worked on my bracelet, went to the island P.X. and got some stuff. Then tonite we played volleyball. We also got our ration of 4 bottles and sat in the tent and sang.

Sunday, March 12, 1944

Went down to Hen Village and did a little trading with the natives. Loafed and read the rest of the time. Went up to the Sub-Depot to see a show. Well it rained, but we just got wet and sat watching the show. Then they stopped and told us that they had picked up Jap subs off shore so no movie. We went back to our area. Two carriers are supposed to come here tomorrow. That's probably why the Japs are here. They must have heard about it.

Monday, March 13, 1944

Well today we had training all day. Read the rest of the day and whipped off a few letters tonite. Total blackout because of the subs. Sat around and sang a little tonite.

Tuesday, March 14, 1944

Had a little training today but not much to it. Did some reading. We were told today that we were going to one of the islands in the Kwajalein group of the Marshall Islands. Rumor has it we leave inside two weeks. Went to the Sub-depot to see a movie tonite. Damn fine show. Got our beer tonite.

Wednesday, March 15, 1944

Well I guess we'll be leaving soon. We started crating our stuff today. Read and just fooled around the rest of the day. I guess training is off since we're moving. Played volleyball tonite. Went to the A.A. guns show. Then saw the one at our area. Tomorrow we bottle the whiskey we made.

Thursday, March 16, 1944

Well today we didn't do much of anything. We're crating our stuff getting ready to go to the Marshall Islands. Played volleyball. We won. Had our 4 bottles of beer. Then we opened up our moonshine whiskey and drank a pint a piece. It was o.k. stuff and we really had a good party.

Friday, March 17, 1944

No mail again today. Somebody's pullin their rope someplace along the mail route. Had day tech duty today. Played volleyball. A big aircraft carrier was in today. About 50 corsairs are based here. They are using them for bombers now. They carry one 500 lb bomb.

Saturday, March 18, 1944

Had a road march today. Hotter than hell. Went to the movies tonite. Air Activity is mostly big bombers. Bombing the Carolines I suppose.

Sunday, March 19, 1944

Well today we loafed around. Went down to the native village. I think they're gettin lighter or I'm gettin darker. That's the sayin anyhow. Tomorrow we pull down our tent. Went to another show tonite.

Monday, March 20, 1944

Pulled down our tent first thing this morning. Had to turn it in. It looked like a sieve. We'll sleep on litters in the dispensary. I guess we move out soon.

Tuesday, March 21, 1944

Well I slept last nite, if that's what you call it. I had two prongs sticking in my back all night. Cleaned out my shells today. I want to send home my package – 2 grass skirts and two head pieces.

Wednesday, March 22, 1944

Well I guess we're going to Kwajalein in the Marshalls. We packed all our bags today. Went to a show tonite. Benny Goodman. It was a pretty recent picture.

Thursday, March 23, 1944

Well we monkeyed around this morning and then this afternoon we got aboard our ship. It's called the Sea Pike. It's a lot like our last ship the Mormacport. We had dam fine chow. Slept on deck but got rained out.

Friday, March 24, 1944

Didn't do anything today, just read most of the time. We pull out tomorrow morning early. Slept down in the hold. It's a fine ship with damn good chow.

Saturday, March 25, 1944
We left Makin at about 4:30pm so we can travel at night. At about 7:00 pm we had a submarine alarm. These aren't the best waters to travel in. We read and played cards all day. I heard we're goin to an island named Carlos about 8 miles from Kwajalein. Kwajalein itself is 93 islands, and then one of the little islands is called Kwajalein. We're going to be near it.

Sunday, March 26, 1944
Well today was pretty nice. We slept most of the day and I did some reading. We dock tomorrow about 4 in the morning. The 1st Bn. is up here somewhere.

Monday, March 27, 1944
Well this morning we had breakfast on the boat and then we came ashore on a higgins boat, onto Carlos Island. Kwajalein is 8 miles from here. Well we went to a temporary area and pitched our pup-tents, then dug in, and looked over the island. A Jap zero smashed here.
   Quite a few remains lying around. Went to a show tonite.

(The Marshall Islands form an area made up of about five atolls, one of which is an atoll called Kwajalein, and within this atoll is an island actually named Kwajalein. The atoll is made up of 93 islands, arranged somewhat like a pear. The pear (lagoon) is so large that it could hold all of the ships in the world. At the north end of the pear were the islands of Roi and Namur, and between them was a north pass. The Marines took and held that pass. At the south end of the pear was the island of Enylabegan, and next to it was a south pass, heavily used. It was occupied and held by the 111th Infantry to secure that pass.)

Tuesday, March 28, 1944
Moved to our permanent area. It's a damn jungle. Well, we started clearing it out (The old engineering Infantry worked all day.) Played a little cards at nite. No mosquitoes. But big red ants. There's a lot more coral rock here than at Makin.

Wednesday, March 29, 1944
Well today we started clearing our area. It's really a job. It's solid jungle. And we have to go from one side of the island to the other. Big trees and plenty of coral to move. We had B ration chow and saw a movie tonite.

Thursday, March 30, 1944
We worked more on our area today. We started blasting trees instead of cutting them. Then we burned our way through the underbrush. What an area. It's really rugged.

Friday, March 31, 1944
Today we worked more on our area. Got some mail. It will take a good 6 weeks to 2 months to fix up this place like Makin. We worked clearing it out all day.

Saturday, April 1, 1944
Well as usual we worked some more on the area. It's still a mess but it's better than it was. I drove the jeep hauling logs and stumps out of the area, and dumped them. This island is only 1 /2 to 2 miles long. The reef is very near shore, about 150 yards. And freighters can pull right up to the dock at Kwajalein Island.

Sunday, April 2, 1944
Well today I worked on the Jeep with Frey, hauling jungle debris away so we could get our tents up tomorrow. We saw a show tonight.

Monday, April 3, 1944
Well today's my 20th birthday. We got a P.X. supply in today and got a bunch of beers and pineapple juice. We put our tents up today. Was it good to get in the old pyramidal tent

Tuesday, April 4, 1944
We had an air raid during the day but the Japs didn't come very near our island. I sure hope that we don't get any raids. We put up railings around our tents.

Wednesday, April 5, 1944
Today we worked on our air-raid shelter. It's one for all 19 of us guys in this detachment. It rained hard as hell tonight. I thought for a while the old tent would blow away. But, no, the rain came in on all of us instead.

Thursday, April 6, 1944
Worked some more today. It's really a job fixing this joint up. But we blasted our way through and made a pretty decent place to put up our tents.

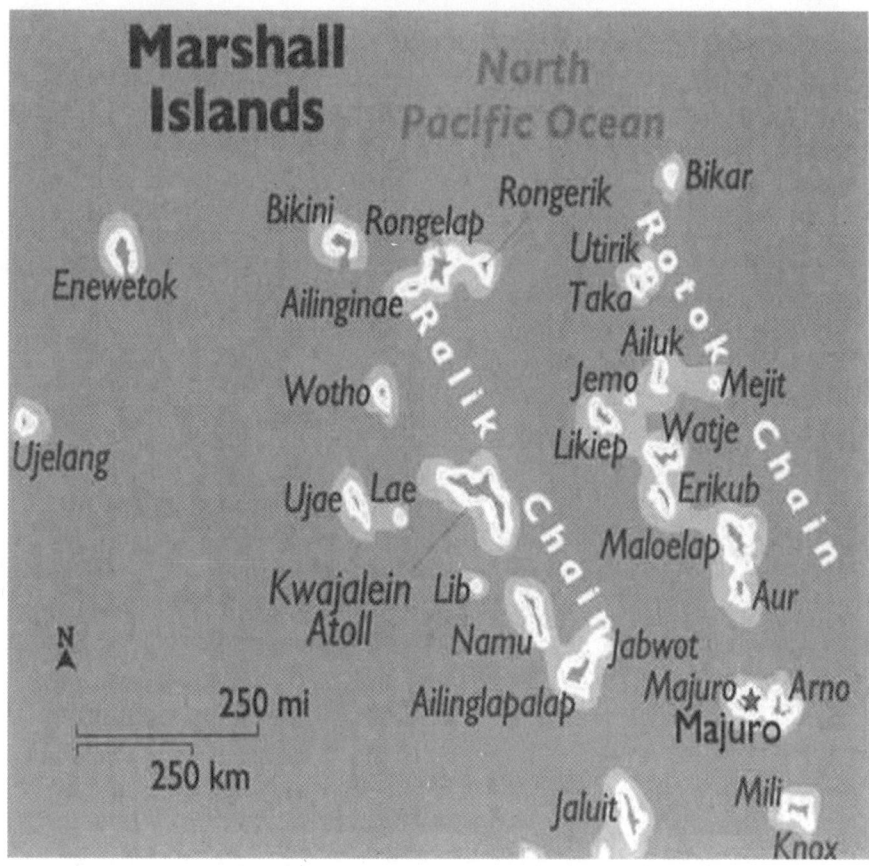

Friday, April 7, 1944

Today we went out and cut logs all day to make a floor so it's raised off the ground. We had to cut 22 logs to the right size and that's a job. Went to a movie tonite. Also, the natives put on a dance tonite.

Saturday, April 8, 1944

Was on tech duty today. Did some reading. Comic books strictly D.C.s. Got paid today. Sending 30 bucks home. Had an air raid tonite. Had him right in the searchlight beam. Played cards tonite.

Sunday, April 9, 1944

Well today is Easter. Went to church and communion. We had all day off. It's the first day off in quite a while. We played some "Red Dog" tonite. Did o.k. Went swimming instead of washing but that's all we can do.

Monday, April 10, 1944

Today we cleared out our area. Went up to the east end of the island. Climbed the Jap lookout tower and you can see everything for miles. There's a beached "waterbuffalo" down there. It's a new landing craft. Has treads like a tank. Looked over Jap pill boxes. Played some cards tonite.

Tuesday, April 11, 1944

Well we didn't do a damn thing all day long today, just loafed. It's hotter than hell in the tent during the daytime. Played a little cards. Went to a show tonite. This island is about 2 miles long.

Wednesday, April 12, 1944

Layed around this morning. Then this afternoon we dug garbage pits and man that's rugged diggin. Came back, swiped some water, and took a bath. Survill, Samford, Weitz, Frey, Haesausller, and I are in this tent.

Thursday, April 13, 1944

This morning we worked on garbage pits. It's a job diggin in this damn coral rock. We made four of them. Then this afternoon we started a well but got about 5 16 feet and hit solid coral rock. Played volleyball tonite.

Friday, April 14, 1944

Worked on the well this morning. Used a trip hammer to go through the coral rock. Just layed around this afternoon. Played volleyball tonite. Captain Kramer has left us to go back to Oahu. It was supposed to be a nervous breakdown. But we all think it's because he and Capt. Demo don't get along at all. Ray Blomker came over on an L.S.T. from Makin where he was in the hospital recovering from a concussion. Tomorrow 2 platoons from "K" Co. and 1 from L. Co. are going out on an L.C.O. to take over a few of the small islands in the Marshalls. I guess they want to clean up the islands over there.

Saturday, April 15, 1944

Well I was on tech duty today. The well should be done in a couple of days. Went to a movie tonite. Had a practice air raid tonite.

Sunday, April 16, 1944

Read this morning and then just loafed around all day. Just wrote a couple of letters tonite.

Monday, April 17, 1944
Today Frey and I went up to the old Jap Barracks and ripped off lumber and made a table for our tent. Now we have something to write on anyway. We played volleyball tonite.

Tuesday, April 18, 1944
Today we went out and scraped up some more lumber and built us a bench (4-sided) to go around the table. Played volleyball. Had a movie tonite, Bob Hope in "Let's Face It." Damn good musical.

Wednesday, April 19, 1944
Well today we finished digging our Air Raid shelter and started putting a couple logs over it. 2 platoons from "L" Co. and 2 from "M" Co. went out to mop up Japs on 4 islands 25 miles from here. They returned because they needed machine guns. They're going out tomorrow again.

(While we were fighting the Japanese here, we were aware that shortly after Pearl Harbor, until the end of the war, 1942 to 1945, Japanese-Americans at home were being rounded up and placed in internment camps out of fear that their loyalty would remain with Japan and not with the US. The first of the camps was Manzanar, but eventually there were at least nine others. It disrupted the lives of about 120,000 Japanese-American citizens, and in retrospect was a terrible violation of their civil rights. Canada, Mexico, and

Manzanar

other countries also had such internment camps, designed to contain and monitor the Japanese.)

Thursday, April 20, 1944

Well the reconnaissance outfit went today and should be back in 6 days or so. Got some mail today. It's slow as hell getting here. Finished the 1st layer of logs on our shelter. Played volleyball. Went to a movie. Played cards tonite.

Friday, April 21, 1944

Well today we really had a racket. We had all day off. Just layed around and read. Got a letter from Daphne about selling the car. Played volleyball tonite. We have Coast Guard on this island now too. Now tomorrow Cannon Co. from the 111th Inf. is coming here. They were on Kwajalein. The Coast Guard has 155mm guns; the cannon co. has 75mm Howitzers.

Saturday, April 22, 1944

Well I was a G-man today. G stands for garbage man. What a stinkin' detail. It's not so hard but it's hot and stinks. This afternoon we had off so we cleaned up our equipment. Played volleyball tonite. We were supposed to have a movie but someone fucked up the sound system.

Sunday, April 23, 1944

Well I had tech duty today. I had it in the morning and then Mclain took it in the afternoon. The recon, group comes back tomorrow. We played some cards tonite. I won a couple of bucks. Then we played solitaire but I didn't do so hot in that.

Monday, April 24, 1944

Well today we didn't do much, just a few details. The recon, group went up to an island and buried 167 Japs. They said that they had committed Hari Kari. They put a gun in their mouth and pull the trigger. That's about all except they got some souvenirs and some pictures.

Tuesday, April 25, 1944

Well today "I" Co. got back. They took an island between Eniwetok and Ponuqe and killed 18 Japs. It's the furthest island in the Marshalls. They got a lot of "J" stuff. Played volleyball tonite. They got a short- wave radio up at Bn. Hq. and they put it on every nite.

Wednesday, April 26, 1944
Went on a lumber detail and got wood to bum garbage with – 3 loads in a 2 14 ton truck. There's enough wood now to build a house. Played volleyball tonite. We haven't had a P.X. order for 3 weeks now. Everyone goes on these patrols.

Thursday, April 27, 1944
Another patrol goes out tomorrow. And then there's one on Saturday, Sunday, and Monday too. Tex is going tomorrow. Worked on the old G-man detail today. Played some volleyball tonite. Went up to Bn. Hq. and listened to the music and news from the States. Then tuned in on Tokyo and listened to "Tokyo Rose." What a dumb broad. She makes the news so bad that no one believes it, and instead of breaking down our morale, she builds it up 'cause the last half hour is just a solid swing session. She comes on with "Hello all you boneheads in the S.W.P. or the C.P.S. area" and makes a few cracks, but if she could hear the cracks that go back at her, she'd shut up fast.

Friday, April 28, 1944
Another patrol went out today. They didn't run into anything. I was G-man again today. That isn't such a bad job. Played volleyball tonite. We were supposed to get our first P.X. order in three weeks. Maybe tomorrow.

Saturday, April 29, 1944
Well we got our P.X. order today. Beer and Coke and it was really good. "K." Co. got back. They got a couple "J"s and one prisoner. "L" Co. got a couple and a prisoner too. We went out and got lumber today for the incinerator. Played volleyball tonite. Today Daphne (my sister) got married.

Sunday, April 30, 1944
Layed around and read most of the day today. We saw a good show tonite, the first one in quite a while. Our generator was broken and just got fixed. Played a little cards. More patrols go out to the small islands. I guess they want to clean the Japs out of these small islands first.

Monday, May 1, 1944
Well my recorder came through today. We got her working and it's going pretty good now. I had tech duty today. The patrol today got three Japs. They were up in trees, on the same island where we buried 169 of them the

other day. O'Neill came over today from Kwajalein Island. He's looking good. We had to swim 100 yds, with clothes on today, and that's no picnic.

Tuesday, May 2, 1944
Well we got paid today. I got the huge total of $17.25, but I have a $30.00 allotment going home each month to slap away in the bank. Went to the show tonite. It was some Russian Film. Played some volleyball and listened to the recorder.

Wednesday, May 3, 1944
What a delightful day. I had K.P. and man that really whacks you out. I wasn't worth two shits on a barnyard fence when I got through. Played cards tonite.

Thursday, May 4, 1944
Well today I had off, so I layed around and did some reading. We saw a damn fine movie tonite "Madame Curie." It's a first run feature. "I" Co. got a recorder from the Jap island they took, and it's set up, so we listen to records before the show now. A big convoy came through the south pass today – Cruisers, heavy and light, 4 aircraft carriers, destroyers – a really big one. They hit Truk last weekend.

Friday, May 5, 1944
Had another day off, so I did some more reading. Played volleyball and wrote a couple letters. Went swimming but some kind of animal got on Survill's and my arm and stung the hell out of it. It raised red blisters but they went away. (This was most likely a Jelly fish and it happened more than once.)

Saturday, May 6, 1944
Well today we loaded lumber again, 3 loads on a 2 !4 ton truck, so that was no breeze. This afternoon we just layed around and read and wrote a couple letters. Went swimming and that's about all. The task force is still in the lagoon.

Sunday, May 7, 1944
Went to church this morning. Pretty good sermon. Worked on the vic this morning. Got it slowed up so it sounds a lot better. Went swimming. Had a show tonite, "The Fallen Sparrow." It's really a hell of a good picture. We're getting all sorts of rumors – maybe to the Carolines when they're hit,

maybe to Australia and then to Burma, India, or China. Or maybe back to Hawaii. No one knows for sure. Two more patrols go out next week.

Monday, May 8, 1944
Well another patrol went out today from "K" Co. They're to meet another platoon and get some Japs on some island near here. Went swimming. It's really nice swimming here. Except the coral will cut the hell out of your feet so we wear shoes.

Tuesday, May 9, 1944
Had tech duty today. Some sailors came ashore from the Naval. Task Force in the Lagoon. They were just back from the Marianas and Truk. We were just bull shittin with them when we had an accident in "K" Co. A guy handed a sailor a hand grenade. The powder was supposed to be out of it. It wasn't. It blew off the sailor's hand and very seriously hurt the soldier.

Had a good show tonite, "Whistling in Brooklyn." Got some mail from Dickey.

Wednesday, May 10, 1944
Today we really did plenty of nothing. Read most of the day. Tonite went up to Bn. and listened to the radio. Came back, did some bullshittin, and hit the old fart sack.

Thursday, May 1 1, 1944
Well today was an odiferous job. I was on G-man. We work like hell for a couple hours in the morning and then the rest of the day is off. Wrote a couple letters. Had a movie tonite. Another carrier came in today.

Friday, May 12, 1944
Well today we loafed around in the morning reading and such. This afternoon we went out on lumber detail and got some wood. The naval task force pulled out today. There were 8 destroyers, 5 cruisers, 4 aircraft carriers. The big one was the "hornet."

Saturday, May 13, 1944
This morning we had wood detail most of the morning. Then we had the afternoon off. We had a good show tonite. I got some mail. The rumors are starting to fly.

Sunday, May 14, 1944
Went to church today. Then swam and did some reading. Had another show today. We had a flare demonstration showing parachute, cluster, and mortar flares.

Monday, May 15, 1944
Went on lumber detail this morning. Worked cleaning out some of the jungle this afternoon. Did some reading and writing. Air Activity around here is almost entirely B- 24s.

Tuesday, May 16, 1944
Walked around the island as I didn't have anything else to do in the morning. Worked cleaning up the island. Had a show tonite. Went swimming. It's really nice but that coral will cut the hell out of you if you just touch it.

Wednesday, May 17, 1944
Had tech duty today. Wasn't much work to that. Played volleyball tonite. Rumors are getting' thick. Listened to the short – wave radio tonite. Air Activity is almost entirely B-24s.

Thursday, May 18, 1944
This morning we went out to get drift-wood for the fires. Did that almost all morning. In the afternoon we worked cleaning out some of the jungle on the island. Had a show tonite.

Friday, May 19, 1944
There ain't no day today. They decided to observe the international date line, so we skipped from Thurs. to Sat.

Saturday, May 20, 1944
Had G-man today. Worked in the morning, but just shoveled out the pits in the afternoon. Played volleyball tonite. Made Molotov cocktails, only we use them for light instead of knocking out tanks. They're made of a beer bottle filled half with diesel oil and half white gas.

They're all wrecked.

Sunday, May 21, 1944
Went to church this morning. Then did some laundry. Went swimming and read this afternoon. Had a damn fine movie tonite. Some bastard clipped 10 smackaroos out of my locker box. That is a dirty trick. Definitely.

Monday, May 22, 1944

This morning we went on the usual wood detail. In the afternoon, we worked on the island but it rained so we couldn't do much. Did some reading. Went to sleep about 8:15 and at 9:00 we had an air raid. Man I couldn't find anything. All my pants were in the laundry bag so I couldn't find them. Then I couldn't find my helmet. It was outside filling up with rainwater. Well, when I did find it and put it on, I hadn't gotten all the water out so I got a free bath. Then I finally got to the hole. Interceptors (ours) must have driven the J's away.

Tuesday, May 23, 1944

Well today it really rained out. The most rain we've had since we hit the islands. It rained steady so we didn't work all day. We filled 4 55 gal. drums with water. Had a show tonite. Had a P.X. order today.

Wednesday, May 24, 1944

Went out this morning on the usual wood detail. Read the rest of the morning. Worked cleaning out the island but it started to rain like hell so we knocked off for the day. Shot the shit and did some reading tonite. Rumors are starting to fly as to where we'll move.

Thursday, May 25, 1944

Had G-man today. That's a pretty good job. You work in the morning and then have the afternoon off. Had a show tonite. It was pretty fair. Read and wrote a couple of letters.

Friday, May 26, 1944

Had tech duty today. So I wrote a letter or so and did some reading. Tonite we had a compulsory training film which is strictly s-h-i-t. The offensive in Italy is going well. Air Activity is strictly B-24s.

(My tent was a tent for music. Let me explain this. I've loved music all my life and I wrote to my dad asking him to find me a little wind-up recorder that I could use overseas. He found one and sent it to me and I became a sort of a music DJ. This little instrument played V- discs at the ancient rate of 33 rpms a minute. But it worked, and that's what I wanted. I carried it with me through the Gilbert Island and the Marshall Island campaigns. (I became one popular guy)

44

Saturday, May 27, 1944
Went out on the usual wood detail for most of the morning and then layed around till noon. Worked cleaning up the island in the afternoon. Had a show tonite but it was so lousy that half the guys didn't go.

Sunday, May 28, 1944
Went to church. Then pitched baseball, played volleyball, and to top it off we went swimming for about an hour and a half. After that I decided I'd had enough exercise. Had a show tonite. Darn good at that.

Monday, May 29, 1944
Went out on wood detail this morning. This afternoon we didn't do anything, just read, layed around, and knocked out a couple of letters.

Tuesday, May 30, 1944
Had a memorial service at the rectory. It was really a very nice ceremony. They had all the natives there. Then we had the rest of the day off. Had a really 1st rate movie, "The Miracle of Morgan's Creek". It was good.

Wednesday, May 31, 1944
Had wood detail as usual, then didn't do anything the rest of the day. Rumors are that 3 more patrols are going out. Did some reading and listened to the "vic" tonite.

Thursday, June 1, 1944
Today we burned trash and junk that was collected. Used gas and diesel oil. Went and did the same in the afternoon. Had a good movie tonite. This lagoon is really gettin busy. There are a lot of ships out there but most of them congregate around Kwajalein.

Friday, June 2, 1944
Went on wood detail today then came back and wrote some letters. Just monkeyed around this afternoon. Tonite 10 L.C.I.s left the lagoon and I don't imagine they're just going for the ride.

Saturday, June 3, 1944
Had tech duty today. Finished up the big work on the ad station. We were supposed to have a movie but something fucked up. Listened to the radio tonite. Air Activity is strictly B-24s.

Sunday, June 4, 1944

This morning 1 did some washing. My bed and mattress cover. We got paid yesterday. I got 5 bucks too much and so did a lot of the other guys in the outfit. Played volleyball this afternoon and then went swimming. No show. The projector's still on the fritz.

Monday, June 5, 1944

Worked on the aid station. We finished that up in the morning. Didn't do anything in the afternoon. Set up a horseshoe court. Had a show tonite. When we came back we saw Makin (our dog) and he was plenty sick. It looked like he was poisoned so we gave him salt water to vomit and a shot of morphine. He is really sick. There's nothin else to do for him.

Tuesday, June 6, 1944

Today we went out for wood. But it rained. Then all day long a huge convoy started coming in. Mostly L.S.T.s with supplies on. Then there were mine sweepers, mine layers. But it was mostly a supply convoy. A small number of destroyers also. Had a movie tonite, pretty fair.

Makin died. Allies captured Rome and invaded Europe.

(We knew what was going on in Europe via the radio. On September 3, 1943, the US invaded Italy and on June 5, 1943, the Allies took Rome. That was followed, a day later, on June 6, 1944, with D-Day, the Allied landing and invasion of Normandy. The war in Europe was heating up and was headed in a new direction.

In the Pacific, the turning points came earlier, but the intense fighting continued. Although the Doolittle Raid on Tokyo preceded this, and was a morale booster, the first major turning point came on June 4, 5, and 6 of 1942, at Midway. There the Japanese lost 4 aircraft carriers and all of their experienced pilots. They never recovered. The second turning point occurred at Guadalcanal in the southwest Pacific. The battle began on August 7, 1942, and continued into the following year. Unlike Midway, which was a sea battle, this was a land battle, initiated and led by the Marines and finished off by the 25th Infantry Division from Hawaii.)

Wednesday, June 7, 1944

More ships came in today but they were more troop ships. Had G-man again today. Played volleyball. I guess that the convoy will go to the Mariannas. It sure has a lot of ships in it. L.C.I.s are right off our island.

Thursday, June 8, 1944

Man today the troop ships really came in. There must have been fifty of them, all other kinds of war and supply craft. We watched them all day. Played volleyball tonite. Rumors are this convoy will hit Guam. I think they will too. It's the next logical spot.

Friday, June 9, 1944

Had wood detail. Filled up 3 loads on a 2 16 ton truck. Then watched about 20 more troop ships come in. This lagoon is solid with every kind of ship. Worked on the island jungle today. L.S.T. and L.C.I.s pulled out about 4:30pm so maybe the convoy headed out. Played some horseshoes and cards tonite.

Saturday, June 10, 1944

Went out on wood detail this morning. Some more of the ships pulled out today. They pull out slowly, only a few at a time. Played horseshoes and some guys off a ship in the lagoon put on a show for us. Read tonite and listened to the radio.

Sunday, June 11, 1944
Well today I had tech duty, not much doing. A pretty big part of the convoy pulled out today. I guess that they'll be hitting something soon. No movie cause the projector's broken. Survill went to Kwajalein to work.

Monday, June 12, 1944
Had K.P. today. Man that's a ball breakin job. The whole rest of the convoy pulled out. Part in the morning and part at night. A U.S. task (carrier) force started to blast the Marianas. But mostly Guam, Saipan, Tinian, and Rota. Ray moved into our tent today, cause we had more room.

Tuesday, June 13, 1944
Went out on wood detail this morning. Got a couple loads. Put up the Captain's tent today. He wanted it changed for some reason. Had a show tonite. It was dam good. Listened to some records and shot the shit.

Wednesday, June 14, 1944
This morning we got some wood and monkeyed around the rest of the morning. This afternoon we worked on the volleyball court. They're still shelling the Marianas. Played volleyball tonite.

Thursday, June 15, 1944
Had G-man today. So we didn't do anything after we'd finished our work. Went swimming down at the dock. Then tonite we had a show. Listened to the vic and shot the shit. Still hitting the Marianas. Figure they should land soon. Saw the new P-61 nite fighter today. Newest thing out. It's supposed to do up to 430 and more. It's got twin fuselage.

Friday, June 16, 1944
Hauled wood and also sand for the volley ball court. Pitched some horseshoes. B-29s based in China bombed Japan proper today in force. They landed on Saipan and the resistance is strong. We beat the officers tonite.

Saturday, June 17, 1944
The patrol came back. They got some more Japs. They were out for 21 days and some of them are still out. The lagoon has quite a few ships left. We played some volleyball and went swimming. Had a show tonite.

48

Sunday, June 18, 1944
Had off today. Played volleyball and went swimming in the afternoon. Saw a couple nurses drive by. They have about 40 at Kwajalein. Survill said that it's easy as hell to get a ride in a plane over there. Had another show tonite.

Monday, June 19, 1944
Had tech duty today. We lost our first volleyball league game to "M" Co. Went swimming as per usual. We had another show tonite. I guess they're making up for the ones we missed. More patrols go out Wednesday. Rumors are now that we'll possibly stay here till October. But it's still in the planning stage. Shot the shit tonite. Listened to the vic. Wrote letters.

Tuesday, June 20, 1944
Hauled wood this morning. Made a washstand this afternoon. Had a show tonite. Listened to the radio and "vic" tonite.

Wednesday, June 21, 1944
Hauled some coral rock this morning. Played league volleyball and went swimming this afternoon. Mail is getting better now. Listened to the news. A big naval battle is imminent between the Japs and the U.S. It will probably be between the Philippines and Marianas.

Thursday, June 22, 1944
Had G-man today, so after the work I read and fooled around up there for a while. There's not much to do in the afternoons. Had a show tonite. It wasn't so hot. The naval battle may be underway now. Had an alert tonite. Must have driven them off.

Friday, June 23, 1944
Didn't do anything this morning. Frank H Jeric. Got a letter from him. He cracked when he went in on the Gilberts. Played volleyball. We won. Went swimming. Listened to the news and the vic tonite. Got some more records from Kwajalein. Had an alert tonite.

Saturday, June 24, 1944
Boy we did plenty of nothing today. I guess it's because we start a training schedule soon. The Naval battle didn't come off as planned, but the J's did lose 14 ships and 620 planes in the Marianas campaign so-far. Had a good show tonite.

Sunday, June 25, 1944
Had off today. We played volleyball this afternoon. Our team is really pulling into shape pretty good. We went swimming again today. Had another good show, read, and listened to the vic.

Monday, June 26, 1944
Today we didn't do anything except exercise. We whipped "K". Co and we really worked to do it. Went swimming tonite. Knocked out a couple letters and listened to the vic.

Tuesday, June 27, 1944
Had tech duty but quit at noon. Took the 1400 boat to Kwajalein. That place is really built, 3 airstrips. They have B-24s, B-25s, Corsairs, A-24s. Everything. Saw some nurses, the first in one hell of a long time. It's about an hour's ride there in a Higgens boat. Those J. pillboxes were really built. They even had twin 5- inch guns built in that had previously been captured at Singapore. Not a tree on the whole island. Went to a show.

Wednesday, June 28, 1944
Came back to Carlos about noon. Worked cleaning up the island again today. Got cold beer for a change tonite. Listened to the news and vic. Then we all had a big argument about everything from soup to nuts.

Thursday, June 29, 1944
Had g-man today. So we did our work and then were through for the day. Had a good show tonite. The casualties from Saipan were buried here. I hear it's plenty rough over there.

Friday, June 30, 1944
Monkeyed around this morning. Played league volleyball and won. Went swimming and got stung by some jellyfish or octopus, anyhow it stung like hell. But it only lasted about two hours. We listened to the vic.

Saturday, July 1, 1944
Had gas-mask drill and inspection. Man those masks are stinkers in this heat. Unloaded floors from an L.S.T. onto the truck and hauled it to the Co. area. Had a good show tonite. Tomorrow we have to work T. S.

Sunday, July 2, 1944

Well today we really worked. We put up floors for the whole darn company. Man that was really a job and a half. Had a good show tonite. Air Activity here is still strictly B-24s although they do have a few P-38's on Kwajalein.

Monday, July 3, 1944

Today we worked all day cleaning up our equipment. Man I had a dust bowl in all my stuff. Had gas mask drill today. Wrote letters and listened to the vic.

Tuesday, July 4, 1944

Has a special program in observance of Independence Day. It was pretty good. Played some cards today. Played volleyball and also had a show. Had fresh meat twice today (a record).

Wednesday, July 5, 1944

I guess the fighting on Saipan is really tough. About 20,000 Japs there but we hold 7/8 ths of the island. Got some printing and developing stuff today. Played volleyball. Wrote some letters.

Thursday, July 6, 1944

Had a big inspection today by some colonel. We really sweated it out for 2 hours in the sun, and man that's hot. We were all o.k. after that. Had a couple lectures. I was on tech duty. Had a good show tonite.

Friday, July 7, 1944

Played another league volleyball game. We had a lecture and then kept working on the island. They're starting to smooth and widen the road. Wrote letters tonite.

Saturday, July 8, 1944

Worked on the printing and developing tonite. We should be able to get a lot of good prints. B29s bombed Japan proper. We hold 9/10ths of Saipan now. I heard that a lot of our B-24s from Kwajalein have moved up in the Marianas. Listened to the vic.

Sunday, July 9, 1944

Well we had to work a while today because Gen. Richardson is coming here to inspect. Fixed myself up a little light. Had a good show tonite. Guess a lot of the B-24s are moving to Saipan. Anyhow that's the rumor.

Monday, July 10, 1944

Had G-man today. Man that's a hot job. But we got it over with. Saipan is almost completed. At least the radio says so. We play a volleyball league game today. Maybe we can win.

Tuesday, July 11, 1944

Had off today. Had a couple lectures. Wrote letters. The main thing on the recorder broke but it might be able to be fixed.

Wednesday, July 12, 1944

Had K.P. today. Man that's a lousy job. I guess it's just a necessary job. Won our volleyball league game today. We fixed the recorder so it works o.k.

Thursday, July 13, 1944

Had tech duty today. Went up to the native village this afternoon. Had a dam good show tonite. That goofy recorder broke again. That spring steel is really rough stuff to work with.

Friday, July 14, 1944

Had off this morning. Played volleyball this afternoon. We won but we really worked for it. More B-24s are moving up to the Mariana's base. A small convoy came in today.

Saturday, July 15, 1944

Had another lay-out inspection today. Then we just monkeyed around the rest of the day. Had a show but I worked on some negatives I wanted printed up. Got quite a few done. Played some crap.

Sunday, July 16, 1944

Did washing today. We're mostly doing our own now cause the laundry is busy with the casualties brought in from the Marianas campaign. Had a volleyball game today. Had a good show.

Monday, July 17, 1944

Did some work in the morning. Played volleyball with "K" Co. today and whipped em. Listened to the news and music. Also did a little printing and developing. There are 13 B-26s here now.

Tuesday, July 18, 1944
Had to clean up all our stuff today cause there's an inspection tomorrow. We had a good show tonite. Came back to the tent and bullshitted.

Wednesday, July 19, 1944
Had an inspection today, but Tex and I were on G-man. Went down to the native village most of the day. Helped them catch fish. They catch them just like they're rounding up cattle. Won our volley-ball game today.

(The members of the village – men, women, and children – formed a half circle around the shore. Then they beat the water with spears to drive the fish toward the shore where they could spear them. They generously gave a spear loaded with fish to me.)

Thursday, July 20, 1944
Well today it rained like hell all day so we couldn't work. Had a good show tonite. Most of the B-24s have moved up to Saipan now and a bit of the activity has stopped. Another convoy pulled through the south pass today.

Friday, July 21, 1944
Today we didn't do much. I had tech duty. It rained harder'n hell today. Caught 200 gals, of water. Ship convoys are really coming in and going out now. Guam was invaded today. Won our volleyball game.

Saturday, July 22, 1944
Today we had off. Col. Kemp is leaving the Bn. to take over the regt, back at Oahu. We didn't have a show tonite. I guess we only get 3 a week now. More convoys are coming in today.

Sunday, July 23, 1944
Today we played horseshoes and did some washing. More ships keep coming in to stop off before the Marianas. Had a show tonite.

Monday, July 24, 1944
Well the Major's getting on the ball. We have every Mon., Wed., Fri., and Sat. afternoon off. I suppose it's because the hot season is starting now. The breeze has almost stopped.

Tuesday, July 25, 1944
We worked this morning. Then this afternoon we went to Kwajalein and saw a U.S.O. show. It was Bob Hope, Jerry Colona, Francis Longford, and Pat Thomas. Man it was really terrific. I guess we've been on these rocks too long. Those white women, well they were really solid. We had a show tonite and beer. It was a real day. Went over on an L.C.T.

(All the kids went swimming, but the high point of the day was always the men's 50 or 60 yard foot race. The "track" was simply a cinder road that ran at the edge of the cliff heading down to the lake. It was a memorable race. One year, my father lost his footing and fell, palms down to cushion the shock, and hurt his hands. Everyone was concerned because my Dad's hands were important--he was a great piano man. Matter of fact he could play a number of instruments – the piano, organ, flute, trombone, and clarinet. He was in the Navy in WWI and played clarinet in the Navy band in Cleveland. He always referred to himself as a "sliver sucker" during WWI. The clambake was marvelous--family, fun, too much sunbathing, and much more. I remember this event with some nostalgia.)

Wednesday, July 26, 1944
Well today we played our second last league volleyball game. We won so we'll have to play "M" Co. for the championship. Just bullshitted and wrote letters. They brought some wounded Japs to the island hospital. "I" Co. guys are taking them back to Oahu.

Thursday, July 27, 1944
Ship convoys are still coming in. A few carriers. They took Jap prisoners back on a carrier. The 1st Bn. is back there. They went back on an aircraft carrier.

(The rest of this entry as well as the one for July 28 are missing.)

Saturday, July 29, 1944
Had tech duty today. Lost the first game in the playoffs with "M" Co. We play them again tomorrow. Celebrated Lott's birthday.

We got together 100 cans of beer. Man what a riot. I guess that's what we all needed, a good drunk. Anyhow it was a lot of fun.

Sunday, July 30, 1944
We had off this morning. We won our game with "M" Co today so the playoff is Tues. Had a damn good show tonite. Had a celebration cause we won. Went swimming.

Monday, July 31, 1944
Had G-man today. Had the bulldozer down there and really did a lot of work with it. Started to play baseball but were rained out. Got paid tonite. Air Activity has slowed down quite a bit.

Tuesday, August 1, 1944
Won the championship in volleyball today. We beat "M" Co. It was really a rugged game. Went swimming. Played some cards. Had a good show. Three L.C.Ls took some of the natives off the island today.

Wednesday, August 2, 1944
Today we didn't do much of anything. Had some training and lectures. No mail. It's slowed up a lot. A small convoy came in today. There are a few P-38s flying around now.

Thursday, August 3, 1944
This morning we had training. This afternoon went to the motor pool and worked on Ray's jeep. He's putting on a protective coat of paint. Had a good show tonite.

Friday, August 4, 1944
Today we didn't do anything. Capt. Demo took off for Kwajalein so we took the day off. Played a few cards tonite. It was purely a social game.

Saturday, August 4, 1944
Played our 1st league baseball game. We won. A fair- sized convoy left for the Marianas. P-38s were flying around. Had a good show tonite.

Sunday, August 6, 1944
Had tech duty today. Played baseball in the afternoon. We won. Had a good show tonite. A lot of the airplanes have moved up to the Marianas.

Monday, August 7, 1944
Well today we started work again with the nose to the grindstone. But I had to go to the dentist in the afternoon. Knocked out some letters.

Tuesday, August 8, 1944
Well we got all ready for inspection today. Then a U.S.O. show came to Kwajalein so they called it off. Had a good show tonite.

Wednesday, August 9, 1944
Had some lectures today in the morning. Did my laundry this afternoon. Almost all of Guam has been taken now.

Thursday, August 10, 1944
Had an alert (ground) today. But was a practice one. Had a pretty fair movie tonite. I guess they'll be running a new movie next time.

Friday, August 11, 1944
Had work to do this morning. Then this afternoon we played ball. We lost to Hq. Co. Knocked out a couple letters tonite. Ship convoys are slowing down.

Saturday August 12, 1944
Had G-man today. We just dumped and covered it over. Had to shovel out the pits. Burned some jungle and some ruined landing barges. We used flame thrower fluid to burn them and that stuff really works.

Sunday, August 13, 1944
Well today we had off so we washed clothes and then played baseball in the afternoon. Had a good show tonite, in the new theater area. It's really a nice set-up over at the show.

Monday, August 14, 1944
Had a couple lectures this morning. Got our equipment ready for tomorrow's inspection. Mail is slower than hell lately. I suppose planes are being used to take supplies to the Marianas.

Tuesday, August 15, 1944
Had a couple lectures this morning. Went to the native village this afternoon. Rumors are we move to Kwajalein next week, just Hq. Co. Had a good show tonite. Got some more pictures today.

Wednesday, August 16, 1944
Did some work in the morning. This afternoon we had off. Played some cards. I guess we move to Kwajalein next week some time. Most of the 24s have moved up to the Marianas. Made another landing in France (southern).

Thursday, August 17, 1944
Painted signs this morning at the pits. Then went to the village. Pulled down the supply tent today. Had a show tonite. It wasn't so hot.

Friday, August 18, 1944
Well today we started pulling down our stuff to move. We just got set up, then off we go. I guess we leave next Thurs. Played some cards today. About 30 transports headed for the Marianas today.

Saturday, August 19, 1944
Played a little horseshoes this morning. Went shell hunting. Played baseball this afternoon. Had a show tonite. For a while I thought we'd get rained out, but it cleared up all right.

Sunday, August 20, 1944
Did some washing today and played baseball in the afternoon Had a show tonite. Wrote some letters. Task force 58 is supposed to come in.

Monday, August 21, 1944
Started packing this morning to move. Played baseball this afternoon. We won. Wrote a couple letters and listened to the radio.

Tuesday, August 22, 1944
Well today we started packing up the equipment to move to Kwajalein. We had to pull down all our stuff. Had a show tonite.

Wed, August 23, 1944
Today we pulled down all the wooden stuff and played baseball this afternoon. Then went back and played some cards tonite.

Thursday, August 24, 1944
Today we really worked. All in all we handled all the platoon's equipment 6 complete times. We loaded it on an SM and 5 other guys and I came on

advance detail to get the stuff here. We really worked. Drove the landing craft right up over the reef. After the work we took off for the show.

Friday, August 25, 1944
Today we unloaded more landing craft and set up our tents and the aid¬ station. This joint is plenty hot. Planes – B-24, P-38, C-54 – everything is about 50 feet from our area. What a racket. Then to top it off they had 90 mm gun practice. Went to the show.

Saturday, August 26, 1944
We worked on the area and started fixing up our tents. The showers are even working. Had A.A. practice. They got three sleeves. Went to the 87th Bomb Sqd. theater.

Sunday, August 27, 1944
I thought we'd be working but everybody went wild so we had it off. All odd jobs around. Went to a show at the Richardson Theater. The Liberators are going out to hit Truk tomorrow.

Monday, August 28, 1944
Worked lining up the tents today. It's hotter'n hell here now, with the temp hitting 140 and over. The Liberators took off today, about 30 of them. They were really loaded down. They're not due back till tomorrow night. They'll stop at Eniwetok.

Tuesday, August 29, 1944
Was down the dump looking for stuff I could use in the tent. We'll use bomb racks for the chairs. They work good. Went to the show tonite. The B-24s pulled out tonite. Paris was captured.

Wednesday, August 30, 1944
Worked on the tents today. Was a little cooler tonite. Got a letter from Daphne. She's having a baby. Went to the show tonite. These Corsairs are really nice. 20 of them flew over in formation today.

Friday, August 31, 1944
Leveled off the Co. street today. There was a heavy cruiser in today. Planes – B-24, B-25, P-38, Corsair, A-24, C-54, C-47, viper cubs. Had a stage show up at Richardson Theater. Good music. We have electricity in our tent now.

Friday, September 1, 1944
Today we worked on dugouts and I went down to the dump to pick up some stuff we could use. The old Jap tanks are really getting beat up. Had a stage show, a Marine dance band, and other variety stuff.

Saturday, September 2, 1944
The 24s went out to hit Truk today. It takes about 30 hours till they come back. I had tech duty today. Went to the show tonite.

Sunday, September 3, 1944
Today we finished fixing up the tent. Then got word that Jack Benny's stage show was here. He had Carole Landis, Martha Tilton, Larry Adler, and June Brunner. It was really a fine show. Even better than Hope's.

Monday, September 4, 1944
Today we loafed and I mean loafed. It was just too damn hot to do anything. Working or lying around you really sweated. Went to the Rich. Theater tonite.

Tuesday, September 5, 1944
This morning we really hit the old shovels. Dug 6 emplacements and put sandbags around them. Then this afternoon we went to the P.X. Went to the show again tonite. Had an air raid alert at 1 o'clock in the morning.

Wednesday, September 6, 1944
We went down to a wrecked B-24 and got some stuff off it. One thing was a small electric fan. There are 112 corsairs in today. About 60 took off, each with a 500lb bomb on it. Then following them about 25 or 30 Libs took off to hit Truk. Had a real wind storm tonite, with buckets of rain also. Read a book or so today.

Thursday, September 7, 1944
This morning we worked around the area. Then this afternoon went down to the wrecked Liberator to get some stuff, switches, etc. Went to the show tonite. They picked up a couple Jap prisoners on a raft off Wojie. So they're in the clink down here now.

Friday, September 8, 1944
Well today we got our stuff cleaned up for inspection. Then we played a little crap this afternoon. Got a few bucks. This field is really busy – everything from soup to nuts using it. Went to the show tonite.

Saturday, September 9, 1944
Had inspection today, which was a royal pain in the ass. Went down and played ball today. The 24s test flighted today so they'll be going out tomorrow. Had tech duty tonite.

Sunday, September 10, 1944
Today was off. Went down and watched a ball game. Frey got his radio back so we all hung around the tent and listened to that tonite. The 24s went out today.

Monday, September 11, 1944
Today a whole slew of Marines landed, about 700, or so the rumor goes. Didn't do much today. Had Ord. inspection. Went to the show tonite. It was really good. Listened to the radio. The 24s came back tonite.

Tuesday, September 12, 1944
Well today we didn't do much of anything. Rumors are flying that we're moving soon. I think so too. Played some crap today. Went to the show tonite.

Wednesday, September 13, 1944
Had tech duty today. The 24s bombed up today so they'll be going after Truk tomorrow. Played some cards tonite.

Thursday, September 14, 1944
Today the B24s went out. Survill and I were in a 24 when she was warming up. That plane's got more dials than anything. It makes a car look like a scooter. They had 10 500lb bombs. Stayed at the tent and listened to the radio.

Friday, September 15, 1944
The B24s came back today. All of the Assault troops hit Halmahera and Palau today. I guess we're going back to Oahu. Anyhow that's what the rumors give out. The new corsairs will be coming in soon.

Saturday, September 16, 1944
Worked around today, in fact K.P. So that tells the work for the day. Went to the show tonite.

Sunday, September 17, 1944

Had off today. Went out hunting shells. When the tide is out there's so much shrapnel left it's like walking on corrugated iron instead of coral. Went to the show tonite.

Monday, September 18, 1944

Today was so damn hot you could hardly keep standing up. We have a new island C.O. His name is Gen. Ross. Went to the show tonite. It seems like there are more planes now than ever around the strip.

Tuesday, September 19, 1944

Today was another scorcher. The thermo must read 130 at least. Gen Ross came around today. We didn't even work it was so hot. Went to the show tonite.

Wednesday, September 20, 1944

Today went out and hunted shells almost all day. It was really hot. The 24s bombed up today so they'll be going out soon. Went to the show tonite.

Thursday, September 21, 1944

Didn't work today. It was so hot. Went around the island. A B-17 (Fortress) landed today from China, also a B25. We've got about everything in the book on the strip now. Went to the show.

Friday, September 22, 1944

Today I worked all day on a coconut ashtray. Wonderful!!!! Went to the show tonite.

Saturday, September 23, 1944

We layed around today. Didn't work. This heat is really getting terrific. Went to the show tonite. Went around the strip looking at the planes and in general loafing.

Sunday, September 24, 1944

Today in the morning I made a bracelet from shells. Played handball this afternoon. Went to the show tonite. A B-24 landed today with a flat tire, the most beautiful piece of flying I've seen yet.

Monday, September 25, 1944

Had tech, duty today. It really rained. Went to the show tonite. We just got to bed and they had a ground alert so we were up half the night.

Tuesday, September 26, 1944
Had work detail this morning but this afternoon we had off. Went to the P/X and just fooled around. A B-17 came in today. It's a low looking plane. Went to the show tonite.

Wednesday, September 27, 1944
Didn't do anything today. We have the new Gen. Ross and so we have to parade for him tomorrow. Over at the boat pool. Went to the show tonite.

Thursday, September 28, 1944
Well we paraded today, and we also got our moving orders. We packed up B-bags. And from all the rumors we're headed back to Oahu for a while. The 96 AAA. is going on the same boat. Went to the show tonite.

Friday, September 29, 1944
Well today we just layed around. Sent out B-bags today and got all the tents torn down, except a few. Played a little cards tonite. Hit the old sack cause we have work tomorrow.

Saturday, September 30, 1944
Today she rained all day but we loaded our platoon equipment on the ship. We were supposed to get on today but they changed it till tomorrow. The B 24s went out today. A group of C-54s came in.

Sunday, October 1, 1944
Got all packed up and loaded onto the ship. Went out on L.C.V.P.s and boarded her. It's a new ship, the Gen. E.T. Collins, an assault transport, and this was her first trip out. It had just come from Saipan and Guam. Had Marines on it. Didn't do much. Pulled out at 2pm.

Monday, October 2, 1944
Well the usual old ocean is in sight today. We have a D.E. escort. The ship is pretty nice, goes about 20 knots. We read and layed around and got dirty and sweaty in that damn hole we live in. Played a little cards tonite.

Tuesday, October 3, 1944
Had a practice at gen. quarters and they had fire power alright. A couple five inchers, three inchers, and a mess of 50s. Played a little cards this afternoon. Tried sleeping on deck but it never fails to rain.

Wednesday, October 4, 1944

Sighted a P.B.X. today so maybe we'll be in tomorrow. I hope. It's really hot sleeping in that hole. Read some stories. That's about all today.

Thursday, October 5, 1944

That plane yesterday was from Johnson island so we don't land till tomorrow. T.S. But we have our stuff all ready to disembark. I have a good old fashioned cold.

Friday, October 6, 1944

Sighted Hawaii today and pulled into the dock at about 9:15am. It really looks good. We got off but I was selected for unloading detail. So we just ate ice cream and coke all the rest of the day.

(We were taking about 40 Japanese prisoners back to Oahu from the Marshall Islands. We would bring them up on deck and they would be hosed down. Often Marines and soldiers would taunt them and say "When we go ashore we're going to hang you." That really frightened them. I don't think they all understood, but probably one or two did, and they probably passed it around. It wasn't really a decent thing to do, in the opinion of some of us – or in the doctrine of empathy. Unnecessarily cruel.)

Returning to Hawaii / Rest Camp

It was time for a break. After a year of campaigning in the Gilbert and Marshall Islands we went to a rest camp on Kauai, one of the Hawaiian Islands. To get from the troop ship to the LSVP, which is a small boat, a landing craft, you had to climb down a rope ladder. The ship was constantly moving from bow to stern and from side to side, that is from port to starboard. It may not sound like it , but it's probably one of the most difficult things I had to do. If you try it sometime, you may find that you have some bruises and a few broken bones. Anyway, I made it to Hawaii.

In rest camp we were based in Kalaheo. There we went to a football game. Everything was just like football in the US except for one thing – no players wore any shoes – no cleats. So they played a tough game. The Japanese, I found, ran the islands during WWII, and there is still a noticeable Japanese presence. Anyway, a Japanese girl, Betty Shimagago, came to the USO and I danced with her a few times. Her mother, who ran

the USO, invited me for dinner at their house; that was probably one of the nicest things that happened to me in the whole damn war. We took off our shoes, sat on the floor, and enjoyed her cooking – chicken Hekka. In 1990 my wife and I returned to Kauai and located Betty, who was then married. Her mother had recently died but we stayed two days spending a delightful time with Betty. She told us that I was the only soldier who had been invited to their home who had come back to visit years later. It was memorable for all of us.

More of the Diary

Saturday, October 7, 1944
Unloaded and loaded up the trucks to go up to hut city where the Bn is. Ate ice cream and coke and cake all day. Slept on the ship. We should be done tomorrow.

Sunday, October 8, 1944
Loaded up and came over to hut city through Honolulu. This hut city is a quarantine station, and it's all red dust. Played crap and dropped more dough. P.S. It was colder than a bitch tonite.

Monday, October 9, 1944
We found out today that we'll have all the rest of this week off, and then next week we go into Jungle training. So we just layed around today. Went to the P.X. That's about all. We're still in quarantine.

Tuesday, October 10, 1944
Well we're getting a new Capt. today and Captain Demo is going to the 2nd Bn. We're still in quarantine. But we can get all the beer and coke we want. Dropped some dough in a crap game. P.S. Played a little cards.

Wednesday, October 11, 1944
We got out of quarantine and we have a pass tomorrow. Went to the post theater tonite. This area we're in is all red dust and little huts, which we live in. I guess it's only for the quarantine period.

Thursday, October 12, 1944
Went out on a 24 hour pass today with Survill. Got a room in the Aula Hotel. Then went to Honolulu and Waikiki. Got some drinks and also a steak dinner at Waikiki. Then tonite we walked around and went to a show.

Friday, October 13, 1944
Got back from town today. Our new captain is Capt. Drisdall. He's a good egg from what I hear. Went to the main theater and service club today. Knocked out a couple of letters.

Saturday, October 14, 1944
Got our bags packed up today. We're to leave tomorrow for jungle training. Went to the PX and got some stuff. We leave tomorrow morning.

Sunday, October 15, 1944
Went out to jungle training. It's really a nice ride out there. Beautiful scenery, mountains, etc. It's about 40 miles from Schofield. I had tech duty today. Had a U.S.O. show with hula girls and singing. Good?!

Monday, October 16, 1944
Had tech duty today. We really worked late tonite. A lot of guys got cut up on the jungle training. I guess it's plenty tough.

Tuesday, October 17, 1944
Man I haven't been so cold as today in a long time. It rained and blew for a long time but training went on. We had bazookas, bayonets, flame throwers, dynamite. Everything. Also had a medical problem. It was really rugged. One of the fellows in Hq. Co. got hit with shrapnel from a composition "C" charge during a demonstration.

Wednesday, October 18, 1944
Went out to a village fight and while we were watching, some clown with a "Tommy" gun threw a dummy down and started spraying it with 45 caliber shells. The bullets ricocheted and hit one of the Lieuts in the arm. Had some more instruction in demolitions and hand to hand.

Thursday, October 19, 1944
Had more training today. It's really a bitch, this course. We went out tonite just looking over the little towns. Had tech, duty tonite.

Friday, October 20, 1944
Went out again today. Had a lot of hip-firing. Fired the light machine gun and the B.A.R. from the hip. Had hand to hand combat. Went out and got some beer tonite.

Saturday, October 21, 1944
Had tech duty today. We go back to Schofield tomorrow. Went out, up the road to a little joint, and bullshitted. Had some cokes.

Sunday, October 22, 1944
Came back to old Schofield today and the old joint really looked good. Took a plenty big bath, and we really needed it. Went and got my recorder and had a little music. Hit the sack early.

Monday, October 23, 1944
They have some Italian prisoners of war here so all day we were shootin' the shit with them. They were caught in Africa 2 years ago. Went to the show. Also we were alerted tonite.

Tuesday, October 24, 1944
Layed around on the old sack today. Had a layout inspection which was a pain in the old proverbial spot. The rumor is we're going to Maui. Went to the show tonite. Darn good. The mosquitoes really are wicked around here.

Wednesday, October 25, 1944
Had tech duty. This new Capt. knows his stuff, but he's strict as hell. They really have the stuff around here – light, heavy, medium tanks, lines of them, and more planes than you could count. Had a Co. party tonite.

Thursday, October 26, 1944
Today we found out we go to amphibious training Sunday, so that will be another week of the Army routine, and it's plenty stiff from all the rumors. Did some laundry today. Went down to the Post theater tonite.

Friday, October 27, 1944
Had nothing to do today so we just layed around. The rumors now are that we're not going to Maui, but some other Hawaiian island. Went to the post theater tonite.

Saturday, October 28, 1944
Had tech duty today so most of the day I was pretty busy. We had to go all through the equipment, which is a stinkeroo.

Sunday, October 29, 1944

Well we turned in our B bags today. I guess we're moving tomorrow to an island northwest of Oahu. Didn't do much tonite. We are alerted so we can't leave.

Monday, October 30, 1944

Well we got down to the ship at Pearl Harbor. That's really a plenty busy place now. We're on a brand-new assault transport, only 9 days out of the states. We passed a battlewagon. This ship is really nice, clean, and I guess it's cause we're the first troops on her. It's the U.S.S. Hendry.

Tuesday, October 31, 1944

Well we pulled up off Kauai and they loaded us in the L.C.V.P. (small boats) and we circled for 1 14 hours. What a miserable ride. Man that was really a shame, but I guess the new boat crews needed practice. We got to our area, and we're really out in the sticks.

Wednesday, November 1, 1944

We did a lot of riding today. We went to the Cos and delivered Barracks bags. "I" Co. is about 40 miles from us, "L" Co. is about 6, and "M" Co. is split up with their mortar and machine gun sections. Went up to the U.S.O. and believe it or not we actually were shootin the shit with some women. The people are really friendly. The Bn. is going to be motorized.

Thursday, November 2, 1944

Today we went down and picked up some vehicles. I'm driving a weapons carrier, a 4 ton truck. It's a bit beat up. It's all just driving though. Went to the U.S.O.

Friday, November 3, 1944

Today we greased, oiled, and changed the oil in the trucks. We're moving to the new area tomorrow. Tex, Coombs, and I went to the Hanapepe on pass. Had a fair time. It's a pretty nice town.

Saturday, November 4, 1944

Well today we moved to our new area. It's all right. I drove most of the day. It's nice riding all right. We really have this moving down pat now. We oughta. It's 5 times this month.

Sunday, November 5, 1944
Today we had off on account of moving yesterday. I guess it went off pretty good. We had a show in the mess hall. The town at the end of the street is Kalaheo. We went to Hanapepe also.

Monday, November 6, 1944
Drove all over the island today, up to L. Co. and then down to I. Co. They're about 40 miles from us. We had a pretty fair time. Had nite tech tonite.

Tuesday, November 7, 1944
Got myself a recorder today, 40 smackeroos, but it's really a nice job. Drove the rest of the day. Taking patients up to the Hosp, etc. Went to the show tonite.

(In Oahu today I not only bought a really nice recorder, but I also picked up a few records somewhere on the island; I can't remember where. With this new recorder I was invited to play music as a DJ at the officers' dance. So I did. I was the local DJ. I played music and they danced. That night I was invited to dance with a couple of the nurses or women that were there, so it turned out to be a pretty good deal for me. After the war, I brought the whole thing home with me, all the way to Cleveland, Ohio, where I lived at the time. I even had it for a couple of years in college when I went back. It worked out great.)

For some reason, which I no longer recall, I stopped keeping my diary at this point. Perhaps I was just tired of writing in it or perhaps I was simply more interested in doing other things. Anyway, the story continues, but without the entries from the diary. A week later, on January 15, 1945, we boarded the USS Telfair in Honolulu and headed out toward the Palau Islands.

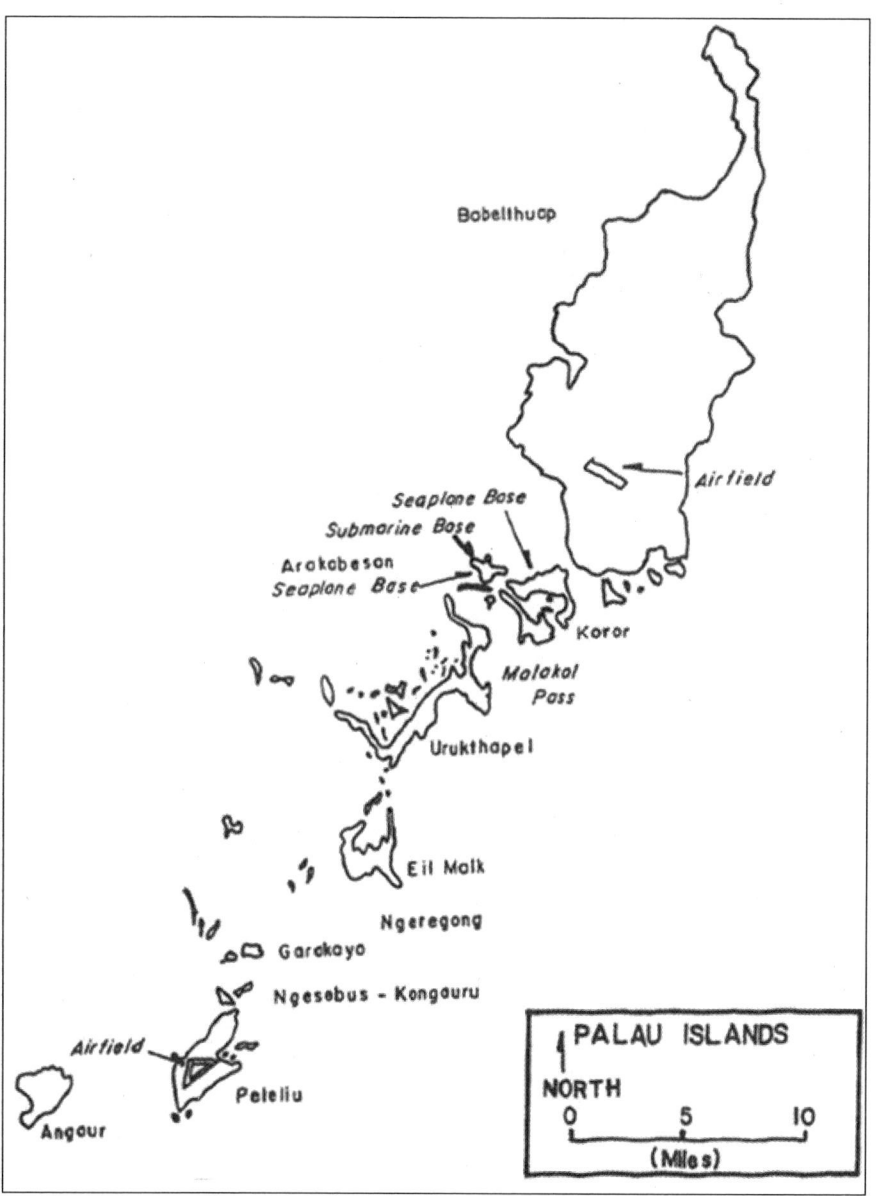

Bobelthuop

Seaplane Base
Submarine Base
Arakabeson
Seaplane Base

Airfield

Koror

Malakol
Pass

Urukthapel

Eil Malk

Ngeregong

Garakayo

Ngesebus - Kongouru

Airfield

Peleliu

Angour

PALAU ISLANDS

NORTH

0   5   10

(Miles)

The Palau Island Campaign and Honorable Discharge

Another Cruise, Patrols – Why Me?
The Last Outpost, Koror: Why Us?
Going Home, Change Is the Rule of Life

We trooped aboard the USS Telfair in Honolulu on January 15, 1945, on our way to the Palau Islands. Life aboard ship was "more of the same." The only interesting departure from other voyages was that this time we went in a convoy of six transports. The entire regiment went this time, two destroyers acting as escorts.

One unusual natural phenomenon occurred on the trip. We ran into a storm about a week out of Hawaii, and a number of waterspouts formed about three or four miles from the ship. They oscillated and moved, four or five of them together, and appeared as a tall column of water that ran from the ocean up to the overhanging low-scudding clouds. Perhaps they were the ocean variety of a tornado. I never found out. They soon disappeared and were forgotten.

We made two stops on the trip, one near Yap and another at Ulithi. At Ulithi there were 12 or 15 aircraft carriers, all lined up in a row. I thought at the time they looked very neat but also rather vulnerable to attack. There were a number of other ships lying at anchor, but the collection of carriers was somewhat unusual.

After a two-week trip, on February 1, 1945, the convoy finally arrived off Peleliu, one of the southern islands of the Palaus. We rounded up our gear, scrambled down the landing nets into the waiting LCVPs, and went ashore. "No messin' around."

The Japanese took the Palau Islands during World War I from the Germans. This seizure was legitimized by the League of Nations in 1920, and Japan controlled and fortified the islands until September-December 1944 when American Marines and Army forces captured the southern islands (see map). The Palaus are 4,000 miles west of Oahu but only 500 miles from the southern Philippines. The islands vary from flat coral atolls in the north to rugged volcanic islands in the south. The natives are Micronesians and because of the islands' remoteness were some of the last to be discovered by the European adventurers.

Peleliu was invaded on September 15, 1944, by the First Marine Division. The island is about 12 square miles and was defended by 10,000 Japanese troops. It was not until early December that the island was declared secure. The United States had overwhelming air and naval superiority during the battle, but the Japanese had learned their lessons well in the Gilberts and Marshalls and were concealed and fortified in a series of caves along what was called Bloody-Nose Ridge. It was an extremely difficult campaign because of the terrain and the heat.

The military role of the 111th Infantry on Peleliu involved five activities: combat patrols through the hills and ridges on Peleliu, bombardment with 155-mm guns of the islands to the north of Garakayo still occupied by Japanese troops, outpost duty, setting ambushes, and taking the surrender of and the disarming of the Japanese troops on the northern islands. We had the usual tasks associated with food, clothing, shelter, fuel, and water, most importantly water. The necessities of life must be realized.

Our battalion area was located just north of the airfield. The medical detachment aid station was set up there, but we also operated a water station near the northern tip of Peleliu on Akarahoro Point. It was just a little south of the causeway that formerly connected Peleliu with the neighboring island of Ngesebus. Huge 155-mm cannon bombarded the Japanese on the northern islands, and they invariably began their shelling while we watched a movie. It was a shattering sight and sound. We would be watching, and WHAM, WHAM, WHAM, the guns would let loose, and their shells would rocket over our heads on their way to harass the Japanese. Shelling didn't occur every night – it was tied to our movie schedule; it couldn't have been a coincidence. We had our own cannon company in the regiment, and I assume it was this group that did the firing.

The terrain of Peleliu Island was very rugged. Short, steep coral rock shot straight out of the ground. In many places these rocky hills went straight up. They were honeycombed with caves, and the fierce battle had turned a jungle into a tangled mass that made walking difficult. The hills were tom up – trees, coral rock, tons of old equipment, unexploded shells – a mess.

Getting into this difficult terrain with its openings, caves, and crevices, and rooting out the remaining Japs was a responsibility of our unit. Virtually everyone went on patrols. There may have been some exceptions, but almost everybody participated. We conducted these patrols from the time we landed until we left the island. It was a daily exercise. Most of the patrol activity occurred on Peleliu and focused on the area called Bloody-Nose Ridge. The job of those on patrol was to kill or capture any Japanese soldiers encountered and look for evidence of more soldiers. That was easy to do; we could leave some small piece of equipment or food and then check it a day or so later. Going on patrol was always a time of some anxiety, and it could be downright dangerous.

I must confess that I often wondered why we were going on patrols at all. It made little sense to me. The Japanese killed or captured were only trying to hide. They may have stolen a little food or equipment but nothing of moment. They were certainly no threat. They could do nothing. But I suppose our officers feared the possible (a suicide attack) rather than the probable (merely a soldier trying to survive).

A typical patrol was manned by eight or ten soldiers from one the "line" companies (I, L, K) and an aidman, and led by a sergeant or corporal. The line company would call the aid station, and Sergeant Neumann would assign one of us to go on the patrol.

Everybody – I repeat, everybody – took his turn, and you just didn't show up for sick call on the day you were supposed to act as the aidman for the patrol. There is a lot of "goofing off" (we called it goldbricking) in the military, but there are times when you take your turn. There was absolutely no pressure to volunteer for any patrol, however. There was an unsaid rule that you went when it was your turn to go, when you were selected. There was never any trouble with this system. It worked.

You never knew what line company you were going with or where they were going precisely. You just reported to their company headquarters and met the group you were going with.

Usually we were taken by truck up to the general area to be scouted. The rest of the patrol was then done on foot. The sergeant would explain our route and check our equipment. Everyone wore a green fatigue suit and helmet, and carried a rifle. BAR or carbine. In my case I carried a carbine because it was lighter and I had to carry the extra gear contained in my medical kit. Nobody wore any indication of rank on his sleeve, and I never did have a red cross painted on my helmet. I thought then (and now) that such a practice – the red cross – was insane. It wasn't needed and was only a target. Nobody in my outfit ever wore insignia in the field.

The average patrol lasted for two or three hours, and we always walked single file, six or eight feet apart. Some patrols killed Japanese soldiers. A few captured soldiers. Still others found evidence of the enemy. And some had no contact whatsoever. We investigated caves, noted booby-trap wires, saw huge unexploded 16-inch naval shells, and were very alert and quiet, as inconspicuous and anonymous as possible.

On one patrol I remember going into a cave that had boards laid over the bodies of dead Japanese soldiers. Whether the cave was closed by bulldozers during the battle, suffocating those inside, or simply the last refuge of enemy troops, I don't know. I do know we went in, looked around, and left. Nobody took anything – it was a grisly scene.

I always liked walking in the fourth or fifth position. It seemed like a good (safe) spot. We would stop on occasion but never grouped up to smoke. When we finished the patrol, we were dismissed, our sergeant reported the results to the company commander, and we went back to our base camp and waited for the next assignment.

Though getting bombed can scare you, patrols seem more related to stress. Noise was the condition of the former; silence, of the latter. In bombing attacks you were motionless for the most part, scrunched into a corner. On patrol you were moving almost all the time. In bombing, you just took it. On some patrols, the troops could dish it out. The patrols were different, and the men who went as aidmen with the patrols were different as well. Edwin Oakley was a big friendly man who looked like Charles Atlas. Leon Roberts was a not-so-gentle cynic from Brooklyn, New York, who always claimed he was going to picket our commanding officer's office after the war with a sign stating 'Many soldiers died under his hands'. Mac McQuine seemed an awfully immature individual, but he had a good-natured approach to life. And Thomas Riller fit my stereotype of the typical southerner – slow moving and talking, not easily ruffled. We all went on patrol. When selected.

On April 3, 1945, John Survill and I celebrated our 21st birthdays together. At the time we were working together at the water station near the north end of the island. We drank all our beer, got a little high, and probably forgot to put the correct chemicals in the water we were responsible for purifying. It wasn't something we worried about very much. The water, or most of it, was sent to ships lying off shore.

Virginia K. Hess

Fighting at Iwo Jima lasted more than a month, but five days into the struggle, U.S. servicemen triumphantly raised the American flag on Mount Suribachi. Of the men pictured here, only three survived the battle.

Iwo Jima & Okinawa

While we were celebrating our birthdays, the war in the Pacific was raging elsewhere. On February 19, 1945, the Marines landed on Iwo Jima. They were under heavy fire from the moment they hit the shore. Intense fighting by three Marine divisions continued until March 26, 1945. By the end of the battle, 7,000 Marines were dead and 20,000 were wounded. But the island was ours. It served as an emergency landing strip for 2,200 B29's.

On the other hand, 22,000 Japanese perished during the battle. Amazingly, some Japanese, who had survived the battle and had evaded the mop-up troops, remained on the island for four more years and did not surrender until then.

But, what most people recall about Iwo Jima is the famous picture of the six Marines who raised the flag on February 23, 1945. A statue of it is located outside of Arlington National Cemetery outside of Washington D.C.

Another important battle took place on Okinawa. The invasion, which involved both the Army and Marines, occurred on April 1, 1945, and lasted until June 22, 1945. It was the largest amphibious assault in the Pacific and resulted in more than 49,000 American casualties, including about 12,000 deaths. It was the last major battle of WWII.

In early April 1945, we heard the sad report that President Roosevelt had died. Everyone was sobered by the news, and all wondered how the new president, Harry Truman, would conduct the war. We knew it was almost over in Europe because our radio reports had American and Russian troops closing in on the last Nazi strongholds. Then, on May 8, 1945, two things happened, one momentous and one of little import. The war in Europe officially ended, and the Third Battalion moved again, this time to the northernmost island in the Palaus held by American troops, Garakayo.

Victory in Europe Day

Long awaited – May 8, 1945, Victory in Europe, or V-E Day arrived. The allied armies converged on Berlin, where Hitler had committed suicide on April 30th. The war was over. Germany unconditionally surrendered to the Allies in Reims, France, and celebrations erupted around the world.

Actually, by the end of 1943 many Germans suspected that the war might already be lost, but they fought on, driven by commitment or fear. In retrospect, perhaps the war had already been lost in 1941, when the United States entered into it, but certainly the battles of Kursk (1943) and Stalingrad (1942-1943) sounded a warning, if not a death knell... If only the war had ended much earlier.

As it was, the end of the war was eventually marked by the division of Germany, including Berlin, into four sections: American, British, French,

and Soviet. It also gave rise to two super powers, the United States and the Soviet Union, and the tensions between the two of them ushered in the era of the Cold War.

Europe lay in ruins and at least 15,000,000 to 20,000,000 died from war, disease, famine, and extermination. If one includes Russia in these numbers, it is more like 60,000,000 – soldiers, civilians, and prisoners. But the full scope of the horrors had yet to be recognized. As the Americans, British, and Soviet troops advanced, they began to encounter the Nazi concentration camps. The Germans did not have time to hide their atrocities. Prior to this there had been rumors about the camps, and some Germans had no doubt been aware of them, but for the most part the rumors had been dismissed as propaganda designed to promote Allied incentive. Overall, the Germans operated at least 1,000 camps, most of them small, or sub-camps, but at least a dozen were large and contained facilities for extermination. This was all part of the Holocaust, and the Final Solution – eliminating primarily Jews, but also Gypsies, homosexuals, the disabled, the mentally ill, political dissidents, etc. Soon these horrors would be exposed to the world.

Ohrdruf was the first camp to be discovered and liberated by the US. It was a subcamp of Buchenwald. On April 12, 1945, Generals Eisenhower, Patton, and Bradly toured the site. Patton, "Old Blood and Guts," who was used to the violence of war, was so sickened that he walked around the corner of a building and vomited. The generals forced the citizens of the town to view the camp and bury the dead, a practice that was repeated in other camp liberations. Eisenhower also made certain that General Marshall in Washington D.C. requested members of Congress and the press to visit the camps and report what they had seen. Afterward Eisenhower stated, "We are told that the American soldier does not know what he is fighting for. Now, at least, he knows what he is fighting against."

Meanwhile the war in the Pacific raged on... perhaps with a little more hope.

By now I had been away from home almost two years and overseas about one and one-half years. I remember thinking, "The war in the Pacific will never end. This is how my life will be led. I shall be in the Army forever." These thoughts didn't really dismay me. I was not homesick at all. I hadn't forgotten my family and friends at home; I was just resigned to living the way I was, as a soldier. I know this may sound strange, but I clearly remember thinking, "This is how life is." It must have been resignation or adjustment; I really don't know. I know it was a fact.

On May 8, 1945, we arrived on Garakayo, a few miles north of Peleliu. The battalion with its aid station was established in the south-central part of

the island, and I was sent to act as an aidman for M Company's machine-gun outpost on the northwest part of the island (see map of Garakayo).

There was also a major dock installation on Garakayo.

A water-purification facility was established, and because of my experience on Peleliu, I worked on this project also. It was a good deal. I was completely on my own, away from every last vestige of authority except for the sergeant who ran the machine-gun outpost. There were about 25 men assigned to the outpost since it had to be manned all night, every night.

The problem was that some of the more tenacious and "intense" Japanese soldiers on the northern islands had in the past built rafts, floated down to the islands captured by the Americans, and then tried to cause as much mayhem as they could. The outpost's task was to shoot them out of the water. I slept in a pyramidal tent, about 50 yards from the outpost. Back at battalion

headquarters, some engineers put up a Quonset hut, a real luxury, but I would never have traded my deal for their fancy tin shack. I told everybody it was terrible out in the boonies, hoping to keep the outpost assignment. I did. I stayed there the entire four months we spent on the island.

I never saw a movie on Garakayo; they were all shown at battalion headquarters. I didn't care; I liked the freedom on outpost duty. There was another "perk". Three times a day a truck drove out from Headquarters with food for all of us, just like pizza delivery today. We played cribbage, went swimming, talked to sailors put ashore on our dock for a beer party, watched the water purifier, and scanned the ocean at night for rafts. Tough duty. It was the best four months I spent in the Army. I read at least a hundred books, and I became a cribbage expert. All I really had to do was to make sure that any injury to the 15 men on the machine-gun crew was promptly treated. Believe me, I tried to take good care of them because I wanted to keep the job.

To add to my good fortune, I received a ten-dollar-a-month raise in June. The rifle companies in our battalion were awarded the Combat Infantryman's Badge, and we were given the Combat Medic's Badge. So each one of us got a badge and a noticeable raise. Our contribution, compared with that of the divisions that frontally assaulted Butaritari, Kwajalein, and Peleliu, was minor. But we took the badge and the money and told ourselves that our efforts were probably worth something.

In early August 1945, atom bombs were dropped on Hiroshima and Nagasaki. In my small unit, there was no question that Truman had made the correct decision. Nobody knew what the atom bomb was, and nobody really cared. It had killed a lot of Japanese, and we hoped it would force them to surrender. That was what concerned us. I don't remember a single person raising the fundamental moral issue of killing innocent people. Perhaps we should have, but we didn't. It's a contradiction I cannot explain. We knew very well that an invasion of Japan was coming, that we would probably be part of that effort, and that the assault would mean millions of causalities. I think the same way today.

Now events began to occur in rapid order, sparked by the near downing of a sailor. Let me explain. From time to time the Navy would put ashore 40 or 50 sailors on our dock so they could swim, sun, and drink beer. Most of them invariably got falling-down drunk. Also, after a few beers, one or two of them would leave our area and go back in the jungle looking for souvenirs. They cared nothing about the dangers lurking there. They were fortified on beer, and after weeks and months at sea, nothing could stop them. We never did this. A few of them always did this.

My Last Day

One such day I was in my tent when Sergeant Brady called me to report that a sailor had just been pulled, half-drowned, from the water. I ran the 50 yards to the beach and found a sailor who had begun to turn blue. I began giving him artificial respiration, and after 10 minutes or so he seemed to be breathing OK. Since the wind was blowing very hard that day, I asked a couple of sailors to help me carry him to the nearest tent so I could continue my efforts in a more protected spot.

We picked him up and started down the path to the tent, but he began to turn blue again, so we dropped him in the sand, and I began applying artificial respiration again. I could see that my technique was rubbing all the skin off his back in the area of his kidneys because the sand was blowing all over us. But I kept it up. He was not going to turn blue on me again. It was a bizarre scene – the patient's coloring alternating between chalky white, blue, and a reddish flush; the sand whipping and stinging our bare skin; everyone offering advice in a chorus that made no sense at all; all surrounded by sailors and soldiers just standing and watching while they smoked and drank more beer.

I asked somebody to call the battalion aid station for help. He reported in a minute or so that they would send a truck. I kept up the only primitive technique I knew for about another 10 or 15 minutes. Somehow, I think with God's help, he was still breathing when the truck arrived. The men from the aid station took him on a stretcher to the truck and drove away. I learned later he survived. I bet he didn't drink a lot of beer on a dock after that.

While the "drowning" saga was going on, a couple of Navy men, souvenir hunters and explorers, went into the jungle. I had just returned to my tent when they came running and screaming out of the jungle. "We saw one; we saw one. We ran into a Jap!" Sergeant Brady and I talked to them. We asked them where, when, and what they had seen, and told them to go down to the dock and get off the island. They did.

Brady decided that it might be smart to set up an ambush and get the Jap if we could. He asked me if I would join him in his little exercise, and I agreed. Why not? I like Brady, and he rarely asked anybody to do anything. After dinner we grabbed our rifles and worked our way back in the jungle to a point about 100 or 150 yards from our area, near the spot the sailors had said they saw the Jap soldier. We huddled down and started looking.

Night fell, and we had been on the ambush only about two or three hours when we heard a call from my tent, the one near the water station and closest to the jungle: "The war's over! The war's over. Hey, you guys, the war's over!" Brady and I looked at each other, shrugged our shoulders, and said in unison, "Let's go!" We got up and walked out of the jungle for the last time.

Admiral Chester Nimitz

General Douglas McArthur

Victory Over Japan Day

September 2, 1945

The Japanese saw two choices in the war: Victory or Death. Despite the fact they continued to suffer ongoing major setbacks, they would not surrender.

The first setback was at Pearl Harbor – December 6, 1941- which "awakened the sleeping giant" and brought the United States into the war. The second was the battle of Midway -June 4, 1942 – in which they lost 4 aircraft carriers, all of their planes, and all of their most experienced pilots. Third was the battle for Guadalcanal – August 7, 1942 – which gave the Allies the use of Henderson Field and kept the Japanese from further expansion.

It is important here to know that the Pacific campaign was divided between two commanders. The Central Pacific was under the command of Admiral Chester Nimitz, who was moving from Hawaii west. He hit Tarawa, which was won at great cost, and Makin Island (in the Gilbert Islands). He then took Kwajalein atoll in the Marshall Islands. Then on June 15,1944 Nimitz ordered the attack on the Marianas Islands which included Saipan, Tinian, and Guam. Here a great land and air assault occurred which is sometimes called the "Great Turkey Shoot" because it cost the Japanese 900 planes.

Later, as the Allies continued island-hopping, inching closer and closer to the Japanese home islands, the Japanese continued to lose ground, confirmed by their losses at Iwo Jima – February 19, 1945 – and Okinawa – April 1, 1945.

Next came Victory in Europe Day, May 8, 1945. Now the focus of the war could shift from Europe to the Pacific, as could the Allied resources. Yet Japan would still not surrender. Even after the fire bombings of Tokyo in March of 1945, the single most destructive raid in history, they remained steadfast, and began planning Kamikaze attacks in the event the Allies reached the home islands.

Meanwhile, the United States and Britain were working collaboratively, at this point, on an atomic bomb. So was Germany. And so was Japan. The race was on for the most destructive weapon yet. But Japan would still not surrender. Soon, the US had the bomb – before anyone else did – and the decision was made by President Truman to use it.

On August 6, 1945, after leaflets had been dropped on the city, warning people to leave, the first bomb was dropped, on Hiroshima. The explosion immediately killed an estimated 80,000 people, and many more would die later from radiation poisoning.

Three days later, on August 9, 1945, a second bomb was dropped, on Nagasaki, killing another estimated 40,000 ... and yet another event occurred; on August 8, 1945, the Soviet Union declared war on Japan.

Finally, Japan's Emperor Hirohito announced his country's unconditional surrender in a radio address on August 15, 1945, and formally signed an agreement on September 2, 1945. The war was over.

After the war, the United States led the Allies in the occupation and rehabilitation of Japan. Between 1945 and 1952 General MacArthur oversaw military, economic, and social reforms. While nothing can justify the cost, events may explain the decision that was made in using the atomic bombs. May they never be used again.

Back to My Story

On August 11, 1945, the big news, which I reported, was that the Japs had accepted the ultimatum. And I mean everybody here really went wild! We broke out our last remaining beers and then got news reports from the other outposts. A few days later, on August 16, 1945, 1 offered the startling insight that the Japanese had surrendered because we had hit them with atomic bombs. Soon I predicted, on August 22, 1945, success for MacArthur in ruling the Japanese. It sounded like he was going to sign the peace terms right in Tokyo, but for sure he'd do what was needed. Finally, I gave a distinctive American touch to the reports on our soldiers and Marines setting foot on Japanese soil. We were all over at the other outpost, listening to the radio broadcast of the Allied landing in Japan, and the way they announced it, it sounded to me like a baseball game. Ah, the brilliant insights of a 19-year-old.

On September 11, 1945, the Third Battalion left Garakayo and went back to Peleliu. We were on the move again. We had no sooner arrived on Peleliu than we were informed that we would leave the next day for Koror. Our battalion was given the "honor" of accepting the surrender and disarming of the Japanese troops, all 35,000 of them, in the northern islands. "Why us?" we cried. "Give this glorious honor to the First or Second Battalion. What if they don't know the war is over?" We tried everything, but to no avail. We were picked, and we boarded an LCI the next day. The LCI is a versatile craft, perfect for the waters surrounding the Palau Islands. They are armed, have a rather "boxy" profile, and they can carry 300 or 400 troops easily. We had three LCIs for our battalion as we left Peleliu.

We threaded our way through many of the Palaus' 200 volcanic and limestone islands as we moved north on our 20 to 25-mile trip from Peleliu to Koror. Only a few of the islands were inhabited.

Most are rocky and jut sharply out of the water. All are totally covered by dense vegetation. Sometimes our transit between islands was so tight

you could almost touch the vegetation on the island. As we approached the island of Koror, the capital of the Republic of Palau today, there was vivid evidence of the naval air attacks and their effectiveness in the scores of sunken ships half in and out of the water.

It was a strange, ghostly sight, especially the barges lying half submerged or run aground. These had been used by the Japanese general commanding Babelthuap to send down reinforcements to his beleaguered troops on Peleliu during the height of that conflict. Actually only a few hundred probably got through because American domination of the air seriously limited the Japanese effort. Another reason the air attacks were so determined was that the American commanders wanted to secure Kossol Passage, just north of Babelthuap, as a PBM patrol-plane base. In any event, there was no doubt that the Japanese naval effort had been aborted by the carrier air strikes. It was a ship graveyard. Our ship approached the main dock on Koror and we could see piles of ammunition, rifles, cannons, and equipment of all kinds piled up on the dock. Tons and tons of military equipment. But no Japanese. Not a living soul. We were encouraged by the stacked weapons and ammunition. We were apprehensive of what would occur next because there was nobody in sight.

We disembarked, spread out, and waited. In about five minutes, from behind a small ridge, a group of 20 or so Japanese officers with their orderlies marched in single file down to the dock where they were met by our battalion commander and his staff. There they surrendered their swords and other weapons to our officers. There wasn't a hitch. It all went off as smooth as clockwork. During the next few days, all Japanese officers and troops were ordered to leave Koror and stay on the huge island of Babelthuap. The two islands had been connected by a causeway (see map), but that had been destroyed by our air attacks, and while I was on Koror, we were always separated by water.

The rifle companies and M Company set up outposts near the causeway, and we moved through what used to be a small town on Koror. It was almost totally destroyed. We set up our battalion aid station next to an old church. Spain had ruled the islands at one time, and it had a look of Spanish architecture. Our living quarters must have been an old hotel or officers' barracks. It was a two- story wooden building, about the length and width of an army barracks back in the States. We built a little shower and were busy treating soldiers and civilians in a day or two.

We ran into a venereal disease on Koror, called yaws, that was nasty. It manifested itself in large "volcano"- type sores on the legs of the natives. We treated it as best we could, but I suspect we were ineffective. There was no penicillin in those days; at least we didn't have it. We "cured" almost everything with sulphur powder. In fact, nothing healed in that moist, humid climate. But that didn't stop some of the more virile troops from engaging in sexual activity with some of the native women and with a few Japanese prostitutes left behind when the troops were forced to evacuate Koror and go to Babelthuap. In the evening it was not unusual to see a soldier going through the rigors associated with an Army prophylactic treatment. These measures to preserve the health of the troops were offered, and given, without question by the medics on technician duty.

Sometimes there were as many as four or five undergoing the treatment. It takes some time, is rather gross and unseemly, particularly since it was done in full view of any casual walker passing by. All they wanted was cigarettes. We had cartons and cartons – they sold for only 50 cents each. The causeway, or what was left of it, became the trading center. In two days I was able to trade a few packs of cigarettes for a Japanese flag, and one day I traded two cartons of cigarettes, one dollar, for an officer's samurai sword. (It's hanging on my gun rack as I write these memoirs.) I could have quickly sold it for 200 or 300 dollars at the time. It was just a lucky trade. I was there at the right moment. The Japanese officer was leading a group of about 100 soldiers from Babelthuap to work. I went up to him, he bowed (they all did), and I pointed to the sword he carried and held out the two cartons of cigarettes. He simply unbuckled the sword and held it out to me, and we exchanged the cigarettes for the sword right then and there. It all took about 30 seconds.

I also had a Japanese carbine. Everyone in our battalion had a rifle or carbine. The battalion commander had sent out an order that all Japanese weapons and ammunition were to be dumped in the ocean and that anyone who wanted a rifle was welcome to come and pick one out. We all did. That was the extent of my trading.

About this time our unit began to break up. Men were being sent home based on points. As I remember it, we were accorded one point for every month of active service, one extra point for every month of foreign service, and five points for every campaign star awarded. I had three stars, one each for the Gilberts, Marshalls, and Palaus; two years overseas; and two and a half years of service. It added up to 65 or 70 points. The old-timers in our outfit like Sergeant Neumann, Oakley, Roberts. McQuine, and Riller were the first to go. I was glad to see them go because I knew our turn would come all the sooner.

Sergeant Neumann turned a problem (his terrible seasickness) into a benefit. It was approximately a three-week trip by ship from Peleliu to the States, and he would never have survived such a long voyage because he was so ill, so the military authorities decided to fly him home – the only soldier in the entire regiment. Mercy does exist.

Sometime in early October, about the fourth or fifth, I received a telephone call, my first in two and a half years. The voice on the other end of the phone said, "Hey, Thob, how about picking me up? I'm down here at the dock on Koror." I had no idea who it was. And the use of my nickname, Thob, was something I hadn't heard for over two years. It was Jack Foley, an old high school friend from Shaker Heights. I leapt into an old Japanese car – we had a number of these as well as bicycles that were left by the Japanese when they moved to Babelthaup – and drove like a fury over the two miles or so to the dock.

My God – there he was, a Marine officer. I've never experienced anything like it since. Somehow I was home. The two years were over. He looked and talked the same. I couldn't believe what was happening. We embraced, shook hands, and embraced again. I just couldn't believe it. Jack said he had talked to my mother just before leaving the States and knew exactly where I was located, so when he arrived on Guam, he hitched a ride on a plane to Peleliu, found I was on Koror, and then hopped on one of the LCIs that plied between the two islands and came up to Koror. It was possible to do things like this at that time. There were few rules, guards, inspections. Nobody cared. If you broke a rule, where could they send you? But a flight from Guam, hundreds of miles away, was something extraordinary.

We talked excitedly for a few minutes, and then, as best I can remember. Jack opened the conversation: "Listen, I can only stay overnight. I have to go back to Guam tomorrow.

How about going down to Peleliu with me? We'll have a nice dinner and drinks at the transit officers' barracks, spend the night there, and then tomorrow I'll hop a plane back to Guam and you can come back to Koror." I didn't know what to say for a minute. Then I blurted out, "Jack, maybe you haven't noticed – I'm a private. Privates aren't really welcome at the officers' club."

Without a moment's hesitation he said, "That's no problem. I've got an extra shirt and overseas cap with gold bars you can put on when we're aboard the ship on the trip to Peleliu. You can do it, Thob. Let's go." I didn't know what to say. I wanted to go, but the consequences worried me. I said, "Jack, I think it's against Army regulations – impersonation of an officer is a federal offense. People go to prison for doing such things." "Who'll know?" he said. "The transit officers' barracks is like a floating crap game – it changes every day. Nobody knows anybody."

After a few moments' thought about what he had gone through to get here, I agreed in an immortal phrase: "What the hell, I'll do it." But first I had to get permission. I didn't think that would be a problem. We hopped in the car and drove back to the aid station. I introduced Jack to our warrant officer, John Rollins, a new member of our unit, and in two minutes had his approval. Off we went to grab the LCI to Peleliu.

Before going on with my story, I want to say something about Jack's and my relationship. We were friends throughout high school. We played ice hockey together, dated the two Harper sisters for a year or so during high school, loved music and dancing, and belonged to the same high school and college fraternities. We were good friends. Jack was 6 feet, about 185 pounds, had a reddish blond tinge of color in his hair, and sharp-chiseled features (somewhat like Kirk Douglas's). He played hockey and football, but his real forte was theater. He was a first-rate actor. During our senior year at Shaker Heights High School, we put on the play Hamlet. Jack played Hamlet, and if you know the play, that is an extremely complex and challenging role to fill. He was super. I had probably the smallest part in the play, Guildenstern.

Jack liked all the girls, and my impression was that they all loved him. He was a complete extrovert, an "operator" with women, always ready to have a party. He was Irish through and through, always a leader. He led

91

by the power of his personality and his power to persuade. He never forced things. He didn't have to. He spent a year or so at Carnegie Tech before joining the Marines. After the war he began making and selling TV commercial spots. He eventually married, had seven children, and lived for years in California until his death in the fall of 1990.

But back to the story. Near the end of the two-and-a-half-hour trip to Peleliu I put on the shirt and cap and became a Marine officer, gold bars and all. Fortunately, there was no saluting; we had given that up almost two years ago. We walked over toward the officers' barracks first because I had to register for a room that night. We decided that since I had no official I.D., I should register as Lt. Richard Black. We picked this name in honor of a mutual friend from our high school days – Dick Black. Black was an agreeable guy and would certainly have approved of our plan. As you can see, real planning was involved in this operation.

I walked in to face the sergeant on duty at the desk, tried to act nonchalant, introduced myself to the sergeant as Lt. Richard Black, and stated that I wanted to sign up for a room for the night. He looked at me, a bit too closely as far as I was concerned, and then pushed the registration form in my direction and went on about his other tasks. I filled out the form, was assigned a room and given a key, and we left. I took a very deep breath as I walked out. We went to our rooms (by now I was really beginning to get into this officer act), cleaned up a bit, and headed for the bar and dining room.

We sat down at a table and ordered some drinks from some poor enlisted man. After I had fortified myself with two or three mixed drinks, I called out to the waiter in much the same tone the others did for more drinks. I don't know how many we had – way too many. I do remember singing old college fraternity songs with gay abandon: "Delta Tau Delta, Delta – you are my safest shelter" et al. We were in superb voice. We forgot everybody else in the room, and there were some from Australia and England. We got louder and better as time and drinks blurred our minds but not our spirits.

Later, much later, we were told that we had better eat if we wanted any food because the kitchen was going to close. We ordered steaks and ate like kings. About 11:00pm we wove our way back to the officers' barracks – full of booze, food, and goodwill. It had been a night to remember.

The next morning, I dressed and shaved, and Jack and I had breakfast at the Officers Club. Then I checked out, and we walked over to the airport. On the way I gave him back the official trappings of a Marine officer. He arranged a ride to Guam, and I watched the plane take off into the morning sun. It was one of the great days of my life. I had been an "officer and a gentleman" for 24 hours. And I spent that 24 hours with a friend I shall never forget. With the plane out of sight, I walked back to the dock, grabbed the first LCI going to Koror, left my life of illusion, and returned to reality. I'll take illusion.

Back on Koror, as the month of October wore on, I lost my wristwatch. My parents had given it to me for graduation from high school, and it had my name engraved on the back. I was getting ready to take a shower one day and tossed the watch in the top of the mosquito bar over my cot while I went to the shower. When I returned, it was gone. To have something stolen was very unusual; we rarely had problems with theft. All of my imaginative detective work designed to recover the watch was in vain, and I gave it up for lost.

As the end of October drew near. Jolin Survill and I finally had the requisite number of points to go home. On October 28 we said goodbye to our friends, left Koror, and went back to Peleliu to get the ship that would take us back to the States. The ship, the Custer, lay at anchor off Peleliu, and we spent October 29 and 30 turning in all our gear. It was a confusing and chaotic two days.

One afternoon I got in a poker game – a rare thing for me to do as I didn't have the stomach for gambling. One of the soldiers playing in the game, I didn't know him at all, ran out of money and offered a watch for sale that he had acquired in another game. The watch was passed around, and when it came to me, I recognized it as the one stolen from my mosquito bar. I pointed to the name, showed him my dog tags, and claimed the watch. He protested and said he had bought it in good faith. The situation became a bit tense, but I offered him five dollars, which he accepted, and I had my watch back. Strange!

On October 31 we were ordered to report to the local aid station to get a flu shot. News had recently arrived announcing a big flu epidemic in the States, and the Army didn't want us to succumb to disease just as we returned home. We all took the shots. In the middle of the night I awoke feeling very sick. I was terrified. If I was really ill, and I was, I knew I would be sent to the base hospital until I was cured. "My God," I thought, "that could be weeks."

I decided to say absolutely nothing. I was determined to get on that ship. That was my ship. I was going home on it come hell or high water. I got up off my cot to get a drink of water and noticed a number of other soldiers who looked a lot like me – terrible. We talked a bit and decided that we all had the flu. Halloween must not be my day. Halloween 1944 was the day the Navy made us all sick by circling the LCVPs for hours off Kauai. Now on Halloween 1945 it was the Army's turn. They gave us the flu. But not one soldier said one word. Not one soldier went on sick call. Not one soldier even asked for an aspirin. We were going to get on that ship, ironically, with "the rising sun in the Pacific."

On November 1, 1945, we boarded our ship for the trip to the States, and we left Peleliu that day heading east. I lashed my Japanese carbine to my bunk below decks, but I carried the samurai sword and flag with me at all times. To put it down for an instant would have meant the end. To make it easier, I wrapped the sword in some old fatigues and carried it slung over my back. When I wanted to sit down, I could just move it to my shoulder. It was no big problem.

At night the ship was brightly illuminated. No more blackouts. We had movies on the afterdeck every night, and I remember well climbing and straddling a boom on the ship and riding it like a horse on the large Pacific Ocean swells as I watched the movie. It was beautiful: millions of stars, the sparkling phosphorescent bow waves, the moon – and we were going home. Any time we made any departure, no matter how slight, from our eastward course, a cry of woe went up, and once or twice the officer of the deck felt compelled to come on the public address system to explain the deviation. It was a long trip, but in two weeks we arrived at Oahu. Nobody wanted to stop, but we needed provisions. We got them and headed east again.

The sailors on board did what sailors always do – scrape and paint. They were going to be aboard a long time. We were going to get off. They carried on with normal routines. Some of the troops started throwing clothing off the ship. I don't know why. Perhaps it was just an act that helped them demonstrate that their days in the service were drawing to a close.

On November 21, 1945, we sighted the United States. To say it was exciting is not enough. For me, there was a rush of emotion; tears welled in my eyes. I remember running and pushing to the front of the ship, the side of the ship, anyplace to get a better look. We were heading for San Pedro in southern California. We pulled in at a dock to the sound of music from a band playing patriotic and popular tunes.

It was unbelievable. We were home. We waved, screamed, cried, almost ran around in circles. We were home. It was a fantastic moment – kind of like one's wedding night. It happens once in a lifetime.

The public address ordered "All troops prepare to disembark." I ran to get my gear from the bunk, but I couldn't get the damn rifle untied. 1 had lashed it to the bunk so tight that I couldn't loosen the knots. "The hell with it," I thought. 1 left it there for some sailor with more patience than I had at the moment and moved to the gangway. A few minutes later I was on American soil. It had been two years and fourteen days. As the popular song of the day said, "It's Been a Long, Long Time."

We went directly to Camp Anza, located near San Pedro harbor in California, where I sent Barbara and my folks a telegram saying I had arrived safely. It was November 22, 1945, and the last time I ever saw John Survill. He was from New Jersey and left that day. There was no big goodbye, just a handshake, a word wishing him well, and a pat on the shoulder. We had seen and said everything we had to say over the past two and a half years.

There was a shuttle flight between the East and West coasts for soldiers who lived in those areas. Those of us who lived someplace in the vast area between California and the East Coast boarded a troop train that headed east through the southwestern states toward Camp Atterbury, Indiana. I remember passing through an area in Arizona, between two ranges of hills, that was filled with thousands and thousands of airplanes. It was a military airplane graveyard, kind of an eerie sight. We talked, slept as best we could, and on November 26 we arrived at Camp Atterbury.

On November 27 we were issued ODs and given the ribbons, stars, and insignia we had earned. The next morning, November 28, 1945, I went through a little ceremony in which I received my Honorable Discharge from the U.S. Army. We went directly from the ceremony to a bus that was to take us to the train. Just before the bus, they had a card table set up, and as I passed, the sergeant in charge asked if I would like to join the Army Reserves. He said, "It's a chance to keep your rank." It took only a moment to say, "No thanks," before I boarded the bus.

The train ride from Camp Atterbury to Cleveland was slow as there were many stops to drop off soldiers. We finally arrived at the terminal in Cleveland where I was met by my mother, father, sister, her new baby, my grandmother, and my girlfriend, Barbara Harper. It was over. My dad drove us all home, and there we talked, had refreshments, and talked some more. My dad finally said he was going to bed and that I could use his car to take Barbara home. That was the first time in my life I had ever driven my dad's car. Perhaps change really is the rule of life.

Epilogue

Shortly after my discharge in December 1945, my father invited me to attend a meeting of the American Legion. I went to the dinner meeting with him and my uncle, Harold Van Schoor. That was one of the few contacts I had with a veterans' group. I have absolutely nothing against them. I recognize the social benefits of membership, the political power they wield, and the good they do for veterans and their families, but I've never been a joiner, and I dislike meetings – all kinds.

Furthermore, I have never established or maintained any postwar ties with anyone from my training battalion or my regular outfit. I think this rather strange. Frankly, I did feel some bonding with the men in the training battalion, but I never felt or thought of our medical detachment as a cohesive unit. My only effort to contact anyone was prompted by these memoirs. On December 19, 1988. a few days after I finished the first draft of this book, I called John Survill in New Jersey, 43 years after I last saw him in California on November 21, 1945. He sounded the same on the telephone, and he said I did also. Perhaps it was a combination of finishing the writing, Christmas, and the desire or need to hear a voice from the past. We had a nice conversation.

Military life was a learning experience for me. I learned something about the world we live in, its geography, people, and cultures. I learned something about human nature and psychology and in so doing learned something about myself as an individual and the values, beliefs, and attitudes that shape my behavior. I learned I could get along ok even when things got kinda rough.

And I learned some things about human relationships – about power, authority, freedom, and equality. I also learned a few "lessons for life" in the Army that have helped me throughout my life, lessons such as the importance of time as a precious commodity (It's so easy to waste.); the importance of not taking life too seriously (I have to keep relearning this.); the importance of self-discipline and accepting responsibility for one's actions (It's all too easy to blame one's misfortunes on external circumstances.); and the importance of being a part of a group (This includes family, church, university, social club – anything.)

Military life was a passage for me, a turning point in my life, and in some sense a transition period. It changed me psychologically and socially. I learned the meaning and the value of freedom, of control over my own life, even when I had little. And my trip on the Mormacport taught me the value of fundamental human equality through gross privilege and inequality for some at the expense of others. Further, my involvement in some meaningless activities in the Army sensitized me to the possibilities that might exist in meaningful work. Finally, I saw little of heroism or cowardice in the Army. What I saw was men doing their duty, simply acting in a responsible manner, sometimes in difficult circumstances. Soldiers put up with a lot just to "get along" with the other men in their outfit. If I have a "clearer perception and livelier impression" of these values today (freedom, human equality, the importance of work, and duty or responsible conduct), then part of the credit rightfully belongs to my experience in the Army.

In August 1990, my wife, Janet, and I went back to Kauai. It was my first visit to the island since the fall of 1944. We went up to Kalaheo so I could show her the town and the area where we were based while in rest camp. We stopped in the Community Center, and I asked one of the older citizens where the former USO was located. The woman pointed across the street and said, "Right over there." I asked if she knew Betty Shimogawa. She said she did, but that Betty's married name was Ihara and that she managed the appliance business now located in the old USO building.

The next day, Janet and I went to the shop, walked in, and saw a woman sitting at the desk. I said, "I'm looking for Betty Shimogawa." She said, "That's me. How do you know my maiden name?" That was it. We began talking and didn't stop for three hours. She took us out for lunch and later invited us to join her at a big Hawaiian wedding and luau held at a resort near the Fern Grotto on the Wailua River. Janet and I had expected to spend an hour or so with Betty. Instead, we spent the day and found a new friend. It was the high point of the trip – all due to the kindness and hospitality that one woman, Mrs. Mitsuyo Shimogawa, extended to a lonely soldier almost a half century ago.

So I bring these memoirs to a close. It has been a marvelous therapy for me, although there was one circumstance where the old war stories reappeared for a few more years.

Let me explain. Years ago, before Janet passed away, we used to go to Florida, to Anna Maria Island. There we had a circle of friends, all "aged" – 70 and over. We had frequent little parties from about 5:00PM to 6:30PM to talk and socialize, but oftentimes the men ended up on one side of the room and the women on the other. When this happened, often the talk turned, somehow, to a story about World War II. Then, as in Shakespeare's Henry the Fifth, when the king spoke to his troops on the eve of the battle of Agincourt, all listened as the storyteller for the evening recalled a particular incident in his military life and, like Henry the 5th, recounted "what feats he did that day."

The Letters

During the war, as I mentioned earlier, I wrote 196 letters home, and much to my surprise my mother kept all of them; she also kept some pictures I had sent, such as the picture of the Micronesian man and his son who retrieved the coconut for me. If you recall, I recently discovered the diary, which I had kept, as well as the pictures and the letters, which she had kept.

On the following pages you will find 16 of those letters, both the originals and, because they are easier to read, typed copies. You may find them interesting, as they represent what I, as a 19-year- old soldier was focused on during the war, but on the other hand, don't expect anything truly profound...

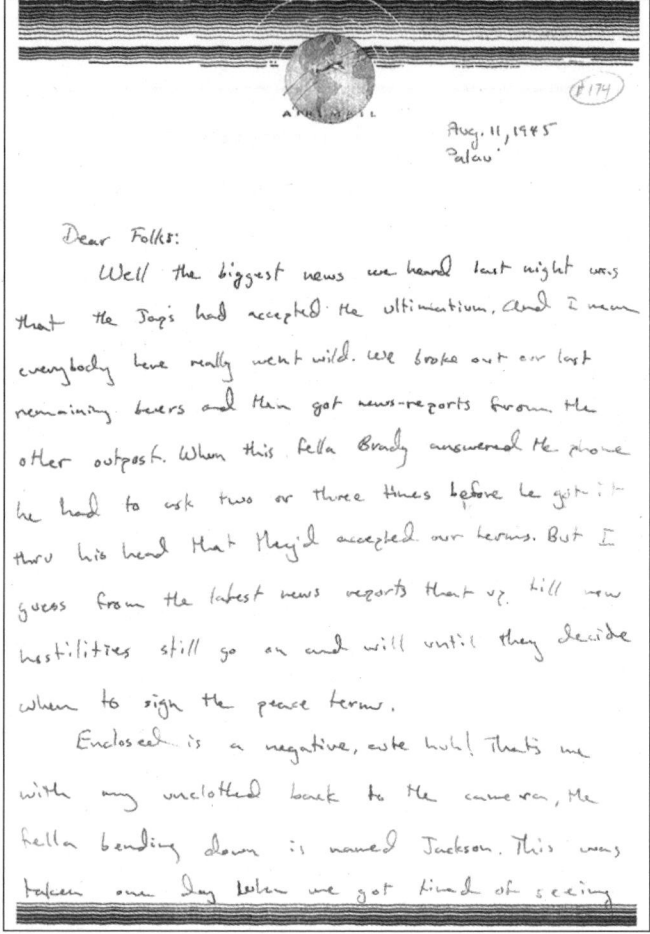

#174
Aug. 11, 1945
Palau's

Dear Folks:

Well the biggest news we heard last night was that the Jap's had accepted the ultimatum. And I mean everybody here really went wild. We broke out our last remaining beers and then got news-reports from the other outpost. When this fella Brady answered the phone he had to ask two or three times before he got it through his head that they'd accepted our terms. But I guess from the latest news reports that up till now hostilities still go on and will until they decide when to sign the peace terms.

it rain around here so much so we went out
and played horseshoes bare — in the rain. I think
after this is developed you'll even be able to see
the rain. It was really coming down when this
was taken.

We had a pretty good meal yesterday we
got a whole bucketload of fish yesterday with
a couple half pound blocks of T.N.T. so yesterday
afternoon Jackson and I spent it cleaning the fish.
Thats a very delightful job. We smelled like a
fish nursery when we got thru. "

Well I guess we'll be going over to the
other outpost to see or rather to hear the latest
news so I'd better sign off. I guess what
everybody around here wants now is to be home
for this years Christmas.

Your loving son
BcS.

P.S. I've taken the negative out it won't pass censorship,
I didn't want you to wonder what happened to it.

Enclosed is a negative, cute huh! That's me with my unclothed back to the camera, the fella bending down is named Jackson. This was taken one day when we got tired of seeing it rain around here so much so we went out and played horseshoes bare – in the rain. I think after this is developed you'll even be able to see the rain. It was really coming down when this was taken.

We had a pretty good meal yesterday, we got a whole bucketload of fish yesterday with a couple half-pound blocks of T.N.T. so yesterday afternoon Jackson and I spent it cleaning the fish. That's a very delightful job. We smelled like a fish nursery when we got thru.

Well I guess we'll be going over to the other outpost to see or rather to hear the latest news so I'd better sign off. I guess what everybody around here wants now is to be home.

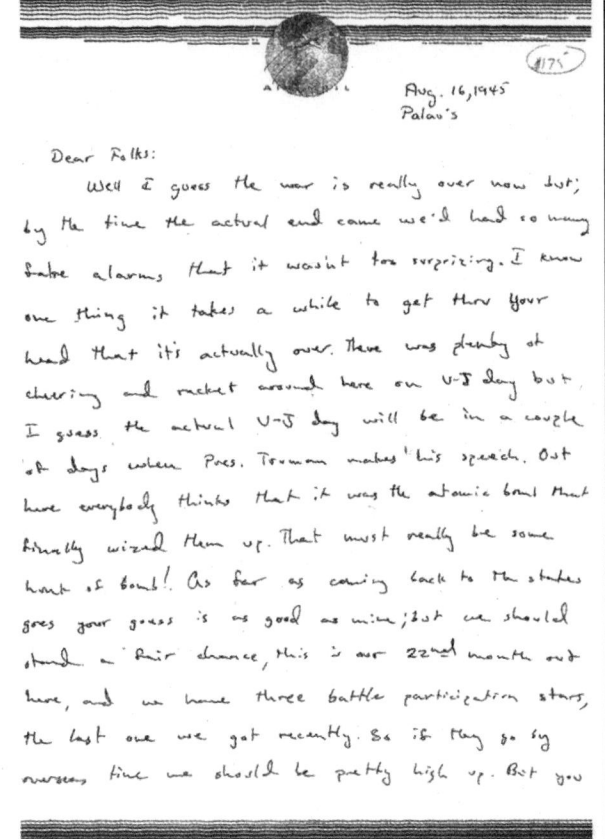

#175
Aug. 16, 1945

Dear Folks:

Well I guess the war is really over now but by the time the actual end came we'd had so many false alarms that it wasn't too surprising. I know one thing it takes a while to get thru your head that it's actually over. There was plenty of cheering and racket around here on V-J day but I guess the actual V-J day will be in a couple of days when Pres. Truman makes his speech. Out here everybody thinks that it was the atomic bomb that finally wised them up. That must really be some hurt of bomb! As far as coming back to the states goes your guess is as good as mine; but we should stand a fair chance, this is our 22nd month out there, and we have three battle

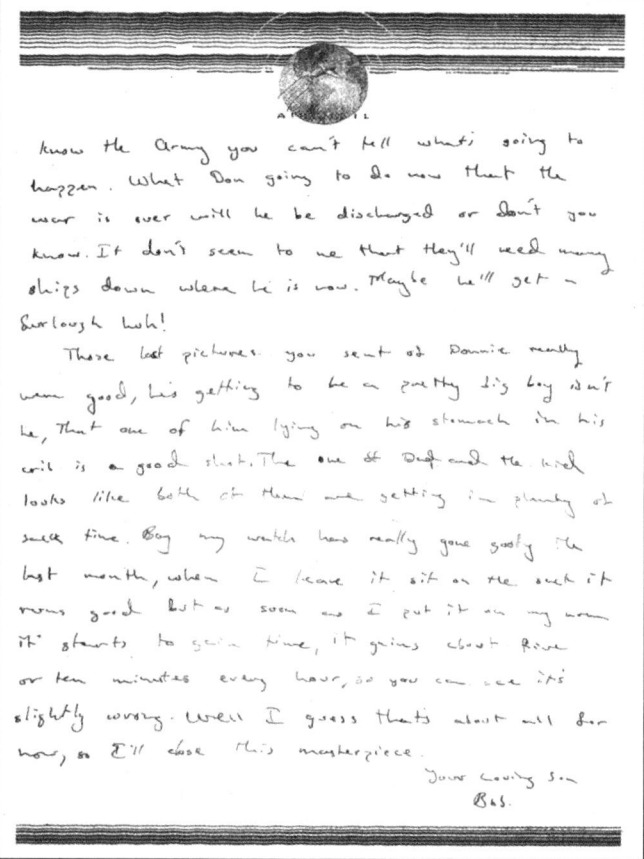

participation starts, the last one we got recently. So if they go by overseas time we should be pretty high up. But you know the Army. You can't tell what's going to happen. What Don going to do now that the war is over will he be discharged or don't you know. It doesn't seem to me that they'll need many ships down where he is now. Maybe we'll get a furlough, huh!

Those last pictures you sent of Donnie really were good, he's getting to be a pretty big boy isn't he. That one of him lying on his stomach in his crib is a good shot. The one of Dad and the kid looks like both of them are getting in plenty of sack time, boy my watch has really gone goofy the last month, when I leave it sit on the sack it runs good but as soon as I put it on my arm it starts to gain time. It gains about five or ten minutes every hour, so you can see it's slightly wrong. Well I guess that's about all for now, so I'll close this masterpiece.

Your Loving Son
Bob

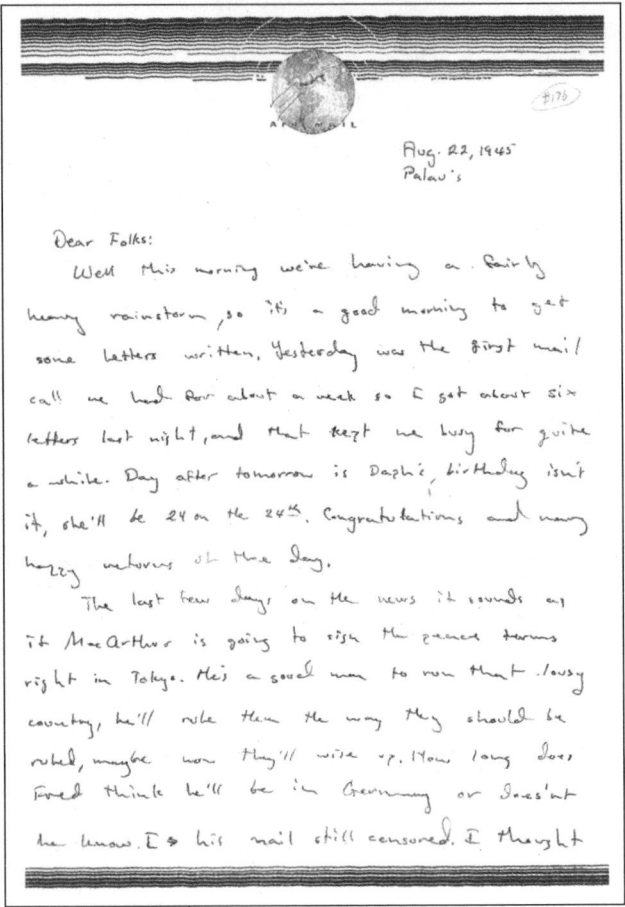

#176
Aug. 22, 1945
Palaus

Dear Folks:

Well this morning we're having a fairly heavy rainstorm, so it's a good morning to get some letters written. Yesterday was the first mail call we had for about a week so I got about six letters last night, and that kept me busy for quite a while. Day after tomorrow is Daph's birthday isn't it, she'll be 24 on the 24th. Congratulations and many happy returns of the day.

The last few days on the news it sounds as if MacArthur is going to sign the peace terms right in Tokyo. He's a good man to run that lousy country, he'll rule them the way they should be ruled, maybe now they'll

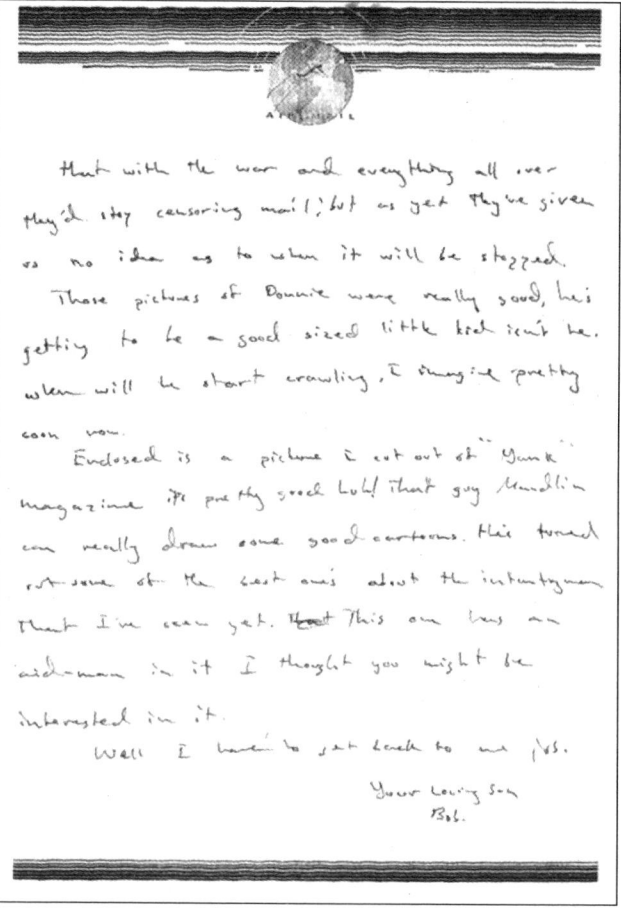

wise up. How long does Fred think he'll be in Germany or doesn't he know. Is his mail still censored. I thought that with the war and everything all over they'd stop censoring mail; but as yet they've given us no idea as to when it will be stopped.

Those pictures of Donnie were really good, he's getting to be a good sized little kid isn't he. When will he start crawling, I imagine pretty soon now.

Enclosed is a picture I cut out of Yank magazine it's pretty good huh! That guy Maudlin can really draw some good cartoons. He's turned out some of the best ones about the infantrymen that I've seen yet. This one has an aid-man in it I thought you might be interested in it.

Well I have to get back to my job.

Your Loving Son
Bob

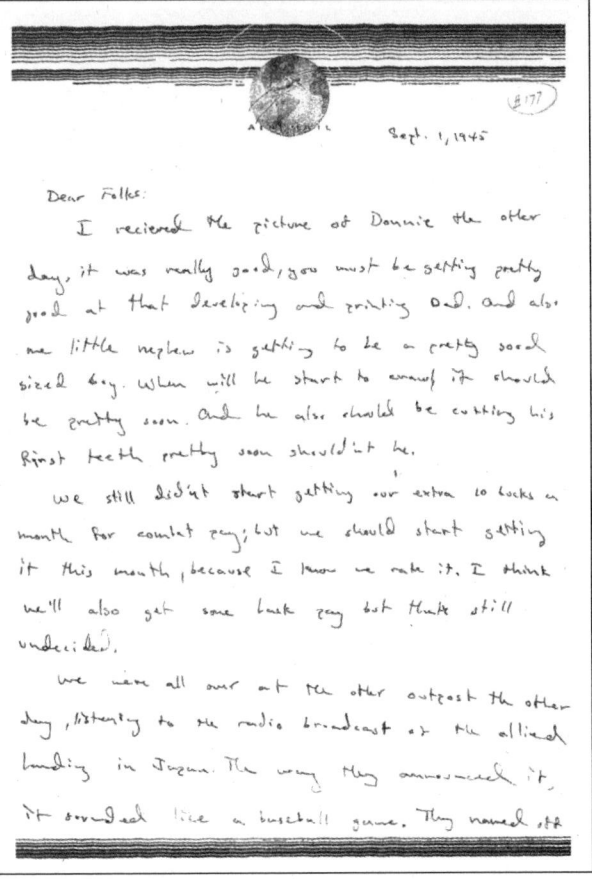

#177
Sept 1, 1945
Koror

Dear Folks:

I received the picture of Donnie the other day; it was really good. You must be getting pretty good at that developing and printing, Dad. And also my little nephew is getting to be a pretty good sized boy. When will he start to crawl? It should be pretty soon. And he should be getting his first teeth pretty soon, shouldn't he?

We still didn't start getting our extra ten bucks per month for combat pay; but we should start getting it this month, because I know we rate it. I think we'll also get some back pay but that is still undecided.

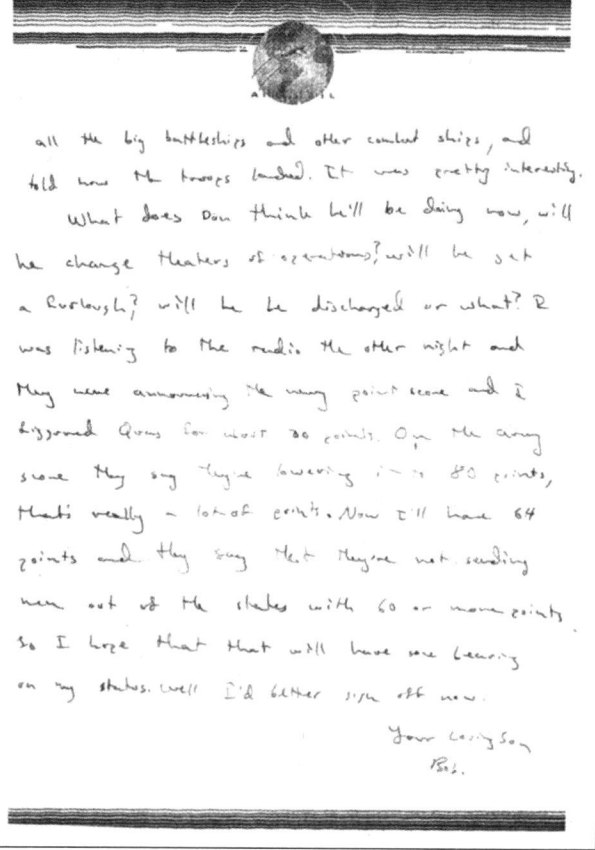

We were all over at the other outpost the other day, listening to the radio broadcast, of the Allied landing in Japan. The way they announced it, it sounded like a baseball game. They moved off all the big battle ships and other combat ships, and told how the troops landed.

What does Don think he'll be doing now? Will he change theaters of operation? Will he get a furlough? Will he be discharged or what? I was listening to the radio the other night and they were announcing the point score and I figured Quas was about 30 points. On the Army scene they say they're lowering it to 80 points. That's really a lot of points. Now I'll have 64 points and they say that they're not sending men out of the States with 60 or more points so I hope that that will have some bearing on my status.

Well I better sign off now.

Your loving son,
Bob

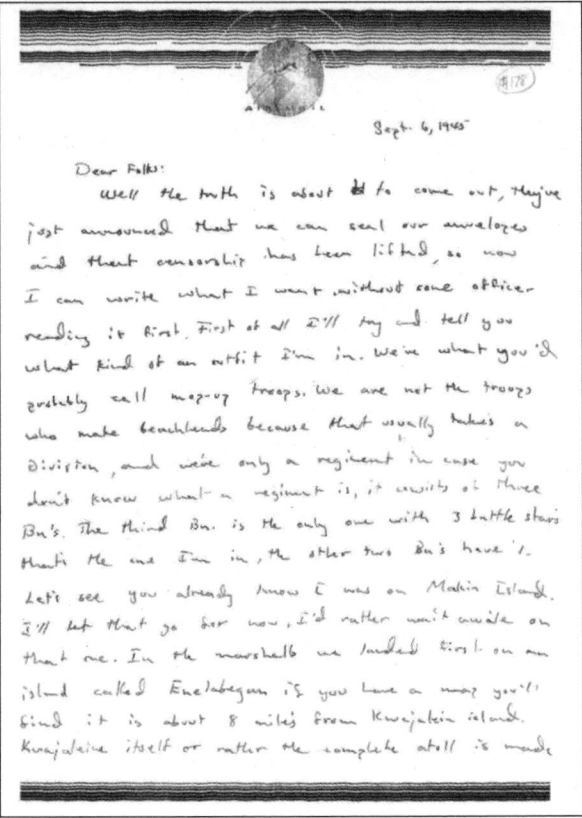

#178
Sept. 6, 1945

Dear Folks:

Well the truth is about to come out. They've just announced that we can seal our envelopes and that censorship has been lifted, so now I can write what I want without some officer reading it first. First of all I'll try and tell you what kind of an outfit I'm in. We're what you'd probably call mop-up troops. We are not the troops who make beachheads because that usually takes a division, and we're only a regiment in case you don't know what a regiment is, it usually consists of three Bn's. The third Bn. is the only one with 3 battle stars that's the one I'm in, the other two Bn's have 1. Let's see you already know I was on Makin Island. I'll let that go for now, I'd rather wait awhile on that one. In the Marshalls we landed first on an island called Enelabegum if you have a map you'll find it is about 8 miles from

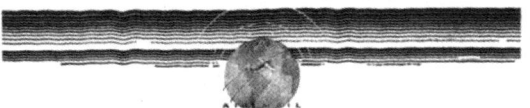

up at 90 different islands. Well you read in the
papers where the 7th Div. took kwajalien. Well what
that means is they took the island with practically
all the Japs on it. The other small islands are left
to troops like us to mop-up all in all I'd say
our Bn. took close to thirty small islands. Don't
get the idea that all of these were big operations,
they weren't they were small! On some islands there
wasn't even Japs only natives. You can't understand those
Japs, on one island we found 157 of them all dead,
they'd committed suicide even before any american
troops landed. Up thru the Marshall islands campaign
the U.S. didn't capture many Japs, but I'd say as an
offhand guess that we captured around 12 Japs in
the Marshalls altogether, big number huh! Guys don't trust them
Then this deal out here, to tell the truth I never
thought we'd come here this dump was invaded
while we were still on Kwajalein; but they gave us
a fast shuttle and here we are. This is the
same type work we send patrols out daily, to get

Kwajalein island. Kwajalein itself or rather the complete atoll is made up
of 90 different islands. Well you read in the papers where the 7th Div took
Kwajalein. Well what that means is they took the island with practically all
the Japs on it. The other small islands are left to troops like us to mop-up.
All in all I'd say our Bn took close to thirty small islands. Don't get the idea
that all of these were big operation, they weren't they were small! On some
islands there wasn't even Japs only natives. You can't understand those Japs,
on one island we found 157 of them all dead, they'd committed suicide even
before any American troops landed. Up thru the Marshall islands campaign
the U.D. didn't capture many Japs, but I'd say as an offhand guess that we
captured around 12 Jap in the Marshalls altogether, big number huh! Guys
don't trust them. Then this deal out here, to tell the truth I never thought
we'd come here. This dump was invaded while we were still on Kwajalein;
but they gave us a fast shuffle and here we are. This is the same type work.
We send patrols out daily, to get -[page cut off]

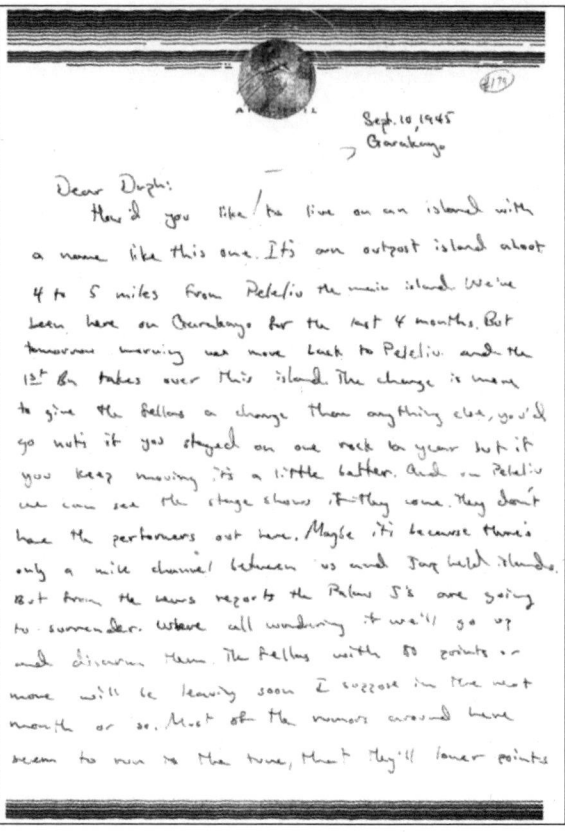

#179
Sept 10, 1945
Garakayo

Dear Daph:

How'd you like to live on an island with a name like this one. It's an outpost island about 4 to 5 miles from Peleliu the main island. We've been here on Garakayo for the last 4 months. But tomorrow morning we move back to Peleliu and the 1st Bn takes over this island. The change is more to give the fellas a change than anything else, you'd go nuts if you stayed on one rock a year but if you keep moving it's a little better. And on Peleliu we can see the stage shows if they come. They don't have the performers out here. Maybe it's because there's only a mile channel between us and Jap held islands. But from the news reports the Palau J's are going to surrender. We're all wondering if we'll go up and disarm

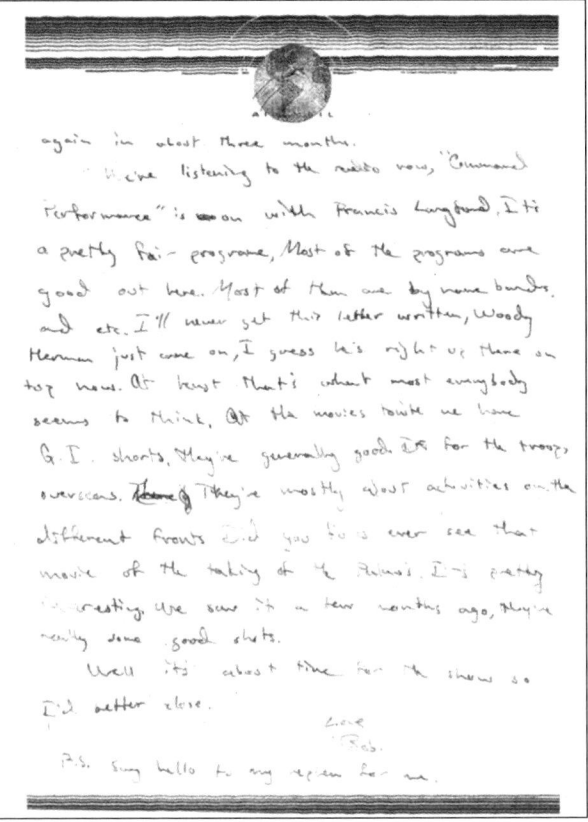

them. The fellas with 50 points or more will be leaving soon I suppose in the next month or so. Most of the rumors around here – [page cut off] – again in about three months.

We're listening to the radio now, "Command Performance" is on with Francis Longford. It's a pretty fair program. Most of the programs are good out here. Most of them are by name bands and etc. I'll never get this letter written, Woody Herman just came on, I guess he's right up there on top now. At least that's what most everybody seems to think. At the movies tonite we have G.I. shorts. They're generally good. It's for the troops overseas. They're mostly about activities on the different fronts. Did you folks ever see that movie of the taking of the Palau's. It's pretty interesting. We saw it a few months ago, they've really done some good shots.

Well it's about time for the show so I'd better close.

Love
Bob

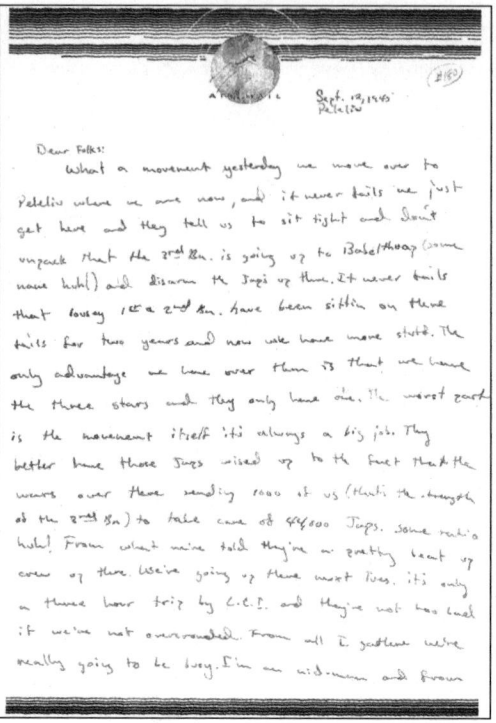

#180
Sept. 12, 1945
Peleliu

Dear Folks:

What a movement yesterday we move over to Peleliu where we are now, and it never fails we just get here and they tell us to sit tight and don't unpack that the 3rd Bn. is going up to Babelthuap (some name huh!) and disarm the Japs up there. It never fails that lousy 1st and 2nd Bm. have been sitting on their tails for two years and now we have more stuff. The only advantage we have over them is that we have the three stars and they only have one. The worst part is the movement itself is always a big job. They better have those Japs wised up to the fact that the wars over there sending 1000 of us (that's the strength of the 3rd Bd) to take care of 44,000 Japs. Some ration huh! From what we're told they're a pretty beat up crew up there.

We're going up there next Tues. It's only a three hour trip by L.C.I. and they're not too bad if we're not overcrowded. From all I gather we're really going to be busy. I'm an aid-man and from what I hear we're practically

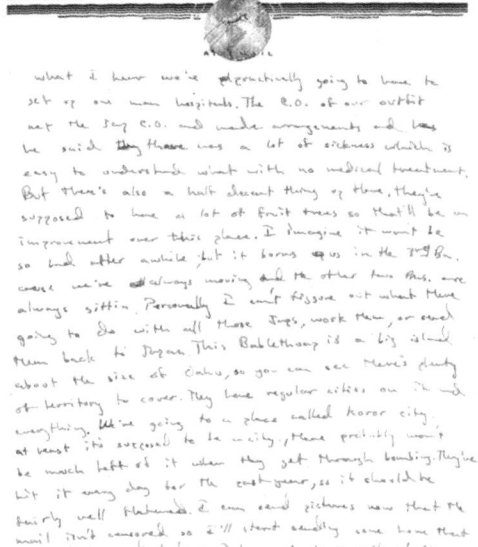

going to have to set up one man hospitals. The C.O. of our outfit met the Jap C.O/ and made arrangements and he said there was a lot of sickness which is easy to understand what with no medical treatment. But there's also a half decent thing up there, they're supposed to have a lot of fruit trees so that'll be an improvement over this place. I imagine it won't be so bad after awhile; but it bums us in the 3rd Bm. cause we're always moving and the other two Bn.s are always sittin. Personally I can't figure out what they're going to do with all those Japs work them or send them back to Japan. This Bablethuap is a big island about the size of Oahu, so you can see there's plenty of territory to cover. They have regular cities on it and everything. We're going to a place called Koror city. At least it's supposed to be a city, there probably won't be much left of it when they get through bombing. They've hit it every day for the past year, so it should be fairly well flattened. I can send pictures now that the mail isn't censored so I'll start sending some home that I couldn't send before. I have about 10 rolls of film left so I should get some good pictures. Well it's late now so I'd better close now.

Your Loving Son,
Bob

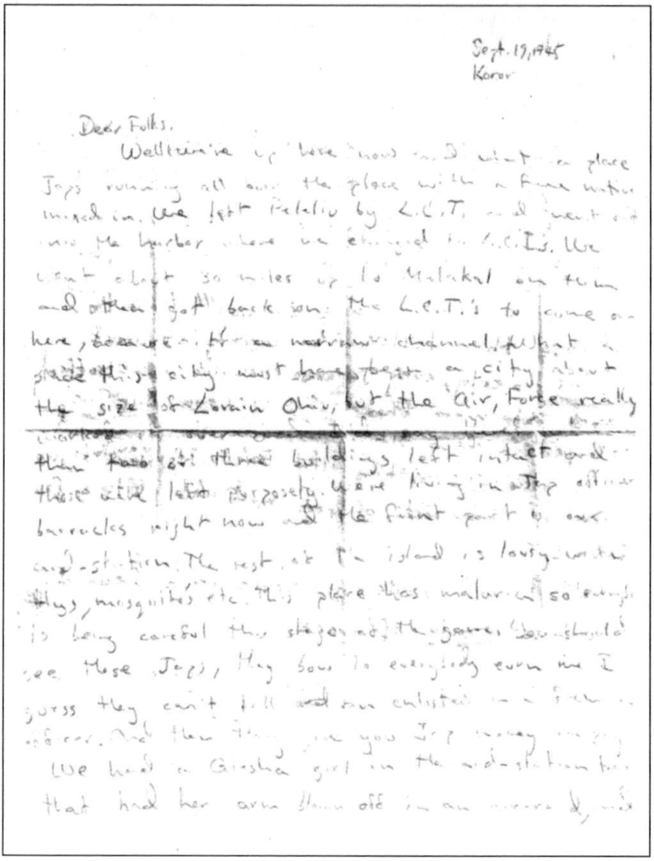

#181
Sept 19, 1945
Koror

Dear Folks,

Well we're up here now and what a place. Japs running all over the place with a few native mixed in. We left Peleliu by L.C.T. and went out into the harbor where we embarked to L.C.I.s. We went about 30 miles up to Malakal on them and then got back on the L.C.T's to come over here, because it's a narrow channel. What a pace this city must have been a city about the size of Lovain Ohio, but the Air Force really worked it over and I'd say there's no more than two or three buildings left intact and those were left purposely. We're living in a Jap officer barracks right now and the front part of our aid-station. The rest of the island is lousy with flies, mosquitos etc. This place has

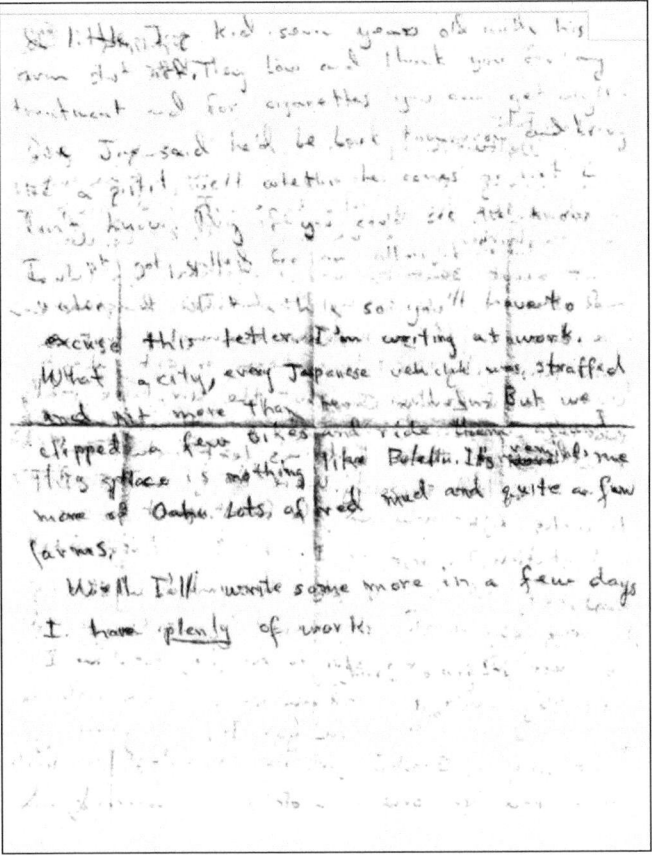

malaria so everyone is being careful this stage of the fame. You should see these Japs, they bow to everybody even me I guess they can't tell an enlisted man from an officer. And then they give you Jap money in payment.

We had a Geisha girl in the aid-station tonite that had her arm blown off in an air-raid, and a little Jap kid seven years old with his arm shot off. They bow and thank you for my treatment and for cigarettes you can get anything. One Jap said he'd be back tomorrow and bring a pistol well whether he comes or not I don't know. But if you could see the-[letter is illegible for 2 lines] – so you'll have to excuse this letter. I'm writing at work.

What a city, every Japanese vehicle was strafed and hit more than [illegible] But we clipped a few bikes and ride them around. This place is nothing like Peleliu. It reminds me more of Oahu. Lots of red mud and quite a few farms.

Well I'll write some more in a few days. I have plenty of work.

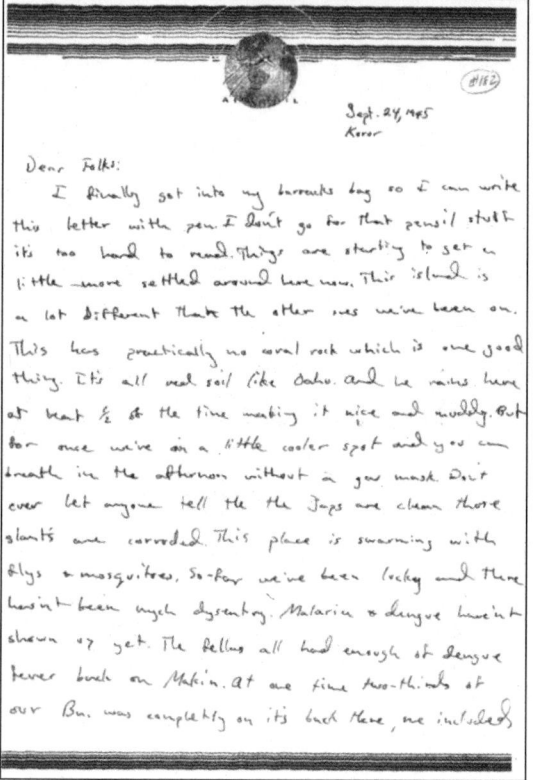

#182
September 24, 1945
Koror

Dear Folks:

I finally got into my barracks bag so I can write this letter with pen. I didn't go for that pensil stuff it's too hard to read. Things are starting to get a little more settled around here now. This island is a lot different than the other ones we've been on. This has practically no coral rock which is one good thing. It's all red soil like Oahu. And he rains here at least 16 of the time making it nice and muddy. But for once we're in a little cooler spot and you can breath in the afternoon without a gas mask. Don't ever let anyone tell you the Japs are clean those slant's are corroded. This place is swarming with flys + mosquitoes. So-far we've been lucky and there hasn't been much dysentry. Malaria + dengue haven't shown up yet. The fellas all had enough of dengue fever back on Makin. At one time two-thirds of our Bu. was completely on

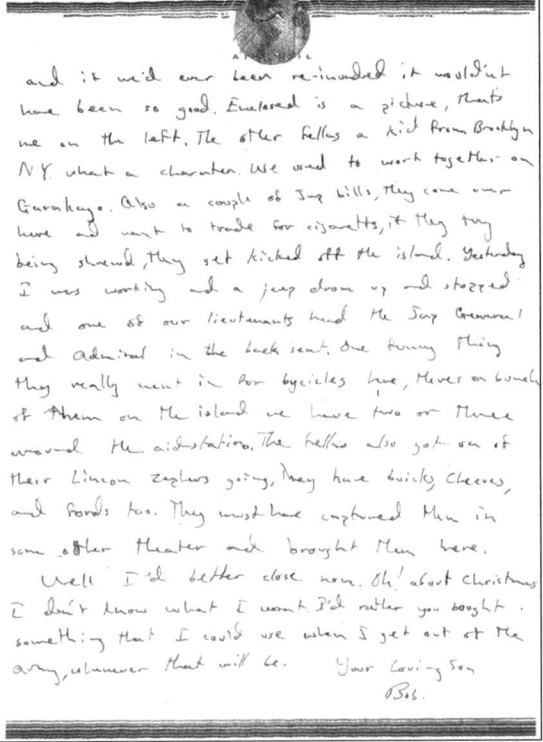

it's back there, me included, and if we'd ever been re-invaded it wouldn't have been so good. Enclosed is a picture, that's me on the left. The other fellas a kid from Brooklyn N.Y. what a character. We used to work together on Garakayo. Also a couple of Jap bills, they come over here and want to trade for cigarettes, if they try being shrewd they get kicked off the island. Yesterday I was working and a jeep drove up and stopped and one of our lieutenants had the Jap General and Admiral in the back seat. One funny thing they really went in for bicycles here, there's a bunch of them on the island we have two or three around the aid station. Then fellas also got one of their Lincoln Zephyrs going, they have Buicks, Cheeves, and Fords too. They must have captured them in some other theatre and brought them here.

Well I'd better close now. Oh! About Christmas I don't know what I want. I'd rather you bought something that I could use when I get out of the army, whenever that will be.

Your Loving Son,
Bob

Sept. 30, 1945
Koror

Dear Folks,

Well all the fellas with 80 or more prints are getting ready to leave now, there's a pretty strong rumor out that they'll be out of the Palau's and headed home by the 13th of next month. Some of the fellas are turning in their clothes and equipment today. Tomorrow all men with 70 or more points become eligible for discharge; but I don't think they'll leave before the end of Oct. then on Nov. 1 all men with 60 or more points become eligible for discharge, that's the group I'm in. I have 64 points, so I have a possibility of leaving here around the end of Nov. that's if I'm lucky. That's about all the talk is that's flying around here, points! One good thing we got rid of yesterday was our gas-masks, that's really a pain to carry around, they're bulky and get in your way and everybody was plenty glad to get rid of them, the guys going home soon are cleaning out their stuff throwing everything away so they won't have to carry it and all the low point men follow around picking the stuff up.

#183
Sept. 30, 1945
Koror

Dear Folks,
Well all the fellas with 80 or more prints are getting ready to leave now, there's a pretty strong rumor out that they'll be out of the Palau's and headed home by the 13th of next month. Some of the fellas are turning in their clothes and equipment today. Tomorrow all men with 70 or more points become eligible for discharge; but I don't think they'll leave before the end of Oct. then on Nov. 1 all men with 60 or more points become eligible for discharge, that's the group I'm in. I have 64 points, so I have a possibility of leaving here around the end of Nov. that's if I'm lucky. That's about all the talk is that's flying around here, points! One good thing we got rid of yesterday was our gas-masks, that's really a pain to carry around, they're bulky and get in your way and everybody was plenty glad to get rid of them, the guys going home soon are cleaning out their stuff throwing everything away so they won't have to carry it and all the low point men follow around picking the stuff up.

> *[Handwritten letter facsimile]*

They have kicked all the natives and Japs off this island now, I guess they don't want them wandering around the place. They let them come over sometimes though to dig potatoes. Next month we get our combat pay but it only goes back to Aug. 15th so we'll only get 30 bucks back pay, that's what is known as a big deal but there's nothing you can do about it.

If you want to sign me up for the American legion, that's o.k. with me because I think it will be a very influencing factor in civilian life. Personally I think the veterans will have a strong head running the country after this war. How is your plant going to do in all this reconversion Dad. Do you have to lay many people off or will they have room for more. I really can't decide whether to go to work or go to school when I get out. Are there any opportunities for advancement where you work, what's the story on your own job.

Well I have to be getting back on the job now, Oh! don't send any more Xmas boxes because I'm getting pretty sure I'll be started home before then at least I hope I am. Well that's about all for today,

Your Loving Son,
Bob

> (#84)
>
> Oct. 8, 1945
> Koror
>
> Dear Folks:
> I really got the surprise of my life the other day, I was sitting around here doing nothing as usual when I got a phone call and who do you think it was, it was Foley. I mean I almost fainted, he was calling right from the dock here on Koror but couldn't get on the island because no unauthorized personelle are allowed on, so I hopped a truck down to the dock and got him in. We stayed here awhile then we took off on an L.C.I. for Peleliu and stayed overnite there, then he had to get back to Guam. You know what he did he just took off from Guam and hopped a plane down here to Peleliu just to say hello, I'll tell you one thing I won't forget that in a hurry. Well our detachment is really getting small now we've only got 9 men left in our platoon that left the states together, a bunch left day before yesterday.

#184
Oct. 8, 1945
Koror

Dear Folks;

I really got the surprise of my life the other day, I was sitting around here doing nothing as usual when I got a phone call and who do you think it was, it was Foley. I mean I almost fainted, he was calling right from the dock here on Koror but couldn't get on the island because no unauthorized personnel are allowed on. So I hopped a truck down to the dock and got him in.

We stayed here awhile then we took off on an L.C.I for Peleliu and stayed ovemite there, then we had to get back to Guam. You know what he did he just took off from Guam and hopped a plane down here to Peleliu just to say hello. I'll tell you one thing I won't forget that in a hurry. Well our detachment is really getting small now we've only got 9 men left in our platoon that left the states together, bunch left day before yesterday, there's

120

how it's working here, all men with 8- or more points will be out by the 15 of this month and all men with 70 points or more will leave before Oct. 31. Then on Nov. 1, men with 60 or more are eligible and they should move pretty fast I hope. There's a pretty hot rumor floating around here that the outfit will be heading for Oahu and should arrive there the middle of Nov. and from there we should be right up on the top to get released. That's about all the rumors now. They let the Japs come on this island to scrape up food so yesterday Survill and I were walking down the road and we turn a comer and who should we meet but about 100 Japs marching up the road. Their officers salute us and say good morning to which we reply Hi. We don't feed them nothin here they get their own chow or none at all. Those bums are really cigarette hungry, they'll trade you a samurai sword for a carton of smokes. So it's a good deal. I think I'll get me one, they're pretty hard to get hold of though you have to make connections. I have a couple of flags and a knife. That's about all. Well I'd better shove off.

Your Loving Son
Bob

(#185)

Oct. 12, 1945
Koror

Dear Folks:

I guess I've been pretty bad in my letter writing, but we've been pretty busy around here, we're getting it fixed of so that it's liveable around now; but it took plenty of fixing. There's plenty of rumors flying around here now, and they're all different. One thing that is almost positive is that a regiment of Marines are going to relieve us here sometime around the 1st of Nov. And then we're to pull out. Now the rumors run that we're to go any one of three places, one is to Saigon; another and about the strongest is back to Oahu and the third is to the states. The Oahu one seems to run the strongest, but nothing is definate yet. I'll be eligible for discharge in 19 more days; but you understand being eligible and actually getting out is another thing; but all the 70 pointers that is men with 70 points or more will be off for Saigon (that's the separation center) before the 20th of Oct that's next week. And then we'll be right on top.

#185
Oct 12, 1945
Koror

Dear Folks:

I guess I've been pretty bad in my letter writing, but we've been pretty busy around here, we're getting it fixed so that it's liveable around now; but it took plenty of fixing. There's plenty of rumors flying around here now, and they're all different. One thing that is almost positive is that a regiment of Marines are going to relieve us here sometime around the 1st of Nov. And then we're to pull out. Now the rumors run that we've to go any one of three places. One is to Saigon, another and about the strongest is back to Oahu and the third is to the states. The Oahu one seems to run the strongest, but nothing is definite yet. I'll be eligible for discharge in 19 more days; but you understand being eligible and actually getting out is another thing; but all the 70 pointers that is men with 70 points or will be off for Saigon *that's

> we're getting some pretty good souvinurs here now, I have a couple flags a small knife and the last thing is a samori sword, it's really a nice sword, I can sell it any time I want for $100.00 but I think I'll hang onto it, there tough to get. I also have some bad news lately we've been getting in some replacements for the high point men, and yesterday I put my watch in my mosquito bar to take a shower and when I came back it was gone, well that's the last I saw of it so I'm just out one nice watch. But if i ever find out who stole it, I'll smash his face in. anybody who'd steal off of a fella in his own outfit is rotten. I know it must be some one of the new fellos but you can't go searching everyone, I'll just have to keep my eyes open. Oh! don't send xmas packages because I'm pretty sure I'll at least be on my way home by that time. well I'd better get back to the grind but I wanted to get this letter off.
>
> Your Loving Son
> Bob

the separation center) before the 20th of Oct that's next week. And then we'll be – [page cut off].

We're getting some pretty good souvenirs here now, I have a couple flags a small knife and the best thing is a samurai sword, it's really a nice sword, I can sell it any time I want for $100.00 but I think I'll hang onto it, there tough to get. I also have some bad news lately we've been getting in some replacements fort the high point men, and yesterday I put my watch in my mosquito bar to take a shower and when I came back it was gone, well that's the last I saw of it so I'm just out one nice watch. But if I ever find out who stole it, I'll smash his face in.

Anybody who'd steal off a fella in his own outfit is rotten. I know it must be some of the new fellas but you can't go searching everyone, I'll just have to keep my eyes open. Oh! don't send Xmas packages because I'm pretty sure I'll at least be on my way home by that time.

Well I'd better get back to the grind but I wanted to get this letter off.

Your Loving Son
Bob

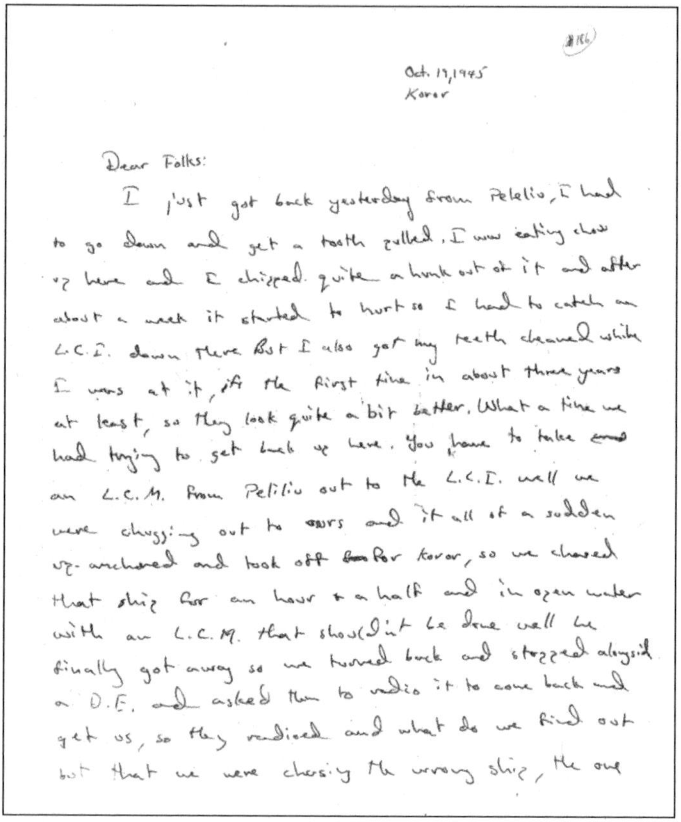

[handwritten letter reproduced below in print]

#186
Oct 19, 1945
Koror

Dear Folks:

I just got back yesterday from Peleliu, I had to go down and get a tooth pulled. I was eating chow up here and I chipped quite a hunk of it and after about a week it started to hurt so I had to catch an LCI down there. But I also got my teeth cleaned while I was at it, it's the first time in about three years at least, so they look quite a bit better. What a time we had trying to get back up here. You have to take an L.C.M. from Peleliu out to the L.C.I. well we were chugging out to ours and it all of a sudden up anchored and took off for Koror, so we chased that ship for an hour+ a half and in open water with an L.C.M. that shouldn't be drue well he finally got away so we turned back and stopped alongside a D.E. and asked them to radio it to come back and get ups, so they

> we were supposed to set was about 100 yards
> away from the D.E. so we finally got on it and
> came up here. ~~Haveit~~
> Haven't heard any definite news on moving yet
> but our 70 pointers will all be out by the 27ᵗʰ of
> this month.
> Enclosed is a money order for #40.ᵘᵘ so you can
> put that in the bank. I didn't get a chance to
> send home a money order last month so I figured
> I might as well send the usual 20 bucks per month, seems
> like I should be over a thousand soon, I've sent home
> at least 50 a month for the last 9 or 10 months! OL!
> I mailed my recorder home so when it gets there
> don't be surprised. That co. hasn't sent me the part I
> paid for yet so it won't operate; but you can clean it a
> little if you want. I'm not bringing the records they're
> to heavy.
> Well say hello to my nephew for me and tell him I
> sure hope to see him before long.
> Your Loving Son
> Bob

radioed and what do we find out but that we were chasing the wrong ship, the one we were supposed to get was about 100 yards away from the D.E. so we finally got on it and came up here. Haven't heard any definite news on moving yet but out 70 pointers will all be out by the 27th of this month.

Enclosed is a money order for $40.00 so you can put that in the bank. I didn't get a chance to send home a money order last month so I figured I might as well send the usual 20 bucks per month, seems like I should be over a thousand soon. I've sent home at least 50 a month for the last 9 or 10 months! Oh! I mailed my recorder home so when it gets there don't be surprised, that co. hasn't sent me the part I paid for yet so it won't operate; but you can clean it a little if you want/ I'm not bringing the records they're too heavy.

Well say hello to my nephew for me and tell him I sure hope to see him before long.

Your Loving Son
Bob

125

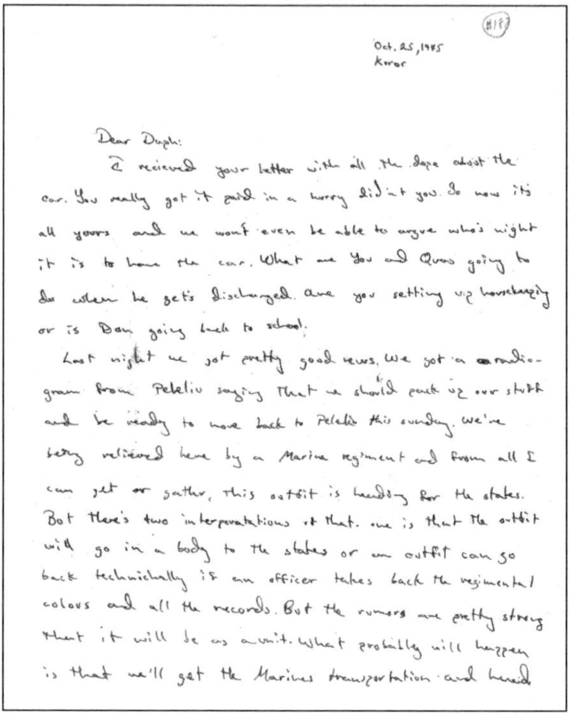
#187

Oct. 25, 1945
Koror

Dear Daph:
I recieved your letter with all the dope about the car. You really got it paid in a hurry didn't you. So now its all yours and we won't even be able to argue who's right it is to have the car. What are you and Quas going to do when he gets discharged. are you setting up housekeeping or is Don going back to school.
Last night we got pretty good news. We got a radio-gram from Peleliu saying that we should pack up our stuff and be ready to move back to Peleliu this sunday. We're being relieved here by a Marine regiment and from all I can get or gather, this outfit is heading for the states. But there's two interpretations of that. one is that the outfit will go in a body to the states or an outfit can go back technically if an officer takes back the regimental colours and all the records. But the rumors are pretty strong that it will be as a unit. What probably will happen is that we'll get the Marines transportation and head

#187
Oct 25, 1945
Koror

Dear Daph:
I received your letter with all the dope about the car. You really got it paid in a hurry didn't you. So now it's all yours and we won't even be able to argue who's right it is to have that car. What are you and Quas going to do when he gets discharged. Are you setting up housekeeping or is Don going back to school.

Last night we got pretty good news. We got a radio-gram from Peleliu saying that we should pack up our stuff and be ready to move back to Peleliu this Sunday. We're being relieved here by a Marine regiment and from all I can get or gather, this outfit is heading for the states.

But there's two interpretations of that. One is that the outfit will go in a body to the states or an outfit can go back technically if an officer takes back the regimental colors and all the records. But the rumors are pretty strong that it will be as a unit. What probably will happen is that we'll get the Marines -[page cut off] – back to Oahu, where the low point men will be screened out. Then those who are eligible will continue on to the states. That's purely guesswork with rumors thrown in, there's only one definite fact, we're being relieved in a few days and we're boarding ships leading towards the states or Oahu. Anyhow I'll be eligible by the time you get this letter so it doesn't make much difference one way or the other. Oh! All our 70 point men have left and Survill + I are the only one's left of the original group that left the states.

Did you get the three envelopes full of pictures I sent about a week ago. I sure hope they all got thru. Anyhow that'll keep you busy pasting for a while most of those are pictures that wouldn't pass the censors, so this is the first chance I've had to send them. Also enclosed in this letter is three negatives, two are of yours truly. That's my samurai sword + flag. Pretty good sword huh! I could get easy a hundred dollars for it; but unless somebody hauls out 200 bucks it stays in my possession.

Well I'd better close now, say hello to my nephew for me, and tell him I hope to say hello to him myself soon.

Love
Bob

> Oct. 31, 1945
> Peleliu
>
> Dear Folks:
> Last sunday we moved back to Peleliu from Koror and now the whole regiment has assembled on this island. We're supposed to go back to the states that is all men with 60 points or more. The ships are out in the harbor now and we should get aboard within two or three days. Course we may get on tomorrow and it may be a week from now, it's plenty snafu. But anyhow everybody's plenty happy that the regiment is headed back. We've turned in our rifles + helmets overleggings and shelter-halves, also part of our clothes. And I mean I'm plenty happy to be rid of that stuff. Well anyhow you might as well stop writing because the letters will have to be rerouted home. In other words I think we'll be back in the U.S. in a while. But don't ever count on anything too much, you can't tell
>
> (over)

#188
Oct 31, 1945
Peleliu

Dear Folks:

Last Sunday we moved back to Peleliu from Koror and now the whole regiment has assembled on this island. We're supposed to go back to the states that is all men with 60 points or more. The ships are out in the harbor now and we should get aboard within two or three days. Course we may get on tomorrow and it may be a week from now, it's plenty snafu. But anyhow everybody's plenty happy that the regiment is headed back. We've turned in our rifles + helmets overleggings and shelter-halves, also part of our clothes. And I mean I'm plenty happy to be rid of that stuff. Well anyhow you might as well stop writing because the letters will have to be rerouted

> about the Army. The Co.'s are packing up all their equipment and they're working all night tonite. To tell you the truth everything is up in the air now. But you might as well stop writing, but if we're here very long or if anything new turns up I'll write again. But otherwise I won't write any-more. But when we get to the states I'll send you a wire or phone if I have time. Right now that's the whole story around here. If anything new comes up I'll let you know. Now dont go expecting me back in a couple weeks. It'll probably be in Dec. sometime.
>
> Well I guess I'd better close now because I want to write another letter.
>
>   Your Loving Son
>   Bob
>
> P.S. You'd better cross your fingers

home. In other words I think we'll be back in the U.S. in a while. But don't ever count on anything too much, you can't tell about the Army. The C.O.'s are packing up all then- equipment and they're working all night tonite. To tell you the truth everything is up in the air now. But you might as well stop writing; but if we're here very long or if anything new turns up I'll write again. But otherwise I won't write any-more. But when we get to the states I'll send you a wire or phone if I have time. Right now that's the whole story around here. If anything new comes up I'll let you know. Now don't go expecting me back in a couple weeks. It'll probably be in Dec. sometime.

Well I guess I'd better close now because I want to write another letter.

Your Loving Son
Bob

P.S. You better cross your fingers

129

PART II

THE INTERVIEWS

There are as many WWII stories as there were participants, and each story is unique to both the person and the circumstances. In 1991 I began interviewing WWII veterans and eventually recorded 44 of them. The idea came from the director of the Centerville (Ohio) Historical Society who, knowing that I was a WWII veteran, thought I might have an interest in doing it.

I learned more from these veterans than I could ever have imagined. More than simply creating a record of their experiences, it became an adventure of self-discovery. What would I have done if I had been placed in their circumstances? What I learned was a lot about them, but perhaps even more about myself. It proved to truly be an amazing experience, as you are about to discover...

Virginia K Hess

Browning The hine Gun

Interview #1 – Fred Hess

Fred Hess was in the Army in World War II in the Pacific Theater. He served with the 24th Infantry Division and participated in three campaigns. He was wounded on the island of Luzon in the Philippines. He is married to Virginia Krause Hess and they have three children-Peter Dane Hess, Kristina Lee Mason and Victoria Lynn Bender. They also have two grandchildren. Fred belongs to a number of groups in the Dayton area- Sister City, Agonis Club, the VFW and American Legion. He owned his own hardware stores for forty years in the Dayton area and at the time of this interview lives in Washington Township.

Could you tell us a little bit about your early life, about where you were born and raised?

Born in Dayton, Bob, and I was the last of six children in the family. And my mother became ill and so she had to go to a nursing home, so I moved with my father to Middletown, Ohio, and lived down in Middletown, and also Hamilton. Later he got a little sick, had problems with his heart, and so my brothers and sisters, were all in Dayton. They came to me and said, you're gonna have to come up with us because you don't have any funds to begin with and Pop doesn't seem like he's gonna be able to help much, you know, watch you and take care of you.

My father was a salesman. He could sell anything, whatever it was. He worked at Dayton dry goods for many years and he worked a lot of different places in sales. He had one thing he sold in Hamilton, Ohio, the people in Hamilton, don't remember, he sold a product called Crazy' Water Crystals. This was made in Texas-- Mineral Wells, Texas, and it was one of those things, it was like, I mean, that type of thing that was supposed to keep you regular, you know. He was a natural salesman. Dayton Dry Goods was his big thing, I think, when it was in town. Anyway I came to Dayton to live with my sister, Ann Hall, and she married Dave Hall, the mayor of

Dayton, and so they took me, from eighth grade on, 'til I graduated and went into the Army. And I always say he was tougher on me than he was on his own sons.

What school did you go to?
In grade school I went to about three or four different ones around town, but I ended up at Colonel White Junior High. Then I went to Steele High School for one year, the last year it was open. And finally I went to Fairview and graduated from Fairview in 1942.

As for work, Dave Hall owned a laundry and I worked in the laundry every summer and on Saturdays without fail, and also during the school year, I would take his father, who was a semi- invalid who liked to take trips, all over and I'd drive him around. I'd get out of the last class in the day and I would go home and take him on a ride to Springfield or wherever he happened to want to go-

I didn't get into a lot of things, I was on the football squad for two years, one year of Fairview, one year at Steele, but that was about it. And then I would take care of him. There were a lot of things I missed, but I was sitting high because not being able to do anything I wanted to do in Middletown, Ohio when I come to Dayton I lived a pretty good life. So because of them, they got me straightened around. Not that I ever got into any trouble but I could have.

I played some intramural basketball on church teams, and I was in a play. I was in the play Anne of Green Gables. I think I was what's known as the spear carrier, I stood at the back you know, but Fairview was a good school. I graduated from Fairview in June of 1 942. Then I went to the University of Dayton for one semester, for half a year in the fall of 1942.

What happened next?
I went to the University of Dayton for one semester, for half a year in the fall of 1942. They said now if you join the ROTC and the ERC, the Enlisted Reserve Corps, you get to finish college. Well, I talked to my brother-in-law, Dave, and he said I can't think that's going to be right, they may think it will be like that, but it won't be, and so he said you might as well either enlist or get drafted. Well, I tried to get into the Coast Guard 'cause I had a friend, you know, that was in the Coast Guard and next I wanted the Navy or something like that. And the one fellow that I knew in the Coast Guard had remarked how nice it was and on top of that here at Dayton you've got

the Air Force in your blood and so I thought, well, I'll try that out before anything happens, before I was drafted. But it turned out that I didn't get in there, I didn't have enough mathematics for what I needed. I was taking mathematics in college but all I had was a semester. And so then I was drafted and I was sent to Camp Blanding, Florida. That was March in 1943. First I went to Fort Benjamin Harrison to get sworn in. And then I went to Camp Blanding, Florida for basic training with the 66th Infantry Division-the Black Panther Division. Camp Blanding is between St. Augustine and Jacksonville, near Jacksonville.

What do you remember from basic training?
Well, I didn't have any problems with basic training at all. I sort of enjoyed it I think. I was young enough at the time and I was with some young, nice guys and the good part of it was with my ROTC training, I became a non-commissioned officer pretty fast. And so I made corporal within two months. And then I became a sergeant after I went to another camp, but I mean I was in a place where it made a lot of difference and I didn't have to do a lot of stuff that some of the people had to do. And Florida, of course, is nice, you know, March and April and it was terrific.

Why did you join the Army?
Well, the story on that is a comic story. Russ Guerra was the captain of the police force and he and I grew up together and went to school, went all through school together. High school, anyway. When we went out to Columbus to be sworn in at Fort Hayes in Columbus we were all in line, and of course, alphabetically, I'm behind Russ, and he kept talking all the time about joining the Army and Navy and I said, I want to go in the Navy. I was dead set against the Army, I just didn't want to go in. If I couldn't get in the Air Force I wanted to go Navy. And so right away we're in this line and a fellow asked Russ, what do you want to go in, the Army or Navy? And Russ says Army. And then the guy says how about you? And I say Navy, Army, I mean Navy. And he said, "oh, too late, sorry, you're stuck. You're in the Army now. It was just a slip of the lip and brain, I think. But it turned out fine.

We went over to Fort Benjamin Harrison, Russ and I, and we were over there for about two weeks to get everything done that we had to get done, to take our tests, IQ test and everything like that. And most the time we were half asleep, I think. But it was enjoyable. And then Russ went to the 99th

Division and I was shipped and joined the 55th Division at Camp Blanding and Russ went to Texas.

Was basic about what you expected or was it more difficult?
I think it was pretty easy, wasn't difficult at all. But it was different in that you only saw part of basic training in the newsreels, and stuff like that, but when you're going through an infiltration course and you're climbing all these walls and things it gets a little bit tiresome after a while. They scare you to death because they always say, don't look up and all this. And it's the same way with the gas drill.

When you go into a house and get the mustard gas thrown at you and you've got your mask and everything on, they say don't take that thing off, or you're going to keel over. Well, I don't know if you would or not, but nobody took a chance. Nobody got sick. We were down there in March, April, and May or June of 1943? We spent most of the summer down there. I think it was June when we left to go to Camp Robinson, Arkansas, the whole division went to Camp Robinson Arkansas, near Little Rock. I was made a sergeant out there, and I stayed a sergeant all the way through the war.

And what was the sergeant's responsibility?
Well, the sergeant's responsibility at that time was assistant squad leader. And the platoon leader was the staff sergeant. He had a rocker underneath, just right, that's exactly what it was. A sergeant was a squad leader, in other words, he led the squad wherever they were supposed to be going. A squad was about twelve or fourteen something like that. We carried M-1 rifles, and carbines, mostly I carried the M-1 rifle. I was also involved with machine guns. It turned out after I got into another division, not another division, but they changed my assignment from a rifle company to a heavy weapons company, Company M. That was when I was in Camp Gruber, Oklahoma. I was there until probably the fall of '43. That's when I went into the Air Force.

How did you get from the infantry to the Air Force?
Well, they had something come up about being able to transfer out of the infantry, if you wanted to, because they needed people in the Air Force for some reason. So I always wanted to be in the Air Force, being from Dayton, so I tried and got transferred to Sheppard Field, Texas from Camp Gruber, Oklahoma.

Would that be in September or something of '43?

I passed the bombardier's tests and whatever had to be done. And everything was fine and I was supposed to leave with the same group I took tests with for California. And I got measles. And they sent me to the hospital. They wouldn't let me out of the hospital for two weeks. This is in the fall of '43? I took training down there and did all that. But then I got the measles so they said we're going to send you back to the infantry because they don't need any more people in the Air Force. So this was a matter of about a month that this happened. After I had the measles they wouldn't let me stay. Back to infantry and I went to Camp Gruber, Oklahoma as a replacement. I was a sergeant, as a replacement, and I knew I was going to be a replacement to go overseas when I went to Camp Gruber and I know I left in September. There I joined the 42nd Division. The Rainbow Division.

That's the only division that I ever knew that gave out a card, an identification card – the Rainbow Division. The Rainbow Division was the division Douglas MacArthur was in during World War I.

They had a history about them, they even gave you a book telling you that this is what a Rainbow Division soldier does, you know, it was a very strict outfit.

And how long were you with them?

Well, I was with them probably for about six or seven months and then I was shipped to California, to Fort Ord, as cadre knowing I was going to be a replacement. We were just sent out, some of the people that were non-coms that didn't start with the division were sent out. I was there all summer and shipped out in September of '44, overseas. I went to New Guinea first and was assigned to a unit after I got there, the 24th Infantry Division. Their insignia is the taro leaf. They call it the Hawaii Division but it was a take off of the 25th, it was formed as a part of the 25th.

What battalion, what company?

At that time I was still in heavy weapons – machine gun, mortar and all, but then after we left New Guinea, they said we're going to put you in the regular infantry into a rifle company. I was put in Company L, 19lh Infantry. I was in the 3rd Battalion then, the MILK Battalion. I, L and K are the rifle companies and M's the heavy weapons company. This is now in October of '44, and we're heading for Leyte. Leyte is one of the islands in the Philippine Island group.

This is to be Macarthur's big return?

Yes, that's where he went because it was probably the one he left from, but I don't know the particulars about Bataan. We didn't know anything about where we were going to land but we knew what to expect. I mean they told us this is what happened when this other unit went in, so be ready for this. We were on this transport with a bunch of boats, ships rather, that were protecting us and we had a lot of suicide bombing. Kamikaze planes. Now a Kamikaze is someone who's been given so much propaganda they believe that nothing can happen to them. And they said the thing you do in life is to kill the enemy in some way or another and give your life if you have to. Take this plane and fly it into the biggest battleship you can find or anything else. But don't expect to come back home. And that's what it was – these planes they were flying, some of them probably couldn't have made it back home. I mean they knew they were gonna do it and were gonna stay out there until they did something, did some damage. They were all suicide pilots. This was on October 20th to the 23, '44.

When did you get up there – just a day or two before that?

Right. Yes, we were about the second wave going into Leyte. But we didn't get a lot of action, as we were going in. We were scared, especially when you see these planes flying around and you know, you're sitting out there wide open and all you've got is a 20mm gun on this LST or whatever it is you're on, or LCI and you're crowded in, you're all crowded in, and you don't know how close you're going to get to the beach. And when that thing pulls up and drops the gangway, you have to get off. You don't waste any time, you don't mess around, you've got your hand and gun in front of you and you're pushing the guy in front of you and he's back of me, pushing me and getting off. And you might get water up to your knees, you might get it up to your shoulders.

How far did you go in?

I got in up to here, (indicates mid-chest level). I'm carrying my M-1. That's correct. And once we got in, everything sort of stopped. They evidently retreated and we didn't have anything else to do. And the funny part is, remember the funny parts mainly, we were given beer rations, and we hadn't had any for a long time. And wouldn't you know that the day we landed on Leyte a boat comes in and brings a beer ration to us. And you never saw so many guys sick and they weren't for anything but drinking too much beer. I had my share too but, I mean, I didn't get sick. But on Leyte, the biggest problem we had was at night time. That's when the Japanese would attack. We got in and moved in and I didn't have to fire my rifle at all. Cause at the time, like I say, we were the second wave and either they had already cleaned it up enough or the Japs had retreated. And so we get in there and it's getting dark. So he said, slit trench, don't forget the slit trench. So we didn't, we started. A slit trench is a narrow trench as long as your body that you dig at least eight inches deep, nothing less or it won't do any good and that keeps anything that's dropped, like if it's a mortar shell or anything like that that's dropped, you won't get hurt, it'll go over the top of you. And so we all did that and that night we had the first attack, that's when they always work – at night.

You were under attack?
Well, mainly it was machine guns and rifles because we were in the woods and so consequently they couldn't shoot a mortar in the woods or it would hit a tree. That wouldn't be effective. We had everybody go in a circle or a defense line as you say, and I know that one fellow had too much beer and he didn't dig his slip trench very deep, but he didn't get hurt- but I do remember him very well.

Well, I tell you, I stayed as close to the ground as I could. I didn't think anything was going to happen to me because I thought that I had been trained well enough that if I got hit, it's just one of those things. There wasn't anything I could do about it. I really didn't think I was gonna get hit. So I think that was the idea that was in my mind, that if I just do what I've been taught to do and trained to do, then I'd be all right. And it turned out pretty much that way. Then after this night we just moved further inland in Leyte, and it ended up that we were pushing the Japanese out of Leyte.

In the subsequent days did you have any fire fights with the Japanese?
Only when you had the patrols out. You take a patrol out and we would run into something out there. You went out with your squad, and like I say, being the assistant squad leader, I was at the rear usually of all these fellows. But the flame thrower was the thing that got them out, they surrendered when the flame thrower started in the caves that they had on the island. They would come out with their hands up and waving a white flag. And so

this was about all of it as far as any action is concerned. Lot of squads go out. We went out all the time. On patrols. A patrol could last eight hours depending on where you had to go. That's probably the most scary part. 'Cause you're sitting out there and there could be a sniper there, could be anything that's fighting against you. I think probably the funniest thing is the way that we were taught and weren't taught. They didn't have any ideas about how the patrols of course really worked- like trying to explain to you how to look after snipers, how to find a sniper is tough.

About how long did Leyte last?
Oh, I would say, probably, we were on Leyte for about a month, a month and a half. Then we were shipped to Mindoro. Mindoro was an island right in the center. We took some casualties there, but the most that we got was later on. We had some on Mindoro which is a small island and they said they had a lot of Japanese there. It turned out there weren't as many as they thought there were, but we had a lot of patrol work there. We went up to Mindoro on an LCI, just one platoon of us-about forty men. We had a lot of patrol work there.

We just sort of mopped up and took a few casualties. We went out on a lot of patrols, a lot of patrols there. And we were there over a holiday, I think it was Christmas. This is still in '44. And we had at Christmas time a couple of Philippine scouts with us. We would go up on these patrols and we didn't have any trouble. These guys were surrendering right and left. The Japanese.

They would surrender because everybody was gone except them. They were in caves and stuff and we got ahold of this one on patrol and I happened to have a Filipino scout with me, by the name of Ben. I don't know why I can always remember his name, but he was with us when we captured this Japanese soldier. We had to hold Ben back because he was going to really do his thing on him, because evidently he'd been tortured or something or somebody in his family had. But we kept him from doing anything until we turned him over to the headquarters – they had a CO down there.

When you were on patrol did you have a flame thrower with you?
Usually a BAR man. Some of these places, where we knew there were hills and a lot of caves, we used the flamethrowers. It takes two guys to take care of a flamethrower. The BAR fellow of course was very important, that is

really a fine weapon. That saved a lot of people, but that really throws out a lot of fire power. After Mindoro we were taken to Luzon by LCIs. That was busy, I'll tell you. The Japanese had everything going there for them, we were shooting and firing as hard as we could. So we get on to Luzon, I mean after a day of trying to get on, and we had some good air support, we had some planes come in and sort of cleared the way for us. And we get into Luzon and that is what changed my mind, it didn't really change my mind, but it made it more strong as to why we were fighting. That I have a bigger cause. There I saw truck loads of American soldiers and they weren't alive. And this is the thing that probably kept you going, I think it kept everybody going. When you see something like that, you say to yourself, we're going to do something, you gotta do something now, you know, up until that time it was the cause that you were fighting for, your country. But now you were fighting for your comrades.

The sight of a lot of dead GIs made you sick.

Then we were just moving over the land and up into the mountains of Luzon and we had another funny incident there. We had some fellows that were a little bit gun happy. We were dug in one night and all at once I heard this firing going on and the guy with the BAR, another fellow with a BAR (Browning Automatic Rifle) was firing, and so right away we were trying to find out what's wrong. The BAR is a beautiful gun. And we heard this going off and we didn't know what it was. Finally we could figure it out – our slit trenches were close enough that we could pass the word down and we passed the word down. Some guy saw some Japs out there and I also saw some Japanese out there and so naturally, the whole night none of us slept. We were just as wide awake as we could be. We weren't even tired then 'cause things were happening. The next morning as soon as it got light we looked out and all that was out there was a great big box, looked like a cardboard box or something. It looked like some soldiers out there, Japanese soldiers, and this guy wasn't gonna let anything happen. He shot the clip. This would be in January of '45.

Were you riding or walking?
We're walking, it wasn't fast. I would say in a day, you could only go maybe ten miles, twelve miles, and so it took a while to get up in the mountains. There was no trucks for us you know, the medics had the field hospitals and they had the only trucks that were there.

How about casualties in your squad now, I mean, how's it doing, how's your squad doing?

In the squad I think we probably lost about three men in Luzon. We lost a lot in the weapons company, because of the fire power they throw out they could be picked off real easy, people could see them and so they were firing at them mostly. That's another thing that gives you a little bit more feeling about helping your comrades and so forth.

I was wounded in an area called Fort McKinley. And it's strange because we have a Fort McKinley right outside of Dayton that was familiar to me. And we were just moving up across rice paddy after rice paddy and I, as I say, was at the end of the line because I was keeping things moving. Anyhow, I heard some machine gun fire and everybody dropped and when somebody hollered I looked up, just put my head up, and a mortar shell landed to my left rear and blew shrapnel all over and some hit me. I still have some shrapnel in my neck – right over here on my side, the side of my head. I was hit by a mortar shell – that's what they tell me, of course, I didn't know what it was, but I laid there for a while until the medic arrived, I kept calling for the medic. I knew I was hit. Oh, yes. Well, I couldn't see anything out of my left eye, I didn't know why, but it was because I was laying down and evidently the blood was running and covered my eye and I didn't realize it. And the medic came and gave me some sulfa and bandaged me up and so forth.

Oh, there's something else I wanted to tell you, but it completely slipped my mind. We were moving up and going over rice paddies and so forth and clearing the way and just trying to get in close as we could to where I think we were going which was toward Manila. See, Fort McKinley was right outside Manila. We were heading straight for Manila.

We'd already been on the mountains and so forth and we were coming down into low lands and the rice paddies and moving in. It was just wide open there actually except for the rice paddies. It's like the hedgerows in Europe only they had just ground and the rice paddies down lower, so you'd have four or five feet to go over a row of mounded dirt. When I was hit, I didn't notice anything except a burning sensation. One thing that did happen and I've told this story many times. I'm awful glad I had that good helmet on. Later they gave me the helmet and everything back including my firearm and I went back to the field hospital, but I could put my fist in that hole in the helmet. It was a huge dent. Like I say, the shrapnel went down, up and down, my neck, After I got back home and got married pieces were coming out. There's still some in there because I can't have an MRL

Do you remember the date you were wounded?
February 15 of 1945. So I had to leave the squad at that time and go to the hospital. Well, they just gave me some more shots I think to calm the pain down and then I was taken to a general hospital on the island and I had a spinal and that's another thing that I always remember. But I had the spinal. I don't know if it affects everybody this way or not, but you're sort of in a daze and I was probably nervous and groaning or whatever, and there was a fellow that sat beside me in the bed and kept talking to me all the time. He was hanging on my arm and kept talking to me and calmed me down. I don't know who it was, could have been an aide. Then I was put on a hospital ship and sent back to New Guinea for a short time. It was only a short trip, but it was a hospital ship so I had plenty of good help. They were taking good care of me real well. When we got back to the hospital in New Guinea and this is where I kept going in and the doctor was checking me all the time. And the best day was when he said, you've got a million dollar wound and I said what do you mean? He says, you're going home. That's the best news I ever heard. This was in April of '45 I think.

Because in May '45 we were coming back on a hospital ship from New Guinea to San Francisco and I think that was when President Roosevelt died. And the war in Europe ends. I was sent to Letterman General Hospital in San Francisco ...

I went in there and the first thing they said to me was what do you want? You can have anything you want. Ice cream, you want milk? I said, milk. Give me a quart of milk, I put that milk straight down. I hadn't had any.

You were a squad leader in your unit. What was your relationship with your men there?
Oh, I had good people, I had real good people. I didn't have to worry about them – there was no problems. What I keep saying through this interview, that I was always the last one, sounds strange, but that was a buck sergeant's job at that time, just to make sure everybody was all right. So if somebody would have been wounded up ahead I would help them out. And they knew that and they would have helped me out. I was back so far at that time that

they didn't know where I was but they were all top notch guys. A lot of people from the south.

I haven't been in touch with any of them for years now, it's been a long time, I think we sort of lost touch, you lose addresses and we've moved a lot. I still know about a few fellows, but they were from the east and so forth. I know their names but I don't see them. I don't go to the 24th Infantry Division just because I never have. I think that's the only reason. But a lot of the people that I knew, I didn't know them well, you get to know their first name, and you know that they're going to take care of you and you of them, and that's what it amounts to.

What happened next? Well, they patched me up and found out what had to have done, and they sent me, it was a nerve injury, to a hospital in West Virginia. White Sulfur Springs, that was the name, Greenbriar. They made a hospital out of that. That was for people who had nerve injury, that's why they sent me home.

And it did affect a lot of my left-hand side. I didn't have power in my left side for a long time. I could walk, I could move my arm, but if somebody asked me to squeeze, I couldn't squeeze. And so they sent me to Letterman, or to Greenbriar and White Sulfur Springs, it's called Ashford General Hospital, it was all Army stuff.

And while I was there I got a pass to go see my brother-in-law and sister. He was a captain at Fort Meade, Maryland. And so we went to Baltimore to see them. Dave Hall and sister Ann Hall came up too and we got together and while we were up there we just went around town and had nice meals and so forth. Coming back on the train I got a malaria attack. I didn't even know I had it and so I ended up back in the hospital again. But after that I had a malaria attack every month for about nine months. I was there at White Sulfur Springs at Ashford General Hospital and I was discharged in April of '45.

Then you were still in the army when the atomic bomb was dropped –

What'd you think of that?
Well, at the time, I was happy they had done it. I didn't know what they were gonna do, and I didn't realize how bad it was at that time. But I knew that they had to do something to stop the enemy.

They were crazy, anybody that just doesn't care about life at all is crazy. That's the trance all these suicide pilots were in.

What happens to Fred Hess then?
Well, I came home. I had a job waiting for me. I could have used the GI Bill, gone back to school at the University of Dayton, but 1 had a job waiting for me and I didn't have the desire to go to college for some reason. All I could think about was making some money and doing some of the things I hadn't done for two and a half or three years. My brother-in-law was a laundryman and I started working for him in the laundry and dry cleaning and so forth. And then I met my wife. I met her on a blind date. A lady that I had gone to school with, that married a fellow who was in the Air Force at Wright-Patt, arranged the date. And I said to her, I'd like to meet somebody, do you have anybody in mind? And she mentioned some names and said I know a lady, a young lady, she said, that you'd probably like really well. She said, "she's been dating another officer but she goes to school in Cincinnati and works down there, but we'll try to work something." We corresponded back and forth by phone. I saw a picture of her and that's all it took. She was beautiful, so I didn't need a million more.

We got together by phone and letters and finally I had a date with her and she came to Dayton and we went out to Lakeside Park to a dance. This was in the summer of 46.

Before we were married, Gini's mother, had some property and some apartments north of town and my brother and I were going to rent one of the apartments. And it turned out that her mother and she were going to live in one of the other apartments in the same building. But it didn't have to go that far because I met Gini before that. And we got married and moved into a duplex off of North Main Street. But then we moved into that same apartment later on.

What business were you in then? I was still in the laundry business for a long time and then when the laundry was sold I became a salesman.
Later I was working with someone and the idea came up about a tool rental business. So I started a tool rental business. We had some money that we had been given when the laundry sold and we thought, well, we'll go into the tool rental business. And that's basically how we started on our own. And then later I went into the hardware store business after that. We were in the hardware business for forty years starting in 1956.

Maybe you could explain your decoration case?
First in the upper left hand is the identification card. The next thing is a little card that they give you when you cross the equator for the first time. This is the one where you're a polliwog, after you cross the equator. And this is my draft

card here. This item right here is money that was made by the Japanese to, for the Philippines to spend. This is my dog tag, the original dog tag. Everybody had to wear those around their neck all the time, you never take them off.

This is the patch of the 24th division. The 66th was the first I was in. This is the Rainbow Division, the 42nd. This is a patch that is given to anyone who has served in the South Pacific. This is the combat infantry badge. This is my sergeant rank stripes and this is the crossed rifles which all infantry people have. These are all experts, rifle and carbine and pistol and mortar. Those are the Asiatic Pacific ribbon and the three stars mean three landings that I was in.

This is a good conduct medal. And here to me are the two main ones – Purple Heart, everyone that is wounded gets a Purple Heart. This is the Bronze Star, they say it's for meritorious service, but I wasn't anymore meritorious than anybody else. But I got it. This is a World War II medal and this is your American campaign, everybody gets a campaign ribbon. This two-striped one right here are for the six month overseas duty.

How did World War II change your life, when you think about it?

Well, it made an optimist out of me, especially since I was wounded. I figured nothing could go wrong after that. If it goes wrong, it goes wrong, but it's not gonna happen, and so this is the way I think. That probably more than anything else. I figure if I got over there and got hit with that mortar shell, fragments of the mortar shell and am still alive, you know, anything that happens just doesn't bother me. If it happens it happens, and of course my wife, Virginia, has a saying about making the bad things work for you, do good things. And it's true. I never thought of it until I met her and married her. That's probably the way I feel.

Tell me about your children.

We have three children. We have a boy, the oldest, and we have two daughters. The boy lives in Dayton and one daughter lives in Roswell, Georgia and one daughter lives in Seattle, Washington. We have two grandchildren, Kyle and Chloe. They are special people. All of them are. We have good family.

Do you belong to any service organizations or anything?

Well, I belong to the Sister Cities here in Centerville. Sports has been a big interest to me and so I belong to a club, it's called Agonis Club. It's strictly a sports club. That's all you do, we have sports speakers all the time and we have outings and we have picnics and we have different things like that. It's just fun. That's the main thing. And the old expression is we don't do anything for anybody, but that's not true. I also belong to the VFW and the American Legion.

Virginia K. Hess

Interview #2 – Ray Hill

Ray Hill was born in Indiana in 1920-a real Hoosier. He retired in 1997 after being involved for fifty-one years with the Seventh Day Adventist Church. He and his wife, Geraldine, did missionary work in the Philippines after the war for ten years. They have four children. Ray then taught agriculture at Andrews University and later was ground superintendent for the Kettering Medical Center. He attended Emmanuel Missionary College (BS in agriculture); Michigan State University (MA in agriculture); and the seminary at Andrews University. Ray was in the U.S. Navy for just over three years, equally divided between domestic and foreign service. He served on a PT Boat in the Pacific Theater and was awarded the Purple Heart medal for wounds received in action.

What were you doing just prior to your military service?
When the war started I didn't want to go to the army, I wanted to be a Navy person, so I enlisted in the Navy and went to Indianapolis and then to Great Lakes in September of 1942. And then I went from there, let's see, to boot training at the Detroit Naval Armory. My parents didn't say that I couldn't go, and they didn't say that I could go. But they supported me.

Then I was sent to the Detroit Naval Armory to cook and baker's school. They made a cook out of me. And I said, if they're going to make a cook out of me, I'm going to be as good a cook as possible. There were twenty-three of us, I was the only one that got to be a third class cook because I had excelled in whatever they said that we were to do in the training. And at baker's school I volunteered for submarine duty, but there wasn't any openings at that time.

A man there said, "How about a PT boat?" "What's a PT boat?" "You'll find out," he said. It was more of a voluntary thing. The PT boatmen were more or less voluntary. And they wanted men from twenty-two to twenty-four. A little older and foolish I suppose you could say. They were told what to do, and they would do it. So that's the way it was.

The PT training was in February of 1943 at Melville, Rhode Island. Melville, Rhode Island is on Narragansett Bay, in fact it's not very far from Newport. Newport is more or less the head of the bay, and we were, oh, maybe five miles inside the Narragansett area. Training was eight weeks which included commando training and training in seamanship and navigation. Everyone got to operate the PT boat – stand at the helm.

How long and how wide is a PT boat?

Eighty feet long, twenty feet wide, and it carried three Packard 2500 HP engines – there were 2500 hundred horses under each one of them. Former President Kennedy was captain of PT109. We were in his area a year after he was there. But his story is a very interesting story. The PTs go fifty knots which was a mile plus an eighth, about sixty-eight miles per hour – pretty fast in the water.

In Melville, Rhode Island we had eight weeks of training and then we were assigned to a PT boat. The first PT boats, six PT boats, were lend-leased to the Russians and we took those across the Gulf of Mexico. We stopped in Miami and went up the inside passage as much as possible. I remember as we got up there we could see the Statue of Liberty and we could see the Hudson River. We went up the Hudson River a ways, and then back and forth-always training to fight the Japanese one day.

Then we came back to New Orleans and got our PT boats and started out across the Caribbean. We went through the Panama Canal and on the Pacific side we waited about, oh, maybe three or four weeks for a ship where we could build a cradle that would fit a PT boat because they picked up the whole thing and put it on the bow of the liberty ship. That's how we traveled when we went on the sixteen day trip to Seattle.

We got to Seattle and we got ready to go north. We got a lot of sea gear and cold weather gear, went up the inside passage to Wrangell, Petersburg, Alaska, and finally to Sitka, and there they told us to stop. They said, "We do not need you in Attu and Kiska. We're going to send you to a hot place, hot in Japanese, and hot in mosquitoes."

So then we came back to the Bremerton Navy yard and got everything on the top deck, it was all new. We never had radar before, we never had a 40mm gun before, plus the other twin turrets. Everything was new. So, it took about two weeks to do that and then we went down to San Francisco. We rode on an aircraft carrier and they placed the PT boat in a cradle again to ride on the top – on the deck of a liberty ship.

While we were down there in the San Francisco area we practiced around Alcatraz. We did it for about a week just to keep in shape, they want you to keep sharp with the operation and everything. Every man at his gun. And about a week later they lowered these PT boats onto a liberty ship, and the crews all went on a troop ship headed to New Guinea. It took us thirty-one days to get to New Guinea.

Then the skipper got us all together, and he says, "Fellows, I'm going to tell you one thing. One half of this crew will not return to the states. One half. In other words eight will not return. Eight will be in battle and will be lost. We'll lose eight of you in the battle." I don't think that he should have told us that. And just about eight weeks later it was true. When our ship was sunk by a Kamikaze, eight men were never found. Eight men – it just blew all apart. I came off with about fifty shrapnel wounds and perforated wounds.

Anyway, first we went up to Milne Bay – that was our base. While we were there we would patrol at night looking for the enemy, and we usually found him too. We had one hundred and twenty-nine patrols, and on twenty-five of those we hit the enemy – enemy ships. We would tackle anything from a row boat up to an aircraft carrier. It didn't make any difference. Course, we'd hide behind an island. And as they got closer we would shoot at their lights.

Could you describe that memorable attack?
Yes. I think on our first attack we were about a mile away – we could see a small craft that was full of supplies and also soldiers. So we opened up. I opened up with my 40mm because they said in any attack the 40mm will surprise and destroy the ship. And then the other guns took the crew. So, that's what happened. We hit the craft and it just blew up – just blew up. And there were people in the water and they were shooting back at us too. I was the gun captain on the 40mm. I was also the cook. I did the cooking and everything. Usually, they would protect the cook. That's about it, but as I opened up and hit it, I had two good hits, the thing just blew up. But the crew, several of the Jap crew, got up so our fifty caliber guns did away with those. Didn't let one go ashore.

See, the Japanese were frustrated because a lot of them had been bypassed by MacArthur. And it was up to us to protect the stern of the task force, and also to stand by if a place had been bypassed to keep the Japs from reinforcing. We had one hundred twenty-nine different missions there including the Philippines. As I said, altogether we hit the enemy, or we escaped from the enemy twenty-five times.

If the enemy was close enough and fired upon us, we would get behind an island. Course, a lot of times they couldn't get close enough, but we could. We could put our bow right up close to shore. We only drew four and a half feet. This was in '44. And we would attack anything from a row boat on up- didn't make any difference because a lot of times they were gun boats. They were enemy ships or enemy boats with troops. We also carried torpedoes, and there were 40mm guns mounted on the PT for shooting at anti-aircraft and we had twin 50s also.

What happened when you went up to the Philippines?

On the 15th of December they attacked, a whole platoon of Japanese. They had gone inland to get away from the shore. Then when we landed there with our PT boats a lot of Kamikazes came. A Kamikaze is a suicide plane. They had the idea of killing themselves. The funeral has already been taken care of. They did it for their Emperor. They take their lives by crashing into a ship.

On PT300, my gun was a 40mm gun on the stern of the PT boat. We had twin fifty caliber, and 20mm- we were actually gun boats. And what I remember was placing four shells into the chamber and then ducking my head. This Kamikaze plane came right in and hit our PT Boat eight feet behind me-right at the gas tanks. We had just filled up with three thousand gallons of hundred octane gasoline, and it just blew up. It blew up. This pilot just kept boring in even though all the boats were shooting at him. But he would maneuver. Every time we would maneuver he would maneuver. What we would head for was a circle, because this was our protection- one boat protecting another. But we just got to that circle when that Kamikaze hit. He hit right here at that gun. I was right there. I actually had to duck my head.

I came to under the water. I could see all the fire around me and I could see the depth charges going off and the guns going off- the shells. I thought I was in hell. That was my first thought. But then after a while, I was shaking my arms and a piece of plywood floated by about four feet square, and I climbed aboard that. I'm sure that a one hundred and sixty-five pound sailor would have sunk that raft, I call it a raft, but my guardian angel must have held up that raft. That's what I hung onto. I could hardly move, shrapnel wounds and perforated ear drums – I couldn't hear.

I had about fifty shrapnel wounds. After climbing aboard this raft, this piece of plywood, another boat saw me and they threw a line to me, but it burned. They threw another line – and it burned. They threw about three or four, and finally they soaked it in sea water, threw me a line and pulled me out of the fiery furnace. Boy, was I glad because I only had about five minutes left. This was another PT boat. A PT boat usually has about sixteen men. If you have more guns you have more than that. But eight of our guys were never found. Eight were killed and blown apart and eight of us survived. This was December 17, 1944. We had three thousand gallons of hundred octane. We had just refueled, in fact, we were doing that when this plane was sighted.

This piece of cloth was a part of the parachute or the clothing of the pilot of the Kamikaze that dived on our boat. Another sailor there picked this up and gave it to me, and I have kept it for fifty-five years. Then I was in the hospital there 'til February 4, 1945 – in our Quonset hospital (a small building) on the island of Mindoro. Then on about the fifth day of February I left. They gave me my orders to report to the receiving station on the west coast of the United States. So, I had twelve rides with twelve different planes going from one base to another and finally arrived in Hawaii. I got a completely new outfit, even a little bit of money that I'd lost. And then I got a troop transport to San Francisco. I left San Francisco after a few months, but now I was coming home.

What are these different ribbons?
Well, this one here is the purple heart – I got the purple heart. That's for being wounded. This is a good conduct ribbon for serving three years in the armed forces. If you're good enough you get a ribbon. And this one is the Philippine liberation medal. This is the patch for our PT boat, and this was the one for the cook. I still got some of the wounds in the arms, both arms, both legs, both elbows, both knees. As far as I know, I was the only one rescued aft. I was glad to get home. This was in, let's see, March of '45. I was in Chelsea Naval Hospital in Boston.

What did you think of the atomic bomb when you heard about it?
I thought it was the thing to do to end the war. It saved millions of lives. I was discharged on October 1, 1945. After the war I came out to Walla Walla, Washington. Went over to Seattle, and I rode a bicycle around Green Lake. And I was watching a couple of young ladies, as sailors do. And

I rode around behind them, and one of them had trouble with her bicycle so I stopped to help. They were going to Walla Walla College after the war was over. My granddaughter just talked to me on the phone yesterday, and this lady, this bicycle lady, is a member of her church up in Washington State. But she was saying that she helped your grandfather go to Walla Walla College. Eventually I went to Walla Walla College, and my roommate said, "Just stay by, just stay by a little while longer." I did and the next week I met my wife. We've been married fifty- three years, and we had four kids and eight grandchildren. We try to see all of them sometime during the year.

Did you go to college under the GI Bill of Rights?
Yes. I got a whole lot 'cause I had forty-eight months service. I was also eligible as a public law sixteen disabled vet. I had forty-eight months of credit coming. Later I earned a masters at Michigan State. Then in the seminary I had training because then we decided we were going to be missionaries in the Philippines. We did that for ten years. I had twenty-eight hundred acres there. It belonged to the school. I was teaching a B.S. in agriculture. That farm later developed into a ranch – two thousand acres into a ranch, two hundred acres into roads and village, and six hundred acres into a farm. I was there from '53 to'63. Ten years. My kids call it home. 'Cause when we first went over in 1953 the boy was two and the girl was four. Two more of our children were born over there.

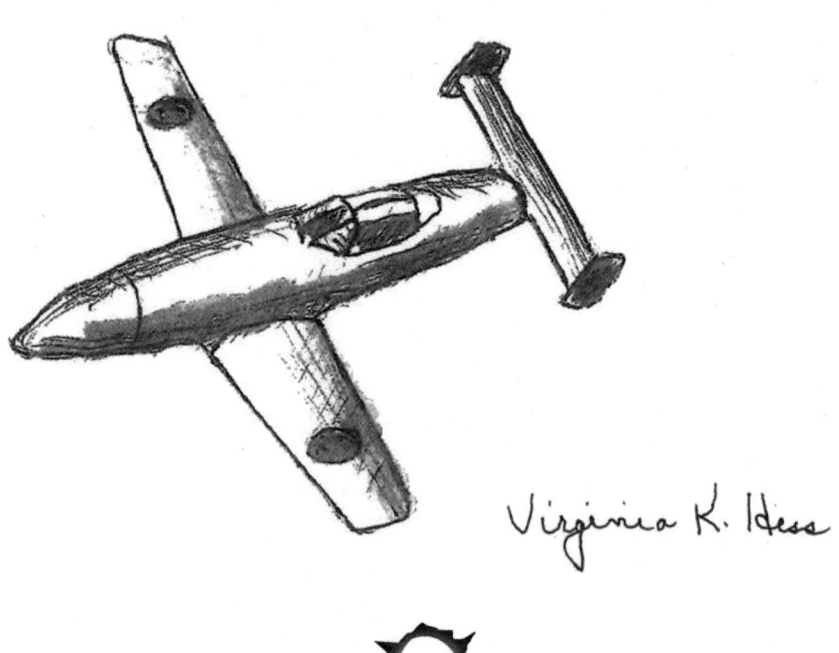

Virginia K. Hess

When we came back I taught at Andrews University. It's our Seventh Day Adventist university and seminary in Michigan – Berrien Springs, Michigan. It's near Benton Harbor, not far from South Bend, Indiana. I taught agriculture there for nine years. We've been down here twenty-seven years. Twenty-seven. And I was ground superintendent for thirteen years at Kettering Medical Center.

When I retired, I worked resource, we call it resource. I had worked for twelve years doing the same kind of work, of course – grass and trees, and everything like that.

Interview #3 – Arthur T. Ensley

Art Ensley and his wife Gloria have three children. Two still live in the Centerville-Washington Township area. Ensley graduated from Central High School in Superior, Wisconsin and shortly thereafter enlisted in the Army Air Corps. He was a pilot on a B-25, an attack bomber, in the European Theater during World War II He flew all of his seventy-eight and one-half missions from a base in Corsica. Ensley was shot down and with the help of partisans worked his way back to allied lines. He attained the rank of captain and served in the military for twenty-three years.

He then flew as a commercial pilot for about another ten years. Ensley is a member of the VFW, the American Legion, and Volabamus, an association of military pilots.

All my life I wanted to be a pilot. So I was one of those people who was blessed with getting the kind of career and profession that I dreamed about and always wanted. I wanted to be Richard I. Bong, I don't know whether you've ever heard of him. He was America's number one ace. He shot down something like forty airplanes. Well, we both came from the same school. He was a couple of years ahead of me and he lived just outside of Superior, in Poplar.

I was accepted as an aviation cadet and I was sent to Maxwell Field in Nashville, Tennessee. And I went through the training there, about two or three months. But what really made it nice was Glenn Miller. That was his last stateside assignment. And when we went out for parade and passed for review it wasn't just some old band playing with a bugle and a drum as most of them did. He put a little jazz into it, you know. We danced to his music several times. This was in the fall of '43. But anyway, that was the highlight of my pre-flight. And then I was sent to the various schools for my flight training.

From primary I went to Cochran Field in Macon, Georgia, and we flew a BT-13 or 15 something, a low wing airplane – a lot of airplane for a kid out of a Stearman to fly. I was twenty-one at the time.

They put us in a higher powered airplane – looked almost like a fighter.

Did you want to be a fighter pilot or a bomber pilot?

Everybody wants to be a fighter pilot. And everybody's working towards it. And I have to admit they took the better pilots for fighter pilots. How they rated them I don't know, but I didn't get a fighter. I got a strafer/bomber which was maybe a consolation prize, you know. Then we got our commission at Moody Field, our wings, and we were officers.

So they sent us out to La Junta, Colorado and all through the training there the attrition rate and the fatality rate raised. So by the time we got through with our training we had lost fifty percent of them from flying ability and maybe three percent from fatalities. There were a lot of deaths coming through the training. We were trained flying the B-25. But no war time stuff, just how to fly it, take it to altitude and this sort of thing. But it was a nice airplane. Everybody liked it . We lost some crews in it but not many because we were just learning to fly that airplane. We were out there three months, I believe, and when I got that assignment I knew I wasn't going to be a fighter pilot. But I knew there was another program going – one that had a solid nose in the B-25. They had adapted it with a French 75, a French type 75 cannon.

Somebody got the idea we could use one thousand pound GP (General Purpose) bombs. We could put four of them in. Then somebody came up with the idea that if the shackles were arranged right we could carry one hundred pound fragmentation bombs – all sorts of different type of armament. Then somebody come up with the idea that we can put six one-thousand pounders in. It's a smaller diameter bomb because it's semi-armor piercing. It's half the diameter of the regular one thousand pounder. So they did everything and tried everything and they had that airplane loaded with six thousand pounds of bombs

When we went overseas we came through North Africa, in Talergma, but we didn't fight out of North Africa. I was sent up to a base in Corsica. All our missions I flew out of Corsica. And we were bombed and everything up there. They'd come in at night and run sneak bombs. We had our slit trenches, we'd run out and get in those slit trenches but, you know, flyboys aren't gonna dig any deep slit trenches. And one night Washing Machine Charlie (slang name for night bombers) came in and knocked out half of our airplanes. They threw basketball size bombs out of it. Boy, I tell you, it actually hit the ground and rolled. Well the next day when we got one of those attacks, all these pilots were out digging those foxholes a little deeper.

Tell me about your first mission?

Yes, it was very good. I went out with the pilot. As I say, I wasn't checked out on the bomb site so I flew missions with the pilot in my crew. Then he went home and I started flying as pilot and they gave me a co-pilot, and it went very well. This airplane that we're talking about was Miss Mitchell. The airplane had no name, it was a brand new airplane when it started flying. Now it's customary that the crew, or ground crew or somebody, puts the name of their girlfriend or wife or anything else on it. But anyway when I got the airplane, that's when I was married to Miss Mitchell – Miss Mitchell the airplane. And I stayed with her through my entire combat career.

When I first got there it was twenty-five missions and you could go home. Hell, you'd get twenty- five missions in a couple months. So they raised it to fifty missions. We were bombing up into France, all the way across Italy, and all the way down Italy. The ground forces were south of Rimini at that time, slugging their way up through the Rimini Mountains, you know. A lot of losses. In fact they were even south of Rome coming up. Theirs was a dirty job. Our job was good. We did lose some airplanes in that mid-Italian area of Italy. But all in all, it was thirty, forty, or fifty minutes to the target, drop your bombs, and come home. Well, the day I got shot down I was up to ten thousand four hundred feet. That was my bombing altitude. They were not doing well on the low altitude attacks so they made us mid-range. They tried to get us as high as possible to minimize the anti-aircraft guns and low enough so that the airplane still performed well. They had loaded them down – they were really heavy. So we bombed generally around ninety-five hundred feet, and if you got over thirteen thousand feet you weren't very efficient. That was our range. And the Jerrys (Germans) and the ack-ack knew that too. I never made a mission in Italy where we strafed. As I say, the airplane just wasn't that adaptable. Now in the Pacific I understand it was pretty good. But we couldn't take that German ack-ack.

Now on a typical mission the squadron would put up eighteen airplanes. When we went as a group we'd go in multiples of eighteen. Eighteen, thirty-six, I've been on missions as high as seventy-two airplanes. Each leader had his own bombsite and you flew in formation, but each plane made its own run and dropped the bombs and then came out in formation with the other elements so they wouldn't be flying all over the sky. You'd sit out there with your box and he'd drop his bombs and you might just turn over two degrees to make your run. And when he dumped his bombs he's gonna be going, so as soon as you got your bombs out, you took your box and took off to catch him, or to get into that formation. The protection was getting all these top guns together. There's two fifty calibers firing up here, two out the side, and two in the tail. The protection was to get as close together with all that fire power and that discouraged some of those fighter pilots. My wing man would be so close to me that it seemed dangerous. I think they'd clear the wings but they would be sitting right tight in there.

We got the fighters knocked out early. But they were always a threat, and we didn't relax because they weren't a threat. The Germans just either moved the fighters out of the Italian area or whatever. We definitely had air superiority. I think they were running out of airplanes. I probably only been hit by enemy aircraft, not hit with gun fire, but attacked would be the word. They'd fly through our formation, and you'd see how close your wingmen were out to each side of you. I liked this slot, I'd always fly a flight right under the flight ahead of me. We'd be right up so close that you could count the rivets and wave at the tail gunner. We stacked them up there.

Anyway, seventy-two airplanes in our flight was a large mission. But it was always eighteen. I flew two missions in a day with eighteen airplanes. Night was kind of a hectic thing 'cause the only time you'd go up at night is if you had two missions that day and something was pressing. By the time you got home it was real dusky. It was hard. We hadn't practiced much at night, you know, and hell at the time I probably only had less than three hundred hours.

What speed would you be flying at in a plane?
I'm trying to think of what the bomb run was. I think our bomb runs were between one hundred and ninety to two hundred miles an hour. We'd take more if you could get it, but generally that's about it. You're maneuvering with a formation and you just can't make a turn here because you got all those airplanes behind you and you have to gradually come over. And when you're evading flak you can't duck out easily. You might just gradually start to turn, to feint away, and then when they start to get your range you might just pick it up two or three hundred feet. And they'd all ease up, and then you'd see the flak underneath you. But by the time you turn around they were up with you again. On some of the longer missions and on the more dangerous targets we'd get fighter cover. I never found it too efficient. They

didn't have the range. We had an RAF outfit that flew Spitfires and we'd pick them up, oh, maybe thirty minutes off Corsica. But they couldn't stay with us to the target. They could probably only get into Italy and they'd have to turn back. A Spitfire is a very, very short range airplane. And the long range airplanes, the American P-51 s and P-47s that had the capability, were being used in the war over Europe.

Could you comment on fear you experienced in war?
Well, you'd go for two or three missions and get a little bit complacent you know. And then when you got a bad mission, and a lot of your airplanes got shot up, and you got shot up, you paid more attention to evasive action. And we had certain target areas that were tough. You'd walk in the briefing room and see the target and know it's trouble. We didn't get it yesterday and we're going back today.

And on those missions, yes, I don't mind saying you had butterflies or bumblebees in your stomach.

Anybody that says they weren't concerned, downright scared, something's wrong.

Once we had come back from Yugoslavia. It was a bad mission and we got shot up very bad. And we were sitting around having our coffee and donuts. That's the last I ever flew Miss Mitchell because we didn't take off on the next mission with her so that was the last time I flew her. In Corsica there's always the hills and the mountains. We were always very aware of those if we were working under a low ceiling or anything. They were a hazard to us, particularly when you're coming in at night and so on, or if we're in heavy dusk.

How about the men in your crew?
Well, we had the pilot, co-pilot and navigator/bombardier. Three up front. Then you got a turret, top turret gunner up in this position. And the bombardier's here and the top turret man is here. They were both killed when we were shot down. Pilot, co-pilot, then you got a radio operator that operates these waist guns. If you're attacked from one side then he goes to that side of the airplane, but he handles both of these guns. Then you got a tail gunner, he's also got a turret. It was a total of six men. Now, if you're on a very exacting target you get hot shot bombardiers. That's if they're really after something – then you take a bombardier with you, a professional bombardier.

What kind of a relationship did you have with the officers and enlisted men?

The enlisted men have their tent area and the officers had theirs. Usually, the enlisted men lived better than the officers because American ingenuity is just something you can't believe. They would make a wooden floor tent with a screen on it – almost like home. Whereas the officers say, "Oh, tighten that up over there," because they weren't gonna be there long. But we had a nice place to live. We went into a bombed out building and had rooms and you could say who you'd live with. I lived with a public relations officer, my bombardier, and my co-pilot lived in another area. And the enlisted crew always stayed in the enlisted area and were probably more comfortable overall then we were. But we didn't live together.

How many missions were you supposed to fly?

Well, when I first started flying it was twenty-five. Then it went up to fifty. And that wasn't bad because the fighter aircraft were being less active and the Germans weren't concentrating their ack-ack unless it was a specific target they were trying to protect. They were really in retreat going out of Italy but they were trying to make the Americans fight for every foot of the way. The ground forces had a rough time coming up through the mountains in Italy. So anyway it went to fifty. And when my crew got fifty I was trying to talk them into staying with me to fly one hundred. I was gonna fly two missions. But I couldn't talk one of them into it. Fifty missions, that's it. They were going home. That was just a difference in make-up – mental make-up. But I stayed on and took another crew, and I also used to fly the make-up crews. If a crew got shot up and there was an odd crew member that survived he'd go on a make-up crew. I ended up with that make-up crew. I volunteered to stay for one hundred. I liked it. Really, I liked it. And I wanted to be a captain. I was a first lieutenant. Went over as second lieutenant, made first, and I was not ready to come home, you know. So you had to do your homework and get the job done real well if you wanted to be captain.

Tell me about your last mission, 'cause you say you had seventy-eight and one-half missions.

Well, I'm on my second crew and this airplane was the queen of the fleet. The engineer, the ground chief, named that airplane. And we didn't like it but we weren't going to argue with him because we had the absolute best airplane in the squadron. I started with it when it was brand new – brand new other than the flight time over. And with the combination of a brand new airplane and a crew chief, a conscientious crew chief – we'd come in with holes in that airplane and the next morning you'd never see it. We'd be up and gone again. So they'd work at night and do everything. It was wonderful. Just fantastic. Phil Ostlie, came from around Minneapolis, Minnesota, I'm jumping ahead of my story, he's the one that maintained this airplane. When he came back to the states and got out he joined the Confederate Air Force, they picked up an old B-25 scrap that they rebuilt into a new airplane. But I'm getting ahead of my story. I was on the seventy-eighth mission with a relatively new crew. We went out and we were on the rail aversion going into the Brenner Pass – that's what we were trying to cut off – anything going into the Brenner Pass. On this mission my bombardier was killed in action. Also Sergeant Knott was killed in action. Knott was in the top gunner turret. The radio operator and the tail gunner got out. The airplane caught fire – a violent and uncontrolled fire. And you went out on two conditions: if the airplane were unflyable the pilot would give them the bell and out they'd go. But you didn't have to get a bell. If the airplane was on fire, if that dude is burning, which ours was – just infernal – you would get out of it anyway you could. I'm glad you brought this up. Flow'd I get in this airplane, how'd it get on fire?

There's so much to tell and it's just like yesterday. Now this wasn't Miss Mitchell that was on fire. As I said when I came back from my seventy-eighth mission we'd been shot up pretty bad. And so the crew chief worked hard and a couple of days later we had it patched and ready to go. Now they did everything except service it, they loaded it with bombs, replenished the fifty-caliber ammo for the machine guns.

And that morning before the mission, that's all I had left was the service thing. They brought the service truck up to pump us full of gas – nine hundred and seventy-four gallons. I'll never forget it. In the meantime we were being briefed. We came out in the jeep, dropped our crew, went to the airplane, and as we walked under the airplane there was some black goop coming out of this thing. Well, they had just been working frantically to get the airplane back in service. But evidently there was a hole left up in the upper section of the fuel tank. And we didn't know it leaked until it was filled full of gas. That's the first time they filled it after they'd gone through this major repair. It didn't look quite that bad, but it was seeping enough so that you wouldn't fly the airplane. So anyway, we had to leave the airplane and go with the spare airplane. Well, now this [the plane they had to leave] was the queen of the fleet. It's like going from day to night leaving your own airplane.

You'd have flak suits, everything perfect in it, even the needles were perfect. Anytime you'd take off and coordinate something or change rpm, everything was just absolutely perfect. So we went down and got this spare airplane. Now the spare airplane was kind of the dog of the fleet. They'd use it as a spare, but they'd also use it on training missions or if they wanted to go on a trip to Rome or something like that they'd use those airplanes. So this is the plane we went to. And I'm thinking – be off the ground in about twenty minutes. So we hit the spare airplane, and went through it, checked it all over. And although we were not very happy with it, we got it ready to go, cranked it up, made take off time, got our formation behind us and so on.

But anyway, one incident that happened, and there's so many things that could happen I couldn't tell them all to you, was the airplane had flak suits – like a lady would have an apron in the kitchen. Only big flak suits, I mean maybe eighty pounds. And it was a bib over the front of you, a bib over the back of you, and they had snaps up at the shoulders. Naturally if you had to get out, your parachute, harness, and everything was under that. So these shoulders snaps worked all right and I got my flak suit on and I was so rushed I wasn't sure if I put my parachute on or not. I was young and foolish. I flew some missions in real hot weather and I said, "Oh, I'll get into the parachute if I have to," but I didn't always really follow the rules. I think that my friends knew me for that. But I got into this flak suit and it's got a snap just like you have on a convertible top – a heavy canvas top. Well, I kept trying to connect those at the chest and I couldn't get them to work. So I just took those two straps, brought them around and tied them in a knot, and then I put another knot in because it kept loosening up. So I was literally tied into my flak suit. That was the only unusual incident on getting that old dog in the air. The airplane flew rather well but we weren't pleased with it, you know – this oil pressure would be up here and this one would be over there, and it just wasn't the queen – Miss Mitchell. So we went out on the mission and it was a rail aversion going into the Brenner Pass. These were vital. The Germans at this time were trying to pull back as much as they could to save it. They had a lot of fight left in them yet down there and we tried to knock these rail aversions in the Brenner Pass to keep it out of service so they couldn't retreat up out of there. Anyway, we were on this mission to go in and knock out one of those rail aversions, but they really had it protected and we had intense anti-aircraft fire. When we started our mission approach, enemy fire kept going even though we're dropping our bombs. We stayed with it and got our bombs off even though the airplane was all beat up. And then about the time we got our bombs off the airplane caught fire. It evidently had leaked enough fuel down into the fuselage, from the fuel they had put in the wings, so we got a collection of fuel in there and it was a hideous thing. So anyway, the two guys in the rear bailed out – the tail gunner went right out the back and the waist gunner went down the bottom and out.

The man in the turret, when I looked back, was completely engulfed in flames. He couldn't wear anything but a chest type parachute. It's a harness and you have a pack, oh, about the size of a three ring binder, you'd snap on you. Well, he had to get out of the turret before he could put his parachute canopy on his harness. The last time I saw him he had it on one side and he had dumped the door out the bottom. But that's the way they found him in the wreck. But it was living hell in there.

How did you get out?

How did I get out? I don't know. The Lord looks out for you sometimes. But right in the top there's a way the crew chief could open that up and get out to clean things and so on – get to the top of the airplane. It's definitely not an escape hatch. And I have to give credit to my co-pilot. When he looked at the situation he pulled the releases and popped that hood. I didn't have to ask him what he was doing. He was going out the top. And you're not supposed to be able to do that because you have all of these obstructions here. Those propellers are turning, there's antennas going from the tail to the main part of the airplane, and one of those antennas could just cut you in two if you hit that in the slip stream. Well anyway, he'd made the decision to go. He stood up on the pedestal and faced backwards, and I was trying to control the plane. He stepped on my hands a couple of times, but we didn't need any briefing because it's never been done before, f here's no procedure to do it. But as he started to hit that position I pulled the airplane up almost to a stall, pushed him, and popped the stick forward. And he said later that he went out of that airplane and it seemed like he had to look way down to see it. Now how did I get out? I have to say I must have done the same thing. I must have climbed up and fought my way out of that. But in the process I was beat up more and I think we had another secondary explosion in the airplane and that might have helped blow me out of it. But I can't say whether I had supernatural strength to get out of it. The Lord was looking out for me because I didn't get cut up by the propellers, or cut up from these top guns, hit by the tail, or hit by an antenna. It's just a miracle I came out of it. But I was knocked out. I lost my consciousness. And I opened my eyes and I saw the horizon and it passed me. And it passed me again, this way. Now in an airplane, if you are in a spin, as you come around you see the horizon, this is the way you right your airplane from a spin. I thought I might be still in the airplane. So, I was reaching for the controls to get with the spin, you know but there were no controls there and I realized I was out of the airplane. I've never been able to determine or never been able to figure whether the seat was with me or whether it was that flak suit that had been giving me trouble, but something was back there and I got rid of that. And I thought, "Oh boy, did I put my parachute on for this mission?" And I reached down and I felt, and I had the parachute. So all I had to do was pull this little release, a quick release, which released these two chest snaps , these two shoulder snaps , and these other two shoulder snaps, and my flak suit would have come off in two pieces. Well, I told you I had it tied with two good knots. And by this time I had been all burned. I was burned from my goggles down to my hands which were burned, the skin was off of them. And I went to untie those knots and it was just almost impossible. I had no feeling except pain, I couldn't tell you where the pain was, but you know what a burn is like. So anyway, I took that first knot and got it out, and there was the second knot and I got that disconnected. Well, normally to get out of that suit you pull this chest cord and it takes these harnesses off. By untying the flak suit, it came up in the back, up in the front, I went on through it, and it caught me in the neck. Well, that didn't really knock me out, but it kind of dimmed me a little bit, you know, what I mean? The lights just kind of go down and come back up again. So I pulled my rip cord and I felt that thud. And oh what a welcome thud that was. And I was oscillating because I evidently had my chute open and I was on an angle as the chute opened and stopped my rapid descent. It was still moving down pretty fast 'cause I had a little momentum, I swung like a kid would swing on the canopy as it came down across the ground and up.

And on the second oscillation, I was worried how am I gonna stop this oscillating, boom, I hit the ground. And I hit the ground extremely hard. I fractured three vertebras, they were compressed, compression fractures. Anyway, I got on the ground and fortunately there was this farm hand who was definitely anti-German and he waved to me. I didn't know what he meant, but in Italy I think that means come with me. I assumed it was and I was gonna come with him. In the meantime I could hear them shooting at us. We were in the river bed. We had about three or four little sectors of the river which was not running at a high level, and we had to wade through those to get off the shore. And he kept telling me to come this way, and I was gonna go that way. And I got up and I ran and carried my parachute with me. I got up on the other bank and one of the batteries that shot us down started using ground fire at me on the ground as I was running. I was about done. I was in extreme pain and he kept wanting me to rush and come. But I can't do it. No. And so he took the parachute off me, covered it with a bunch of stuff, and I went a little further with him. He was alert enough to realize that I was spent. They put their hay up with a pole up through the top and it keeps it from the weather. Evidently, this was being partially used so it had some loose hay and he covered me up with that hay and I laid on my stomach in there. I don't know whether I laid there hours or days. We figured later on that I probably was in there the rest of that day, that night and the next day and they probably got me out the next night. But I dirtied myself and I was bloody, I was hurting, but I laid in that hay and literally slept. I think I must have passed out or gone to sleep. Later he came and got me out.

They were partisan fighters – they were the Ozapos and the Garibaldis. Fortunately, I was with the Ozapos. This was northern Italy. They were still fighting for ground up there, even during the war, you know. These were the anti-communists. The Garibaldis were the reds, they wore red pants and shorts and red wherever they could put it on, red scarf. The Ozapos wore green, they were the Christians but they were partisans too. And I was with them. They were both against the Germans, but they weren't very friendly to each other. One was supplied by the communists and the other one was probably supplied by some of our special forces. We had all kinds of secret stuff going on up there. We went to a house and they cleaned me up and I got something to eat and early the next morning they came and got us again. And they brought a bicycle for me to ride. They asked me if I knew how to ride. I know how to ride a bicycle, let's get out of here. Well anyway, my hands were in such bad shape I couldn't do anything but lay my hands up on the handlebars. And you know their bikes have a handbrake to slow them down. So I laid my hands up on the handlebars and peddled along with them, very slow. I didn't have much strength left. I immediately worked myself into just a terrible sweat. And we had a couple of little hills over into another valley and as we went up I found I couldn't do it. I had to get off. So one guy pushed my bicycle up while I walked up – and they even kind of gave me a pull to help me up. When we got on the other side I thought, "Oh, this is fine, I won't have to pedal." So I was ready to go again and they said wait. They knew what was coming and I should have known, but I wasn't very alert that day. One of them went on downhill and he cleared everybody out of the way. So over the hill I went and down on that bicycle with my hands up here on the handlebars – worthless. And I'll tell you, that was a ride. It kept picking up speed. It actually scared me. Not as much as the airplane did, but it did scare me. Eventually we come to the bottom, and then we did the same thing again. There were three ranges that we covered and I felt I was gonna just lay down on the side of the road. I was just completely exhausted. And we came to a place where the fingers of the mountains come out and then we went over this range, and this range, and over this range, and finally there was a pretty good road. So they said to get down and wait. And along came an ox in the road and a wagon. They expected me to follow along on that bicycle, and they had my tail gunner who had been shot through the legs, and he couldn't walk, in the wagon, along with my co-pilot in that wagon. So evidently, they'd coordinated this thing and we met them at this rendezvous. I said, "'Keep the bicycle," and got into that wagon. It just moved at a snail's pace. But anyway, they took us up into a safe place and we went through all the routine of the escape evasion. And we stayed out of harm's way, and didn't get captured, and eventually walked out. I stayed there about a week and I was in severe pain and I had to receive medical help for my hands. I couldn't use them, they were wrapped in bandages. 1 I couldn't do any of your personal things or anything like that. It was horrible. And after about seven days, I was gone for forty days, we ran into these special service people who were back there causing trouble by helping the partisans. And there was an English mission back in there too. And there was some English major, a pain, but a nice Englishman, and this individual was a pain. So we got a party together and we were going to walk out. Well, I took my tail gunner and he says, "I'm coming too." I said, "All right," and I took him out and walked around a little bit, but he couldn't do it. So I had to leave him back there in the hands of friendly people. So I left him and I had my co-pilot with me and two others from those special sendees. This English major, the American first lieutenant, and we two walked out across the lower portion of the Alps and down into Yugoslavia. And we walked into that area and ran into some more partisans. They were just not very nice. They took care of us, got food for us, but they were more on the communist side. I didn't know this. I was just a kid, I didn't know what a communist was from a traffic cop, you know. But I knew they weren't friendly to us.

They weren't real friendly like the Ozapos. So anyway, we got in touch with a transport outfit in a RCAF Dakota. That's an RC-47, who's gonna come in and pick us out. By this time we had quite a number. So they flew in, and I think there were twenty of us. And they flew in and flew across this makeshift runway and, I'll be darned, somebody parachuted out. I said, "Oh no, they're here to get us and they're going to bail out. Something's wrong with the airplane." Well, their procedure was they flew over the runway, one guy bailed out, looked it over, got on his walkie-talkie, and told them if it was OK to land. So they come in and landed. So anyway they got us out. I was shot down November 18, 1944 at about eleven o'clock, if I remember right, in the morning. I remember the altitude as ten thousand four hundred feet on my altimeter and from that time until we got into Florence, Italy where they had moved our air corps headquarters I was walking out.

But on New Year's Eve I was sitting in a bar with my co-pilot in raunchy, mismatched, mis-sized clothes and uniforms ordering a drink. It was New Year's Eve day. They flew us in and we were gonna get drunk. And we'd been eating horrible stuff and neither one of us could hold a drink. But we covered four hundred and eighty miles.

I never took advantage of the GI Bill because I stayed in the military. They promoted me to captain even though I didn't fly my complete second mission. They took good care of me. In fact, I was a captain when I was shot down, but I didn't know it.

Virginia K. Ness

Interview #4 – Karl Rotterman

Karl Rotterman lives on Springrun Lane in Centerville. He and his wife Anna have two children. His daughter, Diane, is a school teacher in Cleveland and his son, Dan, is a school teacher in Brookings, Oregon. Karl went to Roosevelt High School and later to Patterson Co-op. He studied toolmaking and eventually owned his own toolmaking company for over fifteen years. He was a member of the United States Marine Corps for about three years and participated in three campaigns in the Pacific Theater- Bougainville, Guam and Iwo Jima where he was severely wounded by a Japanese rifleman. He was a member of the 3rd Marine Division, 9th Regiment, Company A.

What were you doing just prior to your military service in the Marines?
Well, prior to my joining the Marine Corps I was in high school. But I dropped out of high school rather young, and talked my parents into letting me join the Marine Corps which I did. I think I was under the legal age – I was only seventeen.

How'd you happen to select the Marine Corps?
I don't know. I suppose because I liked the uniform. I thought it was probably the elite of the military branches, so I wanted to be a Marine. That was in October of 1942. The war had been going on for about a year, and I went down to the post office in Dayton and talked to the sergeant, and he decided that if I passed the physical why I could go in. So I went to Cincinnati on the train and went through the physical examination and passed it.

And then within a couple days I got my orders through the mail to be at the train depot on a particular date. And after the boo-hoos of mama and papa, away I went to Parris Island, South Carolina. And that's where I started into boot camp. And I'm sure lots and lots of people have seen the drill instructors at Parris Island. Our drill instructor, our main drill instructor's name was Sergeant Feinstein. Looked like a mountain of a man. Had a voice like a cannon. And he ruled the roost. When we went in he said he was going to be our little god for the next four months – and he was. Every word he spoke you jumped.

I think there was like fifty men in the platoon. That's as near as I can remember. Most of them made it, but there were a few who fell out during the course of the boot camp due to sickness. And then at the end of our boot camp time we had our graduation, and the day after the graduation they had an outbreak of spinal meningitis on Parris Island and quarantined the entire island. So we were there a month and a half extra in training.

The rest was the ordinary boot camp type thing. You had to have guard duty and we had lots of long hikes. And back then in the Marine Corps you boxed every day. And Sergeant Feinstein always put the biggest guy against the smallest guy. Everyday. Every morning we boxed. Toughen you up I guess. But I'll never forget the fellow that he put me against. We called him typewriter. His name was Smith I think, we called him Smitty. Anyway, he was a great big heavy set red-headed fellow about twice my size, and Feinstein would put me in with him. And we only boxed like two rounds, but he beat me something fierce. I never could hit him. But anyway, I lived through it.

What about indoctrination – building the esprit de corps?
I think that in the Marine Corps from day one they continually hammer that into you. At that time it was hate the Japanese. And they did many things that really built up a hatred for the Japanese. One time we had what they called field days where you take everything outside, all the beds and everything else outside. And you have a bucket, and you take a bucket of sand, and you take it inside and throw it on the floor, and then you take a brick and you scrub the floor with a brick. They call it holy stoning the floor. Then you wash it all out. And it usually happened at one and two o'clock in the morning. So this one particular time we got it all done, and before we put everything back into the barracks, Sergeant Feinstein said, "Everybody empty your bucket of sand." So everybody emptied their bucket outside and he said, "Put them buckets over on top of your head." So we put the buckets over our head. And then we lined up against the walls and he came along with his swagger stick and cracked the bucket on every guy's head. Said, "You look like a bunch of damn Japs." Which was psychological, I guess. Hate the Japs. We were a very close knit group. You had to be the best

and your drill instructor instilled in you continually that you're going to be Marines when he gets done with you. When you leave here you're going to be a Marine, and Marines are known for excellence. And they constantly hammered that into your head, so that by the time you got to graduation you looked sharp and you felt sharp.

Next I went to Cherry Point, South Carolina, because my assignment from boot camp was supposed to be in the Marine Air Corps. So they sent me to Cherry Point and we were in what they called a casual company – waiting for another assignment from Cherry Point. But then they sent me to Memphis, Tennessee which was the Naval Air Technical Training Center.

And about half way through that school, each day names would be listed on the bulletin board. You were to be on the flight line at such and such a time, and you had to draw a parachute, and they were using Stearman airplanes. And, of course, eventually my name came up and I was on the flight line. And as I said before, I learned to fly an Aronca before I went into the service. So I was a pretty hot shot pilot I thought. Then this sergeant took me up in the Stearman, and by the time I got back down I was so sick that I couldn't even get out of the airplane. He did all kinds of acrobatics – everything. That Stearman, as I'm sure you're aware of, that dam thing can do anything. It can go upside down forever I believe. Anyhow, he did all kinds of fancy stuff and he let me do a little bit, but very little. And when we got back down, like I say, I was sick and I more or less fell out of the airplane.

I finally got back to the barracks and within a day, about two days after that, my name appeared on another list – I was being transferred. And they transferred me to New River, North Carolina for advanced infantry training. That was the day they decided I wasn't going to be a pilot. From there I went to California for five or six weeks. Then we went to Camp Matthews out of San Diego, California – down toward Camp Pendleton to scout and sniper school, and from there I went overseas.

Did you leave San Diego on a troop ship?
Yes-on the Lurline, a converted cruise ship. We went to Auckland, New Zealand. That ship was so fast that they said we were not in danger of submarine attack by the Japanese. This was beginning the spring of '43. Anyhow, we went to Auckland and did some training there. When I got to Auckland I was put in a unit and we joined the 3rd division there. Then we went from there down to Guadalcanal and did a little more training. At that

time the Bougainville campaign was ending so that by the time we got to Guadalcanal they felt that we were able to go right on into Bougainville and do some mop up.

Now Bougainville is a small island, very swampy except for the runway which was a fighter strip only. The weather is hot and the island is loaded with every kind of crawling thing. It was Thanksgiving day, November 25, 1943. I was a member of the 3rd Marine Division, 9th Marine Regiment, 1st Battalion, Company A, 1st platoon. The Company Commander was Captain Conrad "Bulley" Fowler, and my platoon leader was Lt. Zimmer (subsequently killed on Iwo Jima).

This was my first experience in combat in what we called, "The Battle for Grenade Hill." I carried an M-l rifle, two bandoliers of 30 caliber ammo, a web belt with more clips of ammo, three hand grenades, two canteens, my K-Bar knife, a first aid packet and we wore light green dungarees. The 3rd platoon was the attack platoon and they were pinned down at the base of the hill. The second platoon guarded the left flank, and my platoon, the 1st platoon, guarded the right flank. We did this to keep the Japs from coming around behind us – flanking us. The fighting took place during this one afternoon and all night. The next morning the Japs had left the area. Most of the fighting was done with M-ls and BARs. There wasn't much use of mortars in this battle because of the canopy of foliage that really prevented it and the swampy terrain. Captain Fowler was wounded. We called him "Bulley"-we never called anyone by rank. He wore no rank insignia and neither did we-never. That was my first experience in combat. On Guam, our next campaign, I was a scout.

What was your role as a scout?

Well, without getting into a whole lot of detail, in the jungle type warfare that we were in, everything is not a straight line. One day you're fighting in one direction, and the next day you're fighting in the opposite direction because the jungle is so thick and so overgrown and almost impossible to get through that you can walk right by the enemy and won't even see them. And the heat is almost overbearing. It's hard to imagine that you can be in such a position and live through it.

The 3rd Marine Division were the assault troops. I think there were some army infantry in there too, yes. That was a long campaign- that was

I believe twenty-eight or thirty days. But then after the Guam campaign, after we declared the island secured, and we made our camps, there was still a great deal going on each day. They'd continually be finding pockets of resistance and holed up Japanese so that they decided that we should do it all over again.

So they broke all the camps and everybody went back, all the troops went back to the beginning beaches that we had started in, and covered the whole island a second time. And we did almost as much fighting the second time as we did the first time. Like I say, you walk right by the enemy and can't even see them. Here's a few photographs that are interesting. Here's one that shows the amphibious assault- where you go in on amphibian boats. And this one is where they're relieving the troops to go back for some R&R – rest and relaxation. If you can relax in the jungles, why, you're pretty good. I wasn't there prior to the invasion, but Agana, the capital of Guam, was a pretty nice little city before the fighting took place.

What did you think about your air and Navy support during this particular campaign?
During the Guam campaign I thought it was excellent. Back then, not having the communications that we have today, all of it had to be by wire. The men had to run with rolls of wire in order to go from telephone to telephone. And running through the jungle with two guys holding a pipe through a big role of wire was tough. And of course the Japs are right behind you shooting and cutting the wires in half as soon as you lay it. Communications were tough. But we could communicate with the ships and call for air strikes and bombardment. On Guam they did a real good job. 'Course on Guam the anticipated point of assault was in a bay on one side of the island. And it was supposed to be a big secret. They sent decoys into a bay to try to make the enemy believe that's where the big assault was going to take place when really it was over on the other side of the island. And so the big assault took place on more or less an area open to the ocean. But somehow or other we all figured that it was not much of a secret because they were waiting on us when we got there.

You were a scout. What does one do as a scout?
Well, the most dreaded call being a scout was when they sent the word out, "Scouts out and draw fire." Now, that means you go out and let the enemy shoot at you. And we do that so we know where they're at. As nearly as

I can remember that first campaign on Guam lasted a month. The second one, the second phase of the same campaign, that was probably, oh, a couple of weeks. We simply went back to the beaches, started over, and did the whole thing again.

This paper was really handed out at Bougainville. (Holds up paper) It was given to us. It's basically Japanese phrases for Marines-that is, how to tell them to surrender, to lay down their arms, to halt, whatever- all in Japanese. And if you studied it you would probably be able to converse a little bit in Japanese, not much, but a little. They thought it was gonna do some good I'm sure.

What did you think of your officers and your non-coms?
Most of the officers and the non-coms were great people. They were excellent. After the Guam campaign they started getting in some of what they called sixty or ninety day wonders. These were the lieutenants that were coming in to replace the ones that didn't make it. Some of those must have been hurried through officer candidate school or something because they were not the greatest. They did not have the experience and they were trying to be leaders. And some of them tried too hard.

They didn't have the experience and they wouldn't rely on the ordinary lowly PFC or private because they were the officers, and they were supposed to be in charge even though they didn't know what was going on part of the time.

We stayed on Guam for six months when I was still in the 21st Marines. We were way up in the hills of Guam where they had carved a patch out of the jungle. And the flying insects and everything else up there in the jungle were terrible. I got dengue fever a couple of times up there and then I got transferred into the 9th Marines as a replacement. Now the 9th Marines had a beautiful spot down on that bay that I spoke of before – right out on the beach. And it was just fantastic. It was just like Waikiki Beach in Hawaii. We had a beautiful spot there and we stayed there six months and did training. One little incident occurred there. One of the new lieutenants who came over had taken over our platoon because our platoon lieutenant had been killed. At that time they were just beginning to get grenade launchers for rifles. Well, we were gonna go out and practice with them, as well as bazookas, and we went out to a range someplace on the island where we were gonna train with these grenade launchers on our rifles. Well, they also made the grenade launcher for a carbine which was a little bitty rifle. And so I was chosen, for what reason I'll never know, to use the grenade launcher on a carbine. You put a blank cartridge in and you put the grenade in the launcher part. I got it all rigged up and I set it on the ground and held it, and I was gonna fire it. But this new lieutenant said, "No, no, no, that's a shoulder fired weapon. You fire that from the shoulder." Well, he's the lieutenant. So I fired it from the shoulder and wound up with a big black eye, a bruised jaw and everything else. And the dag-gone carbine came apart in the process – the stock fell right off. It has a brass ring or something to hold the barrel to the stock but it flew off and the thing flew apart. The grenade went, fortunately, but I sure got hurt. It's a wonder I didn't break my shoulder. But I held it tight because I knew that thing was gonna kick. Boy, it did, and then after that it was decided that maybe you should put that on the ground. I never did see anyone use one in actual combat.

But anyhow, we were on one end of the island after our six months stay doing training and everything. We put on several night time exhibitions of fire power for different admirals that visited the island. And then it came time to leave. Of course they never told you where you was going for your next campaign, but our colonel decided that we should march from our base camp which was on one end of the island to the other end of the island where the ships were waiting to pick us up. It was a pretty long haul. And so we marched and marched and finally we got to the ships.

And after about, I don't know, a couple days outbound they started bringing out the topographies of the island where we were gonna go. And we were scheduled to go to Okinawa. But we were gonna be stand-by for Iwo Jima. It was the 4th and 5th divisions at Iwo Jima, and we floated around out there for a couple of days. But they were running into so much resistance and needed flame throwers so bad that it was decided that our unit should go in early which we did.

Here's a picture – it could be me, but if it isn't me, that's exactly the way I looked when we went to Iwo Jima. A flame thrower weighs around sixty-five pounds. I weighed about 140.

Were you afraid under fire?
Absolutely. Scared to death. Shook and shaked so much that sometimes I couldn't even eat.

I think I was just as scared both places-Guam and Iwo Jima-especially on Iwo Jima. We were trained in the jungles and Iwo had no jungles. Iwo was wide open, flat volcanic ash. No jungle whatsoever. We didn't hardly know how to act because we were trained in the jungle which I think was a big mistake. And as I said before, we were scheduled to go to Okinawa. That's jungle. But we were up on Iwo where there's no jungle and it was different.

How long were you on Iwo Jima before you were wounded?
Six days. A rifleman got me in the head. We were prime targets. Carrying that flame thrower is like painting a target on your back because they wanted to get you. The only reason I was there was because they sent the flame thrower units in early. The rest of the division was still on the boat. But they needed them badly, so after being wounded I was put on a ship, I can't even tell you if it was a hospital ship or what it was, because at that time it was nip and tuck.

And we went to Saipan first. There was a hospital on Saipan and they put us in the hospital in Saipan, and we were only there for maybe a week I guess. And then we got aboard a ship and went back to Hawaii, to Pearl Harbor, and I went in the hospital there. Had a couple of surgeries there, well I had surgeries on the ship and then a couple of surgeries in Hawaii. And then I left Hawaii and went back to the United States, San Francisco, and went into a receiving hospital in San Francisco.

And there I was diagnosed with psychoneurosis and locked up. But the psychologist that analyzed me was crazier than I was. They didn't keep me there very long-they called it psychoneurosis anxiety. Then they let loose of that and put me in an ordinary ward. I think I was in the psycho ward maybe three or four days.

And from there they transferred me by train up to Seattle, Washington – to a hospital up there. And up there a Navy captain, Captain Hill, was the chief surgeon, and up there I had two more surgeries. They were starting to put me back together. I stayed in Seattle and that's where they gave me the purple heart in a little ceremony.

And I don't really remember how long I was in Seattle. Perhaps three or four months. And all the time, of course, I wanted to get home. Then they finally transferred me to Chicago – to Great Lakes in a hospital there. And while I was in Chicago, in that hospital, the Japanese surrendered. To back up a ways, when I was on my way from San Francisco to Seattle on that train trip, that's when Franklin Delano Roosevelt died. That was in April of '45. That's when he died. When I was on that trip. And of course Harry

Truman took over and he decided to drop the bomb. And I was in Chicago when all that took place.

What do you think about dropping the bomb?

I was glad they did it because everything seemed to be pointing towards an invasion of Japan, and that would have been lots and lots more people dead. I was glad they dropped it, even though it was a terrible thing – it ended the war. I was discharged then from Great Lakes in October '45.

Did you take advantage of the GI Bill of Rights?

Yes I did. Back in the beginning, as I told you, I did not graduate from high school and I felt that I needed something. So I took advantage of the GI Bill of Rights. Got everything all signed up and went to Patterson Co-op in downtown Dayton and spent my four years studying to be a toolmaker. And I became a toolmaker. That's all I ever did for all of my working life was be a toolmaker.

Eventually I owned my own tool company. I had my own tool company for about fifteen years. But one of the recessions took us down pretty low so I sold out and retired. But the main reason that I retired, at that point in time, I was only fifty-five, was because I developed colon cancer due to the stress of the business. It was in 1985 that they operated on me for colon cancer and gave me one year to live. And this is 1999 and I'm still breathing.

Looking back fifty-five years, how do you think that World War II changed your life?

Pretty dramatic. A total change. I'm not the same person I was prior to the war for lots of reasons. We have a reunion every two years up in Canton, Ohio, where members of the flame thrower units gather. Now our numbers are dwindling. I think there's only four of us left. In the past two years two of them have passed away. So either there's gonna be just two of us this time, or perhaps three, because someone has said that they found another one. So our numbers are getting real small.

After I finished my Patterson Co-op schooling I was employed at Master Electric Company in Dayton as an apprentice toolmaker. And I was assigned to their research and development department which was kind of an exclusive little area in the factory, all enclosed with glass, and we did the research and development. And there was a hallway that ran the length of our little enclosure, and right on the other side of that hallway was the engineering offices. And the girl that I married was a secretary for an engineer in those offices.

And a couple of years later we had our first baby which was Diane. Later we decided that the only way I was ever going to be able to retire was start my own business which I did along with another man. And our tool company was called Triad Mold and Die. And we stayed in business there for about fifteen years.

Virginia K. Hess

Interview #5 – Will Frazee

Will Frazee was drafted into the Army in January of 1943 and served with the 69th Infantry Division in Europe as a rifleman. He was in the service just over three years with sixteen months overseas. He attained the rank of sergeant. Frazee and his wife Barbara are the parents of three children. After the war Frazee used the G.I. Bill of Rights to earn his bachelor's degree and a law degree from Ohio State University and later an M.S. degree in economics from Columbia University. Frazee worked as an aide to the mayor of Kettering, Ohio, but in 1958 moved to Centerville where he still practices law. He's a member of the American Legion, Post Five.

Would you comment a little about your life prior to your military service?
Well, I was born and raised in Dayton, Ohio, went through the Dayton public schools and graduated from Parker Co-op in 1941 with a major in tool and die. Then I became an apprentice, an apprentice toolmaker, in a General Motors plant which happened to be a war plant located in the northern fringe of Dayton – in Vandalia at Arrow Products. Arrow Products was making a convertible pitch propeller and hub for the P-51.

When did you go into the military?
I went on active service in January of 1943. First I went to Jefferson Barracks, Missouri. And this was January, you have to remember, and Jefferson Barracks was an old, old army camp perched on a bluff above the Mississippi River. And it was so damp and so cold that even the marrow of your bones was cold. That was a miserable experience in basic training – to be in hutment at that old army camp. The hutment had lumber sides up four feet high and then on top of that was a tent.

There I had an opportunity to volunteer for airborne. And after I finished basic I went to Westover Field in the 881st Airborne Engineer Battalion.

177

Airborne was all volunteers, they had a very high esprit de corps. It certainly was in contrast to what I experienced in the infantry. It just seemed to be an exciting thing to do. I liked being in an all-volunteer outfit. I thought that would be good and I thought I would experience some interesting combat in the airborne because they were quite active. Also you got to fly overseas instead of taking a boat because the B-17s that they were flying overseas would have airborne troopers in them. So you got to fly to England instead of going on a surface ship and risking the German subs.

There's paratroopers and gliders. Which group were you in?
Slightly more than half were glider troopers – I was a glider trooper. I was not what we called a jump man. I picked gliders. Flights in gliders were part of our training. The flights were terrifying. It was a CG4A glider manufactured by WACO in Troy or Piqua – I can't tell you which. But it was a fabric glider and it had aluminum spars. The front hinged up so when it was in position the air pressure of gliding held it shut. The only way to get out of that glider was to walk to the rear of the tail section where they had omitted some spars and you simply stepped out, the fabric would give way and you would fall out of the glider. Actually, the front of the glider was like a clamshell. That's how you got in, but you could not get out that way. If you had a smooth landing, like on an airstrip, then everything worked, you know, then the front came back up. But if you were airborne, you could only get out by going to the rear of the glider by falling through the fabric. The glider was supposed to hold eight troopers, but if you had a jeep in the glider or another piece of engineering equipment like a small grader or something of that nature then you had to reduce the number of troops.

Well, we were getting ready to go overseas, we were in the final stage. Then out of the blue came orders that I was to report for a program called Army Specialized Training Program (ASTP). And so that was quite a lark, but I was only there nine weeks. Then they decided they didn't need twenty-seven thousand engineers and linguists and they sent us all to the infantry as buck privates to start over.

Then I was sent to Camp Shelby, Mississippi. It was late spring of '44. At Camp Shelby we were back in hutments. I was assigned to G Company, 2nd Battalion, 272nd Infantry Regiment, 69th Infantry Division. Well, I trained with them until we left for overseas at the end of October in 1944. I went overseas as a private and in France I was promoted to PFC. I was a rifleman. I was a rifleman in a rifle squad, of a rifle platoon, of a rifle company, of an infantry rifle regiment. It was rifle all the way. They said take care of your M-1 and it will take care of you.

We were in a convoy of ships so big that as far as you could see to the horizon it was all ships. We could not see the edge of the convoy it was so large. It swung south of the Azores in an attempt to avoid German submarines. And when we got south of the Azores which is a little off kilter as far as getting to Southampton, England goes, there were submarine attacks and we were ordered below.

And we heard all of these depth charges going off and we hoped that that old freighter could sustain that because we didn't see any possibility of getting up on deck if one of those hit. It took us nineteen days to get over to England.

Well, when we got to England we saw our first bomb damage because the warehouse area of Southampton was mostly unroofed and the docks were beat up. We boarded trains and we went to Winchester, England, and were quartered in hedgerows in Nissen huts. Winchester is in southern England, the famous Winchester Cathedral is located there. We were there through Christmas of '44.

When the Battle of the Bulge broke out they took about twenty percent of our personnel and sent them over as replacements. So we were reduced by about twenty percent in personnel and firepower and people who had trained with us. When we got to France they replaced those soldiers with repo- depo people – the replacement depot people. And they sent us cooks and bakers and truck drivers and gasoline tank fillers and a little bit of everything. These were people who scarcely knew which end of the gun the bullet came out of. And so we took those people under our wing and tried to teach them as much as possible because we were going to have to rely on them when we got in combat.

Anyway, we went to Le Havre where we debarked very crudely – at Le Havre that is. We went over the side of that ship on landing nets and climbed down the landing net into an LCI. And the LCI took us there. A few people fell from the landing nets and didn't land in the LCI and those were the first men we lost. They were either drowned or crushed. This was early January of '45.

When we got the division ashore we were put in cattle rack semis and taken to a place near Soisson, France, and they said, "there's a rest camp there and you're going to be in the rest camp." When we got there, there was nothing but a muddy hillside where the quartermaster had thrown tents off into the mud and we had to set up that camp. We had to erect those tents to have protection. It was bitter cold and very windy.

Then toward the end of January, around the 20th, we rode 40&8 boxcars up to a quartermaster truck company in Belgium which took us up to the line, the front so-called, in Belgium. And we relieved the 99th Division which had been shattered by the German onslaught in the Battle of the Bulge.

They were down to about a regiment and a quarter of the normal three regiments – so we went into the line and replaced the 99th. We put three regiments in place of a regiment and a quarter, which shows how heavy a buildup, was going on in the Battle of the Bulge at that time. This was very late January, probably up to the 25th, 26th, or 27th.

This was our first combat. We were supposed to replace them at 4:00 a.m. in the morning but they were substantially pulled out by midnight and so we took over and in my regiment, by 8:30 in the morning, forty-two men were dead. These casualties were due mainly to German snipers. We were well trained and well equipped but we were combat green. And as a result some men, thinking themselves out of range and being out of normal range, fell victim to German snipers. There was very little artillery fire – although it did claim a couple of people. There was heavy mortar fire but there was no small arms fire at all. So they were lost in various ways. I think it was the penalty of being green troops and assuming too much.

How far were the Germans away from you?
Well, they were in the Siegfried Line and from our front we could see the Siegfried Line. We could see the pillboxes, we could see the apertures in the pillboxes. I don't know, a half-mile or something like that, maybe a third of a mile. And there was a gravel road there which was called the International Highway – a fancy name but not much of a road. And that was the border between Belgium and Germany, that road – the International Highway, so called.

I was frozen stiff for a number of reasons. We had winds of fifteen to twenty-five miles an hour, it was sub-zero, and we had been instructed to heavily dub our combat boots to waterproof them. So we had put on all sorts of this greasy substance called dubbing which did indeed waterproof. The problem was it also penetrated the leather, made the leather very dense, and made it a thermal bridge from the outside temperatures to our feet and to our toes. And having no galoshes at that time to help insulate us our feet were frozen and we were frozen most of the time. The weather was horrendous. It was as much a problem as the Germans. We were losing people to trench foot and we were losing people to frostbite.

What were your emotions at this time?

Well, I think you wondered if you were going to make it. The Germans were awfully good soldiers and certainly had a lot of experience compared to us. Although I will say this, the 69th Division was reputed to have expended more live ammunition in training than any other unit. They were emphasizing that before they sent our units over. And so we had a lot of training sessions with live fire where we would move forward under live fire or we would move forward behind artillery. They did a magnificent job of training us at Camp Shelby. The camp was horrible and the living conditions were miserable – it was full of snakes and chiggers. If you could count on your body four hundred chigger bites you were eligible to go to the hospital. Less than four hundred chigger bites you weren't. But the training itself, in expending ammunition and in putting us unrealistic situations, was truly magnificent.

That helped a lot but it didn't overcome our inexperience – we were still green troops when we went in the line. But I'll tell you, you learn quickly or you're not there. For us it was three to four weeks

I suppose. Remember, you're highly motivated to learn. We found that the army was very poor about bringing up hot food, they just sort of didn't. They gave us combat rations, mainly K. rations. We found that they were always willing to bring up ammunition and we had plenty of it. We found that specialized things like white cloaks to help conceal us in the snow were not available. They were available to the Germans and the Germans wore them but we didn't have them. We found we had no galoshes. We found that a heavily dubbed combat boot was a tremendous conveyor of heat out of our feet and into the air. We found that it was vary fatiguing – the heavy packs we carried. I opted for a pack board. I had to carry the squad cooker and the nested aluminum pans in return for getting the pack board. So I had it a little easier, but the conventional packs were not really well designed.

What about fear when you're in combat?

I think you slightly get used to it. Of course the thing you learn is to keep firing whether you see a target or not. Lay down heavy continuous fire. That was the best thing to keep Jerry's head down and to get Jerry in the mood to pull out and retreat and give up what they were defending. So we had to learn that, but we learned it. We'd been told that before, but we lapsed, you might say, when we actually got into combat.

But we did learn to lay down heavy fields of fire and would only save three clips and stop firing when we got down to three clips. We each had to carry two bandoliers of ammunition and each bandolier contained eight clips. And the ammunition came forward to us riflemen in the form of bandoliers. You sling the bandolier over your head, it crosses your shoulder, it is made of cloth, and it contains eight filled clips of M-1 ammunition – thirty caliber.

Then we went in an attack mode and we were preparing to attack the Siegfried Line. We crossed this gravel road called the International Highway and my rifle company walked right into a minefield. And a couple of men stepped on mines and one medic attempting an evacuation stepped on a mine.

So we were ordered back out and we turned around and we tried to put our feet in the same footsteps we had made coming in. And we had an ignominious retreat back over the International Highway and into the woods. So we were there two days and the Siegfried Line was breached about fourteen miles north of us by another outfit that swung in behind it. And finally we were able to go through the Siegfried Line unopposed. And so we regrouped on the other side.

Our first billet inside the Siegfried Line was in a little frame constructed German house that didn't amount to a hill of beans – but it had a basement. So we went into the basement and we found that the concrete wall facing toward Belgium was about eighteen inches thick. And the concrete wall towards Germany was only about six inches thick. And they had stepped the basement widows so that you could fire out at an angle. We were astonished at that. This little innocent house had been converted into a strong point.

Were you in combat until the war ended?
Until the war ended. It ended a little early for my division because we were the first to meet the Russians at the Elbe River. We made the historic link-up. We had captured Leipzig and had advanced past Leipzig and gotten to Torgau, at least a group of four men, a patrol, had gotten to Torgau. The body of the division was still back about eight or ten miles. And we made that historic link-up on the 25th of April. So the war for us was over on the 25th of April. We had met the Russians.

What's the difference for the combat infantryman between fighting in a city and in the countryside?
Well, I would say street fighting is about twenty times more scary than in the open countryside because there's only a certain number of doorways to get into. They can rake those streets with machine gun fire. Yes, it's pretty much pure terror fighting in an urban environment. All the buildings are

masonry, therefore if a bullet happens to hit a building, it glances off and it's still active, you might say.

From time to time we would run into tanks, but that was rare. The big thing we would run into would be the 88s. They had ringed their cities with these weapons. Even relatively small villages, like five thousand people, would have emplaced 88mm anti-aircraft guns. And these anti-aircraft guns could be leveled and could send time-fused shells right into us.

So we developed a technique where we would get in place, but stay hidden. And at the crack of dawn, when we could just begin to make out each other and not cause any unnecessary deaths from friendly fire, we would get up, we would throw off our pack, some men even threw off their helmets, and we would race as fast as we could toward these emplacements. We did this because they could only cut the fuse so short, and therefore there was a protective zone from the emplacement out to where they could cut the fuse the shortest. And we had to get up into that protective zone as fast as we could. I would say the protective zone would be perhaps as much as three hundred yards. They couldn't cut the fuse shorter than that. If we got in that zone we were pretty safe. We wouldn't cany any bandoliers because you had plenty of ammunition in your belt and bandoliers would flop around and all. And we would go up over the emplacement and we would stand there and pour our fire into the emplacements, and frankly kill off all the crews – you know. And it worked almost every time. And those enemy crews, even though they were armed with small weapons, would never come up to the bank and oppose us. Well, we were usually in overwhelming numbers.

We were strafed once – in my entire combat experience we were strafed only once. And when I say we, I don't mean that any bullets landed near my outfit, my rifle company. But the plane came and was intermittently hopping and strafing and going like a roller coaster. And when he went over us we had no problem with it, you know, because he was not firing, he was going up when he went over us.

When you met the Russians at the Elbe River, did you actually shake hands with them?
Oh, absolutely. They were supposed to stay on their side of the river. That was the diplomatic agreement as we understood it. We were supposed to stay on our side of the river. Well, we went into these towns. I was in Mockrehna which was about eight miles short of Torgau. We would go in and we would take the best houses for our billets, skipping the other houses because there

were plenty of houses in regard to our number. Well, the Russians came pouring over the river and they took the houses in between the ones we had rejected. So their company street was our company street. And it was something else. We found a totally different culture in the Russians. Totally different – as soldiers. They were, shall we say, unstrained. They had fought the Germans for longer than we had. They had come back through their ruined cities and villages, those the Germans had leveled with demolition [charges] and burned out, and had even leveled the walls with demolition [charges]. They had hatred, a burning hatred of the Germans that we did not possess. And so they treated the Germans very, very badly. They even treated their own troops, we thought, very badly. What happened on our company's street was a Russian officer came back about two in the morning and didn't know the password. The Russian sentry insisted he give the password. The Russian officer didn't know it and couldn't give it. So there was this confrontation, the sentry would not let him pass. So the Russian officer pulled out his side arm, an automatic pistol, and shot the sentry dead. If that had happened in the U.S army that officer would never have gotten out of Leavenworth.

And also they had these huge cast iron kettles on wheels, they used steel wheels, and they used to build a fire under them. And they would go out in the middle of a pasture with a sledgehammer and knife and they would hit a cow in the head and hit it repeatedly with a sledgehammer until finally the cow would go down. They would then strip the hide off, they would take the entrails out, they would cut up the meat and throw it in this big cast iron cauldron – whatever. Those things must have been eight foot across, you know, eight feet in diameter and they were at least six feet high – probably seven. They would build a fire under it and they would fix their food. Many of them had German army equipment – cartridge belts, and many of them had trousers. They had cotton tunics of the Russian army, but trousers of the German army. They truly lived off the land. We had an elaborate supply chain, you know, we got cartons of eggs. Even when we were at the front we received pork chops, we received all sort of things like that. They lived off the land. They had no discernible supply chain at all for anything.

After V-E Day in May we were told we would go to Marseilles and we would be shipped through the Suez Canal and we would be part of the invasion force for Japan. But of course that never happened with V-J Day coming. So I finally came home and was discharged a PFC. That's not much of a military career, to go in as a private and come out thirty-seven and a half months later a PFC.

Did you take advantage of the GI Bill then?

Yes. I didn't go back into tool making even though I loved the trade, even though I was proud of being an apprentice toolmaker. Still, I thought, the army's gonna pay for this, you know, this country's going to pay for this. And I used every day of my GI Bill. Every single day of eligibility. I went to Ohio State. I took a bachelor's degree in business, I took a law degree, and then I went to Columbia University in New York City and took a master's degree in economics. Then I became a senior research analyst because of my degree in economics. I became senior research analyst for the city of Columbus. And I was in that position for a little over a year.

Then I went to the village of Kettering and I was there sixteen and a half months. Then I moved to Centerville in 1958. I practiced law here and I got married in '49.

How do you think being in the Army changed your life?

Well, I would have been a toolmaker for General Motors all my life and that's not a bad life. And I certainly don't know whether I improved it or not. But I would say that toolmakers have a higher standing in society than do lawyers, you know. They say that there are two lawyer jokes, all the rest are true.

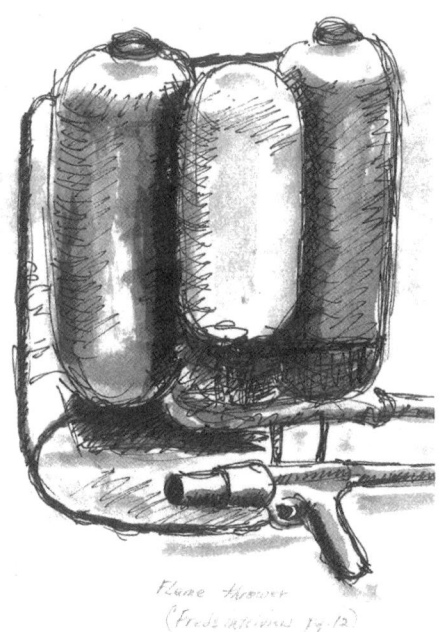

Flame thrower
(From interview pg. 12)

Interview #6 – George Cooper

George C. Cooper was born and raised in a small town in North Carolina. He entered the Navy in June of 1943 and was subsequently commissioned as an ensign-one of the "Golden Thirteen"-the first black officers of the United States Navy. He attained the rank of Lieutenant J.G. before he left the Navy in 1945. After his discharge he returned to Hampton Institute where he had done his undergraduate work. Later he earned an MA in personnel administration of Columbia University. He and his wife Margarett have a daughter, Peggy Davis, who is a professor of law at New York University. He now lives at St. Leonard's retirement village.

George, where were you born and raised?
I was born and raised in a little town in North Carolina, Washington, North Carolina, population about 8.000 people. It's on the east coast of North Carolina. Right on the Pamlico River. I'm from a family of thirteen-including my mother and father. Eleven kids. I'm in the middle. And incidentally, the only one left out of the whole family. Just buried my last brother about six months ago.

My father was a sheet metal worker by trade. And there's a little bit of history there. He worked in a sheet metal shop that was owned by a hardware store. And in eastern North Carolina, the big thing for sheet metal in those days was putting roofs on houses, metal roofs, and building tobacco flues. They used those in tobacco barns to cure the tobacco. They were probably thirty inches in diameter, and they went around the perimeter of the bam on the inside of the wood. They no longer do that now.

Now we had, as I say, a large family – there was eleven of us – a large family. He went to his boss one day and said, Mr. Mallison, I need to make more money. And the man said, well, Ed, I just can't pay you any more money. He said, well, then I'm going to have to leave. I'm sorry. I gotta leave because I gotta have more money, my family is getting larger and

186

larger. And this man said to him, if you decide to leave and there's anything in this shop that we're no longer using that you think would be helpful to you in your new venture, you take it. And he used what he picked up out of there as the beginning of his own shop.

And he began his own sheet metal business right in the same town. I was the only one of his boys who even went near the shop. As a matter of fact, I had a sheet metal shop after I got out of college. And it was a real close relationship between him and me. Very close relationship. And I think that that's a part of his life and my life that's quite interesting.

My mother stayed home. And in addition to that, we put a garden. It's a small town with a lot of empty lots, and we had a garden in almost every empty lot within a radius of a half mile. And we had to get up early in the morning and take the produce downtown and sell it. We lived twenty-two miles from Greenville. As a matter of fact, they wanted to put the college in Washington, and the power structure would not allow it. They went to Greenville, and that college made Greenville.

Did you do any traveling prior to military service?
Very little traveling prior to my military service, except that I had brothers and sisters who lived both in Boston and in New York City, and I went to visit them. So I traveled a little. I'd done some traveling up in the state of Maine where my brother was a member of a camp that came out of Washington, and we used to go up there every summer and camp with him up in Maine. They had their own camp, had their own lake and everything.

Incidentally, I was born September 7, 1916. So I was eighty-three years old day before yesterday. I went through high school in Washington – obviously a segregated school at that point in time. And then I went to Hampton University-Hampton Institute it was called then. It's now called Hampton University-that's where I did my graduate work. Went to Columbia for a masters, and did additional study at Ohio State. As a student I was slightly above average.

The main thing I did in high school was the debating society. I enjoyed that tremendously, came out of Hampton with a degree in what they called at that time trade education which qualified me to teach my trade. And I took sheet metal work at Hampton, and that was the reason, or one of the reasons, that my father and I parted company afterwards. I went back after school to work in his shop with him, and having gone through the thing at Hampton, I could draft anything I wanted to draft and I could layout anything I wanted to layout. Where he had learned his the hard way. If he had to do something he would tear the old one apart and trace it. I thought that was a waste of time. Finally we'd have so many arguments, I found an opportunity in an old town called Wilson, North Carolina that needed a sheet metal worker-a sheet metal shop. And he said, George, I'm gonna tell you like Mr. Mallison told me, if there's anything in my shop that you can use, you take it and God bless you. So, I did. I was in my early twenties.

OK. So I had this shop in Wilson. And my ambition was to manufacture metal caskets. And I just could not scrape up enough money to buy the equipment that I needed to do it. So, I was reading a trade magazine one day, and I saw an ad in the paper where they needed a teacher for aircraft sheet metal work at Wilberforce University in Wilberforce, Ohio. I answered the ad and was invited to Columbus for an interview. I walked into this gentleman's office, and he said, are you George Cooper? And I said, yes. And he said, well, we made a mistake. I said, I don't understand, I'm George Cooper. You got my letter, I answered your ad. He said, I don't believe you because I've never seen a black sheet metal worker do what we want done. So, I said, I've come a long way for this interview, and I think that there ought to be, if you're going to be fair about it, at least some test you could put me to in order to tell me that I can't do the work you want. He said, that's fair enough. And this gentleman gave me a set of blue prints for a metal locker like they use in school rooms, you know. And he said, we've got a complete shop. You take these blueprints and you go down to Wilberforce. If you can make this locker for me in a week you've got the job. I called him Tuesday afternoon and told him he could come and look at his locker. I got started on Monday. I was done the next day. I called him to tell him he could come and look at the locker and I got the job.

So, I worked there. At that time they called it NYA – National Youth Administration. And they were training these kids for defense work, in part for the defense industry. I stayed there, and I really did not want to go into the service. I didn't want to go into the armed forces because I didn't think I would like it. And this was a way to stay out. I got a call one day from the naval training school in Hampton Institute where I had done my undergraduate work, and it was the captain of Class A training school for the US Navy. And he needed an aircraft sheet metal instructor because they were training them to be blacksmiths in the Navy. So, I said, well, I'd be interested in coming, he said, would you be interested in coming down for an interview. I said, sure. They sent me a ticket and I went down for an interview. This was in the early 40s.

So, I went down and I said to him, I said, captain, I'm here because I'm interested in doing civilian work in the war, I don't want to go into the service. He said, well, I checked you out fairly thoroughly. I discovered later that he had indeed checked me out. And he said as long as you can do this job for us you'll be working for the Navy, and I think I can keep you out from going into the service. So I took that job.

He used that shop to get anything he wanted out of Washington. For instance, out on my porch there is a metal, copper, brass thing that has feet on it and magazines stuffed in it. I used to make, in the shop, little coal scuttles this high. And he would take items like that to Washington and lay them on the admiral's desk and walk out with anything he wanted for his school. He was a very shrewd man and we enjoyed him thoroughly.

So, I took this job and enjoyed it. I was able to have my family with me. We had an apartment and everything. I was married the year I graduated from college, in 1939. We met at Hampton. I was graduating from there that year. She was there that year in the graduate school of library science. She had graduated from Wilberforce and was there at Hampton for additional work in library training as a librarian. And that's where we met – on the football field at one of the football games. We married that same year-1939. Her home was in Hamilton, Ohio incidentally, right down the road from here. Her parents are there, and we were married there.

Now, to get back to this story, Commander Downes came into my shop one day, and he said, George, I can't keep you out any longer. He said, we need you here desperately, and you've done an excellent job for us, but the Navy needs you for something else. And I can't tell you what it is, but I have sealed orders for you. And if you do what I think you will do, you will never be sorry. So, I said, Commander, you know I have all the confidence in the world in you, so let's go with it.

I was ordered to Great Lakes. I reported to Great Lakes and went over to Camp Robert Smalls at the Great Lakes Training Center. Downes said, if you enlist in the Navy I will promise you that you will never be sorry. That's how I got in. And then one day after that he came and brought my orders, sealed orders. And I went to Great Lakes with these sealed orders which you'd better not open, as you know. This was in 1943. So, I go to Great Lakes, and they escorted me to Camp Robert Smalls which was the black recruit training camp at Great Lakes.

Camp Robert Smalls. Let me back up a minute. Great Lakes Naval Training School is the biggest training facility-the biggest one in the world. It's in Chicago-just outside of Chicago. We were escorted to Camp Robert Smalls which was the recruit training camp for black enrollees. We were set up in a barracks which became our school building and our housing. Now, over on the main side of Great Lakes, they had every kind of facility in the world to train officers.

We discovered that evening after we got there that we were sent there to find out whether or not blacks could be trained as officers in the Navy. We didn't even know each other because we had come from all over. We didn't know how we got there or who had recommended us. Obviously, Captain Downes had recommended me. So, everything we did was done in that barracks-a segregated barracks – except swimming. This was an experiment that was set up by the Navy to see if black people had the ability to become officers of the United States Navy.

A little history about that, too. At that point in time, one of the well known black women in the United States was a lady by the name of Mary McLeod Bethune who was the president of Bethune College [Bethune-Cookman College] in Florida. President Roosevelt was using her as a consultant on black education – Negro education. She and Mrs. Roosevelt became very, very good friends and this relationship lasted for years. Until one of them died, as a matter of fact. The story is that Mrs. Bethune convinced Mrs. Roosevelt to persuade President Roosevelt that the Navy needed black officers. So we were pulled together.

There was sixteen of us to prove whether or not we could make the grade. The second night we were there, we got together after lights out and decided that despite the fact that we didn't know each other, we were all there for the same thing, and at that point in time each of us represented roughly ten thousand black sailors in the Navy. There were no officers. We would either make the grade thereby paving the way for others to come or we wouldn't. So we decided we would not try to compete against each other. We would study together every night after lights out. And as fate would have it, one of each of these gentlemen knew something about every subject they studied. That was pure luck-and he would drill the rest of us on the subject. On the subject in which he was an expert. We went through that course, and at that time they called us, these officers in training, 90-day wonders. They trained us to be officers in 90 days. At the end of 90 days, our grades were sent to Washington. The very same day, there was a message back from the Bureau of Naval Personnel saying you sent grades up here indicating these guys had come out three-tenths of a point higher than any class in the history of the Navy. There is a mistake. They cheated. Send them back through it again. They didn't believe it.

And we actually started the following day, going back through it. The same courses. The same course of study. The third day somebody in Washington said, if they were that good the first time around what the hell do you think they're going to do the next time around. And they decided that they would commission us.

When were you commissioned then?
I think it was in the fall. Well, anyway, Great Lakes, as I say, was the biggest training base in the world. And they had these classes coming out all the time as officers. We were all commissioned ensigns in the United States Navy, except that there was no ceremony whatever. Each of us was called over to the office on the main side – individually. This is the official picture for that class. And I am here, front and center.

Now, instead of the graduation exercises they held every thirteen weeks for white candidates, we had no exercise. We were called in to Commander Armstrong's office individually. And there's a little story behind that when I got my call. I went into the commander's office, saluted, naturally. At ease. He said, you are what we call a hell raiser in the Navy. I said, commander, I haven't even been on report since I've been in the Navy. What do you mean, a hell raiser? I don't understand. He said, did you hit a little white boy in Washington, North Carolina when you were six years old? I said, yes, sir. I said, he called me a nigger at the wrong time, and we fought. I said, I think he won, but we did fight. And I instigated the fight. I said, if that's what you call being a hell raiser then I'm guilty. I did not know that he had my commission on his desk, at that time. Well, he subsequently handed me my commission, gave me the glad-hand shake, and that's how I was inducted into the officer corps of the United States Navy. And each of us went through that same process. The FBI had gone back to everything we'd ever done, each of us.

I was then ordered back to Flampton, and I'm sure that was at Captain Downes' request, as his personnel officer at naval training school which was incidentally naval training school to train blacks for billets in the Navy. All of the trainees were black. The ships company was two-thirds white. I was personnel officer for that base.

What does one do as a personnel officer?

One of the main things that one does is to watch over the discipline for the sailors that are enrolled in that institution. See, this was a school, a class A training school. Another thing that one had a responsibility to do was approving all leaves. I have always operated on the principle that the best way to win friends and influence people is to work on a one to one basis. As you can imagine, with me being the only black person among a thousand naval officers uniforms a lot of things happened. As I said, three-fourths of the instructors were white enlistees who were training these guys that just came out of boot camp. And as you walked across the street of Newport News, some people didn't salute you. And invariably, when that happened, if it really got to me and I thought it was something that needed to be corrected, I would find a way to have that man come through me personally for something. One of the things that I used frequently, there's always somebody dying in somebody's family, was when somebody's got to have an emergency leave to go home. My yeoman could do it all. But I said have him come by and I can sign papers in the office. So I bring him in and he, hopefully, recognizes me as a human being rather than the black s.o.b. he thought I was when he wouldn't salute me yesterday on the streets of Newport News.

One day, one of them came up to me and said, I've heard about you sons of bitches, but I never thought I'd see you. And he was this close to me-in my face. That's the one time I lost my cool because my wife and my daughter were at my side. And I reached back to hit him. He was ready to beat me to death, and I was gonna beat him to death right there on the streets of Newport News. And my wife grabbed me and said, George, it isn't worth it and he isn't worth it, and she saved my commission. And we had, you know, experiences like that all the way through. In those days, everything was segregated. Every institution was completely segregated.

Well, I stayed there for a year and a half, and then I was scheduled to go overseas-to Okinawa. And I went over to the Norfolk Naval Yard to have the only real physical exam I had from Uncle Sam. When we were at Great Lakes we used to go to one of the other camps where they had a swimming pool to teach abandon ship drill. There was a tall thing rigged up where you jumped off into the pool and learned to abandon ship. Some fool had left a bar of soap there, and I stepped on it and fell in that pool. And my back is still in bad shape. So I went on temporary duty, I mean, restrictive duty.

And that's really the reason I stayed at Hampton, and stayed stateside the whole time.

So when I was finally ordered to Okinawa, I went to Norfolk and got the first real examination I had and they said, we can't send you, we're going to have to discharge you from the service. So, I got a medical discharge in 1945. And that represented my stint in the Navy- about three and one-half years.

What did you do when you got out?
When I got out of the service, I went back to Hampton Institute and was hired there where I had done my undergraduate work. I was a director of the department-director of the veterans' bureau they called it. All of these guys are now coming out of the service, coming back on the GI Bill. So, I directed that program for two and a half years and then was made director of their trade school, because I had graduated from that trade school. There we taught all of the building trades and machine shop etc., etc. They had fourteen different trades. And I worked at that for a while. While I was there I did graduate work at Columbia. I took a year off interim period and earned an MA in personnel administration from Columbia University on the GI Bill.

How do you think World War II changed your life?
I'm sure it changed my life considerably. Because in my earlier life I was something of a hell raiser. And I think that having married the lovely young lady I did back then and the influence she had on me, led me to change my whole philosophy of life. This happened while we were in the Navy. For the most part, at least. Also, because of some of the things that I confronted in the Navy. Because as I say I was the only black, I stood out like a sore foot everywhere I went. You know. And it was something that you had to respond to twenty-four hours a day.

One example. I was officer of the day. And they used this naval training school to train white officers in how to manage black troops. I was officer of the day, one day, and I go to the airport to pick up this man, and he said oh, my god. Do you live on the base? I said, yes, sir. He said, do you live in bachelor quarters? No. He said, where am I going to stay? I said, you're going to stay in BOQ, bachelor officers' quarters. He said, do you live there? I said, no, sir. He said, well, I want to see the captain tonight. I said, sir, it's impossible to see the captain tonight, it's after midnight, but he will have the orders for you at 08:00. If you are there you can see them. I refuse to take you to his house. I'll take you to BOQ-those are my orders. He said, well, where do you live? I said, we have an apartment, fortunately-because I'm married. He said, O.K., if you don't live there, I'll go to BOQ. I told him the skipper always comes early, so if you come a little bit early you may be able to see him before quarters, but I'm not going to take you to his house. We went into quarters at 08:00 and the skipper said: George met a man at the airport last night who came here for this training program, and he was here when I got to work this morning, said that he had never seen a black naval officer, and he hoped he would never see another one. He said, between the time he and I talked at quarters at 08:00, I've been in touch with the bureau of naval personnel, and he's been transferred already. That man was transferred to Alaska. Five months later in the BOQ officers quarters he said, you remember that man who said he hoped he'd never see another black officer? He never will. They found him frozen to death in Alaska.

Maybe you'd comment on this book?
There was a naval historian at the naval institute by the name of Paul Stillwell, and his forte was oral history, naval oral history. And that's all he does, as a matter of fact. And he uses these oral histories to do a lot of writing from them. As a result, he has published innumerable books, this being one.

The Golden Thirteen, Recollections of the
First Black Naval Officers.

Paul became interested in our story and got permission from the naval institute, from his bosses, to do an initial interview with a few of us to see if it made sense to try to go into it in depth. He decided he would do it. Paul visited each of us wherever we lived on at least three occasions. He came up with a book like this on each one of us which represented a compilation of our interviews. And from that book he produced this one. You have to recognize that being the first black officers of the United States Navy, we were 90-day wonders, we had not been trained in navigation, we had not been trained in engineering, we were just guys that came off the streets, that this country shot quickly through a training program and made officers.

Four of these guys were assigned to the ship that came out of the harbor of New York City, the USS Mason. And the skipper of that ship turned those four officers into real seagoing officers for the Navy. Two of them worked for recruiting command. Two of them worked in some sort of medical function, although they were not doctors. Two of them were lawyers, these two guys, White and Goodwin were lawyers. Incidentally, White subsequently became justice of the supreme court of the state of Illinois. And they worked in the law end of the Navy.

Who wrote the foreword to this book?
It was written and signed by Colin Powell. There was a young white petty officer in the Navy by the name of Glen Witt whose home is right here in the Dayton area-in Drexel, west of Dayton. Glen Witt got interested in our cause, and he started talking us up throughout the Navy. At that time he was a detailer in the Navy and he assigned men based on their capabilities to various billets throughout the service. He fell in love with this book. I got to know Glen when I was serving as president of the local chapter of the Navy League. During that year I instituted a program where we would honor, on a monthly basis, a recruiter of the year, and he was one of the recruiting officers here. Glen then became an advocate of this group. It was because of him that those of us who still lived while he was active would go to various bases throughout the world literally. We were doing primarily black history month interacting with black sailors and anybody else who was on the base.

Glen Witt was responsible for this reunion. He's a chief petty officer. Glen had the best gift of gab I've ever seen on anyone. He would walk into an admiral's office and tell that admiral what he wanted and he usually came away with it. He therefore engineered a reunion trip for us on the USS Kidd. Now the USS Kidd was one of three ships built for the Shah of Iran, but he didn't take it. He backed out. So the Navy took them and converted them into Navy ships. They decided they would do this, they would have the reunion on the Kidd-one of those three ships.

We were taken out of Norfolk, Virginia on two helicopters, and the third helicopter was media. Just prior to that the New York Times wrote a story on it-that we were going to be going on this cruise. We got an opportunity to see what changes had been made over all these years and it was a lovely cruise. It brought us all back together. It was a beautiful ship. As a matter of fact they would not allow the media in certain areas as it was so plush. They didn't want it on television. The ship wasn't made for the Navy, but they didn't take the stuff out after the Navy took it over, and it was the last word in terms of everything. Well, one of the guys who was not with us when we went aboard read the New York Times, called the New York Times, and said, I'm a member of that group. We thought he had died years ago. And the next day they flew him onto the ship. This [picture on back of book] is the way we greeted him when he got off that plane. We thought he had been dead for years. And we didn't even know what that helicopter was coming in for. Jim Harr stepped out of this helicopter 'cause the skipper really knew it. He had us all there to greet him.

Now, of the thirteen, how many are still alive?
Five of us. Three in Chicago, one in Indianapolis, and I'm here. For about fifteen years, we met annually with an organization called the National Naval Officers Association which is an organization for black naval officers. And the minority office of the naval recruiting command sponsored us to go to these conferences. And I suppose the only way to explain it is to say it. When we went they would throw out the red carpet. Because these men, now some three thousand strong, black officers in the Navy, were meeting annually with seven, eight, or nine- thousand officers there. Frequently different officers because of their duties, perceived us as being the ones, the trail blazers, that paved the road for them. And they appreciated that tremendously. We have traveled literally all over the world. The same Glen Witt, for instance, called home one day and said, may I speak to George. And my wife said, he's not here but he'll call you back when he comes in. She says, where are you calling from? He says, I'm calling from Edinburgh. I'm calling from Scotland. She said, you mean Scotland, Tennessee? He said, no, Scotland. She said, well he won't call you back over there – you call him back. He'll be back in about an hour. He did in fact call me, and he invited me over, because he was stationed over there. Come over here and speak for their black history week. And we went over and had such a good time that the next year they invited the whole damn crew. And we did that kind of thing on bases all over the states and the world which also gave us an opportunity for my wife and I for a trip.

Could you tell us a little bit about your daughter?
Peggy lives in New York, our daughter, Peggy, lives in New York. We're very proud of her. She's a full professor of law in the law school of NYU. And just eighteen months or two years ago she published her first book. And she is doing very well. And we have one granddaughter. A year ago she graduated from Brown with a major in theater and is working in New York

City- working with disadvantaged youngsters and their parents developing videos that they develop and then show on public television in New York City. And in terms of acting, our granddaughter just finished taking the lead in a small movie-what they call a festival movie. These private companies make these movies and take them to film festivals and try to sell them. We're proud of our daughter and granddaughter.

Virginia K. Hess

Interview #7 – Marie Morris

Marie Morris was a member of the Army Nurse Corps. After her husband was killed in Europe she enlisted in the Army and served in the Philippines and in Korea. Morris graduated from Middletown High School and took a BS degree in nursing at the University of Colorado. She stayed in the service and retired in 1960 at the rank of major, having served in Germany, South Korea, Japan and the Philippines. She lives with her second husband at St. Leonards in Centerville, Ohio.

Marie, where were you born and raised?
I was born in 1910 in Jamestown, Ohio, and I spent my grade school from one through the eighth grade in Xenia, Ohio. I went to high school in Middletown, Ohio and graduated in 1929. I had two brothers and one sister-they were all younger. My sister came next and then my two brothers. I also played basketball and was on the basketball team.

I actually lived with a family in Middletown, Ohio, not in my home. The husband managed the Middletown journal paper and I made my home with them for seven years helping them out. So I didn't have a lot of extra time to be running around because I helped the wife with household chores and things like that, babysat, and what have you.

I never really traveled a lot. But when this family went to visit her father and mother who lived in Columbus, Ohio, I always went with them, see, that sort of thing. But, mainly, it was local, because I was near Cincinnati, Ohio. I went down there sometimes.

Anyway, I graduated from high school in Middletown and after high school, I went to the university- went to nurse's training at Christ's Hospital in Cincinnati, Ohio. And I finished there in 1932 as a registered nurse. And then following that I went to the University of Cincinnati, took courses, and did private duty for a number of years. And I also worked quite a little bit at Children's Hospital in Cincinnati doing private duty. Following that,

I went to the University of Colorado, but this was after I had already served a year and a half in the military, in 1946. Well, I continued with that until, doing my private duty, until, actually, I went back into the service in, let's see, what year was that that I went back in? In 1949, I think it was, I went back into the service.

Did you get married in the 1930s?
Yes, I got married. It was in August, I think it was August 14. What year was it, though? It was before the war. We lived in Cincinnati. He was a school teacher. He taught in the schools there and I was a nurse. He didn't want me in the service, and so when he was called up we hadn't been married very long. He was drafted and was sent to England for training purposes. He spent about two years over there. It was right after he was drafted that we got married.

What happened to him over there?
Well, they got prepared for D-Day, of course, and he landed on Omaha beachhead the 12th of June, 1944. And he already was prepared for G2 work, that is, bringing back information on the enemy. And he told me that at the time that that's 96% casualty which I didn't like to hear, of course. But, he made it until October 11, 1944. He'd gone out, this was before the Battle of the Bulge, and they were going into Luxembourg. He had another friend with him in another jeep that was also a school teacher, so there was no question about who he was, or what it was. He led the way, and as he did so he hit a land mine. Took the driver's seat right out of the vehicle. He was on his way into Luxembourg, I can't tell you exactly the city or anything, but he was killed on October 11,1944.

Well, it was about eleven or thirteen days later when I was finally notified that he was killed in action. But one of the other school teacher's wives had already written me and said that a school teacher had been killed. And so they knew that that was my husband. And I called her, not knowing that she knew it. She said, Marie, I didn't want to call you because I didn't know whether you'd been notified or not. So, that was the way it happened. My current husband, Marvin, and I went over there, and we spent six years there, and while we were over there we took a trip. He's buried in Belgium, it's an American cemetery, and it's a beautiful cemetery. Well, they had to do that, because they couldn't bury him where this happened, because there wasn't an American place to put him.

What happened to you then?

Well, let's see, in '44, yes-well, it took me a little while to make up my mind that I actually wanted to go in the service. I don't recall exactly the date that I called the Pentagon and requested that I be put on the list to be taken. But it was, let's see, I went in in March of 1945. It was before the 12th of March, I know that. About five months, something like that. I decided to enlist.

I went in as a nurse, but in the early part of this they gave us a salary, and we didn't have rank. And then they decided to give the nurses rank comparable to the male personnel. And I worked up from the base to a second lieutenant, first lieutenant, captain, and finally a major. I went first to Fort Knox, Kentucky. And I took my basic training there. We had formations, and marching-that type of thing. And then the chief nurse asked me if I wanted to see foreign duty, and I said yes – that's what I came in here for was to take care of the soldiers.

So, then she made plans for me to be placed on the list for foreign duty. I wasn't at Fort Knox very long. Probably a matter of a month or two. From there I was in different installations. They had an orthopedic ward in Indiana-Fort Benjamin Harrison near Indianapolis. I was in charge of one of the wards there dealing with injured servicemen. By the time they get there, there is nothing like warlike activities. It was no more than a clinic. That's about what it was. They had a few hospital beds, maybe twenty was the most hospital beds that they had there.

Then I started overseas in the summer of '45. I shipped out on the US Comforter which was a naval vessel. We had 500 nurses on board and we were headed for the Philippines. I was out on the water two days when the atomic bombs were dropped. We were on our way to the Philippines. Well, they were preparing to go into Japan, to invade, the Americans were all ready to invade Japan.

And this is where Truman gets involved. He didn't want that, and it's a good thing that Truman could foresee what was going to happen, because the Japanese were dug in up there in Japan, and we'd all have been dead. President Truman was in Potsdam, at the Potsdam conference, and this is when he found out that we have an atomic bomb.

Anyway, we got over to the Philippines. When I got over there, we had to be taken off of the ship and put on small boats to go in Subic Bay, because there was so many ships sunk there that you couldn't get in. The nurses were housed in the, oh, what's the name of that- where they house the religious people-a monastery more or less. But we were housed there. And then while we were there we got our food through these canteens in lines, they lined us up, you know, and put us through the line. We also had to take malaria therapy which was Atabrine. If you didn't take it, they knew that you didn't take it because you didn't turn brown.

Later, we were taken from the Philippines to Japan-we actually flew into Japan. It was January of 1946 I think, it was cold weather. We didn't do much really. That was it. After the Japanese surrendered, they gave all of us that were thirty years of age or older an opportunity to come back to the states. So I came back and I got out of the service. I had been in a year and a half. And I went back to private duty, and so forth, until I got settled again.

Did you continue your education?

Yes. I did that on the GI Bill. I finished up in, gee I even forget what year that was. But I went back and got my Bachelor of Science degree and my public health certificate at the University of Colorado in Boulder. I went there because we had an intern at Christ's Hospital, and I had been there, of course, and I asked one of the doctors if he knew of a good nursing school to go to – to finish my degree. And he said yes. He said go to the University of Colorado- you'll like it. I thought, I haven't been out there so I guess I'll do that. So, I did, was out there a good two years or more and got my degree.

And then what happened to you?

I was where the cadets train – at West Point. I did floor duty there, and then we went from there to Fort Lewis in Washington. And there's where I met Marvin, my second husband, and we went to Korea. We were in the Korean conflict. We were there all the way. For every conflict they had over there we got a star put on us. I had five stars. We got to Korea before November.

Finally I retired in '60, 1960. After we left there we were at Fort Hood, Texas, and I had six years in Kaiserslautern, Germany. I was at the headquarters with the surgeon general, and Marvin was at the headquarters with engineer corps. I visited all of the American schools, and more or less helped the teachers and the superintendents, and so forth, to understand the regulations and see that they got what they needed.

Could you comment just a bit on how World War II changed your life?
Well, I tell you, the loss of my husband is something that becomes a part of you, but you have to adjust to all of it. And of course by being in the service I traveled extensively. And that part I did enjoy, to a certain extent, because we've been all over Europe. But some of the other phases – I can't see war at any time.

And I will say this, too, that if you ever improvised anything, and I mean improvised anything, that's what you do when you're in those situations. You're thrown into them, you don't have this, you don't have that, you have got to use what you've got up here [points to her head]. And the doctors even found that some of the things that they did over there really weren't authorized, or wouldn't have been authorized to do, but they turned out very, very well. We used regular tap water and dipped hands and arms if they got burnt so they wouldn't dry up, you know, and leave scars. And they got along fine with it. So, some of the things turned out real good. But all in all, it isn't something I looked forward to.

Virginia R. New

Interview #8 – Peter Granson

Peter A. Granson was a surgeon in Dayton, Ohio (he died 9/23/00) and practiced medicine in the area for over thirty years. During his career he was Chief of Staff at Kettering Memorial Hospital and President of the Montgomery County Medical Society. After high school he attended Cornell University where he graduated in 1939. When the war ended he returned to school where he earned his MD degree from Temple University. He and his wife Tee had four children. Granson served three years in the Army (2 years and 2 months overseas and 10 months in the states). During WWII he was company commander of the 107th rifled mortar company, a chemical warfare unit. He served 138 straight days in combat in the battle for Italy, much of it in close support of infantry where his mortar platoons fired both white phosphorus (WP) and high-explosive (HE) shells at German troops. He was involved in both the Anzio and Salerno assaults.

Where were you born and raised?
Well, I was born in Canton, Ohio and lived there until I was twelve years old. Then we moved to New York City and I went to high school there. After graduating from high school I went to Cornell University in Ithaca, New York where I was a pre-med student. And after leaving New York, we moved back to Canton, Ohio, and I went to work for the Republic Steel Corporation as an industrial chemist. This was in 1 940 and I was there until the war started. After Pearl Harbor I enlisted and went into the army. It was the Monday after, the next day after Pearl Harbor, that I enlisted. Because I know I was inducted on the 4th of January, 1942. I was single, but had an AB degree from Cornell.

Where did you do your basic training?
At Fort Leonard Wood, Missouri. It was in the Ozarks. In fact when we got there the camp wasn't really completely built. Believe it or not

it was an engineering camp. So I was trained as an engineer and when I finished my training there I was sent out to Camp San Luis Obispo in California with the 7th, I guess it was the 7th division. Yes. Now this was an engineering outfit and I was supposedly a combat engineer. We learned how to blow up things and what have you, and we went through our basic military there.

Then I was sent to the Mohave Desert for desert training. So we all felt we were going to go to Africa. By that time I decided I was going to try to go to OCS – just got tired of doing dishes – I did enough of that in college. Well, not only that, but that's how I got through school, I washed dishes. I was a "potwalloper." That was the guy who took care of the great big pots. But I decided I'd go to OCS and it was in Maryland at Edgewood Arsenal School which was the chemical warfare school. And I thought, "My gosh, here I am a pre-med and I'm going to be doing something in a lab somewhere." But this was not to be.

We left there as second lieutenants and I wound up at Camp Rucker, Alabama attached to a chemical warfare outfit which had a 4.2 inch mortar. And of course it had nothing whatsoever to do with chemical warfare. Actually, the Germans had a bigger mortar than we had- they had a 100mm mortar, and you could actually see those shells coming through the air. But this was a rilled barrel.

That gun could really shoot those shells you know. Our field manual told us that we were only allowed to shoot these about eleven hundred yards. And the first thing we did the first day in combat, we realized that that manual was antiquated, outdated, and useless. So we just got rid of it and we started experimenting with our ranges, and we found that we could really propel that shell a long distance. And I told you we used to shoot the same targets as the 105 Howitzers. In this little diary you'll find that we fired some of those rounds over three thousand yards.

When did you finally ship out for overseas?
Well, it was in the spring of '43 – we went to North Africa. We landed in Oran. And from Oran we went to a little place called Bizerte that is near Tunis. Then later we shipped out of there for Italy. We were in North Africa from about April to September and then we went to Italy. The North African campaign ended shortly after we got there. We never saw any combat in Africa. None. That war was practically over when we got there so we saw no combat in North Africa.

Well, from there we got ready to go to Italy. We landed at Salerno on September 8th of '43, and then joined the 45th division which was an Oklahoma National Guard outfit, a good outfit. From there we were attached to Darby's Rangers and went up to Casino, just north of Casino, and stayed there until we went to Anzio.

When we hit Salerno we set up our guns. The field manual said that the company headquarters was to be behind the guns. The guns are supposed to be in front, but we soon realized that that manual didn't make much sense because we were completely at the mercy of all the artillery that they were firing. The Germans were firing artillery all over the place. And this little place had some cactus plants around it, and the shrapnel would just go right through this cactus. It was the only time I really saw Hollywood's version of war. Because, while we were being shelled there was a tank battle going on to our right, German tanks and our tanks just milling around shooting at each other, and then from our rear came our own tanks shooting at us-- which wasn't too much of a surprise because they didn't know what was going on. But that was the last time I really saw a so-called Hollywood version of war. After that it was just dirty.

Was it an opposed landing?
Oh, yes. Oh my, yes. In fact, there was a little town, let me think, maybe it's not on this map. It was Agricola. And the Germans could see everything we were doing. And there was a town over here, let me see if that town is Agricola – yes it is. All we had was a foothold on the beach. And the most unusual thing about that landing was when we landed there was this beautiful Greek temple in a place called Piester, that's the name of the town or the area, and the Germans wouldn't shoot at it and we wouldn't shoot at it. It was left intact. It was kind of a rule, and we respected them for that. They would not deface that temple. They could have destroyed it, but they didn't. I don't remember how many divisions were involved, but the 45th was one. We went into action right away, right away, yes. We had forward observers to select targets.

You're an officer, you wouldn't do that would you?
Oh, yes. Oh, my yes. They loved me, especially at Anzio. You simply had to be able to see the German lines. Well, our targets were troops, tanks, artillery, whatever. Whatever we could see. If we could see any gathering of troops we would fire.

Oh, we had adequate ammunition, but in those days our shells came packed in cosmoline. Do you remember cosmoline? Can you imagine trying to clean those shells because the quartermaster didn't do it, we had to do it. And if we had to really fire a big mission, it took forever to clean that cosmoline off. In fact, sometimes when we couldn't get it all off we'd actually get some fire on those shells. But we were lucky, we only had one hang fire that exploded in the barrel. That was due to defective ammunition but other than that we got away scot-free. Finally they decided they would clean the ammo for us in the rear areas. So we started getting our shells in these aluminum containers.

My company consisted of two platoons and we had four or five officers and I think there were one hundred and twenty-five enlisted men. We had troops on the guns, we had our cooks, and we had our supply people. Control of the air really was up for grabs. The Germans were more in control than we were at that moment. But it didn't take long before we ruled the skies. And we were not strafed or bombed at Salerno. But the artillery was terrible. Well, number one, you're supposed to dig a fox hole or slit trench. And it's amazing, we had trouble getting the guys to dig slit trenches in the states, but we had no trouble getting them to dig them when we got overseas. They were anxious to dig. And as long as you were below the level of the ground, unless it hit right on you, why, you were safe.

What about casualties?

At Salerno? Oh yes, we lost some people. Some we lost even before we went into combat from so- called combat fatigue. Some couldn't take it. Couldn't deal with it. I had one officer who trained with me at OCS. He got sick on the first day that we landed at Salerno and we didn't see him until we got up to Anzio. He came up there, he was there one day, and he got sick again. And he finally came back and I was the company commander then. Well I kept him around the headquarters a couple of days, and finally I said, "Larry you've got to go back to your platoon." I got a call in the middle of the night from the sergeant, the platoon sergeant, and he says, "This guy is out of it." So I said, "Send him back." I wanted to court-martial him, but he got back to the hospital and some psychiatrist got a hold of him, and he got sent back to the states. And he had the nerve, after we took Rome, to come and say goodbye to us. I could have shot him. I felt very badly about this guy because he never tried. I mean, he was never really subjected to combat. He decided he didn't want any part of it.

But I remember I had one officer who at the time was a forward observer, and this was about a year after we'd been in combat. I was going up to his observation post to see him and I saw him corning back towards me, and all he did was just give me his pistol and he kept on walking. Never said a word to me. But I couldn't get upset with him because I knew he'd been through it. But this other guy had never been through it. You didn't have much use, it's a strange thing to say, but you didn't have much use for people that didn't stand up – do what the rest of us did. But, this guy didn't even give himself a chance to find out whether he was a man or a mouse.

This photograph was taken in the field eating my lunch – a little c-ration. And believe it or not the k-rations weren't bad, particularly if you got the canned cheese. We'd put it on our little Coleman stove and heat it up, and then take those great big bricks that they called crackers and break them up, and just dip our cheese.

We also actually had a company barber. We tried to keep the guys as neat as we possibly could. The only thing I allowed them to grow was a mustache. I couldn't grow it myself, but I didn't complain about the mustache. But I did complain about the hair.

Well, this photograph is a prize – this is my jeep. I called it the Baltimore Lady after a young lady that I knew in Baltimore, Maryland. And in fact, we corresponded all through the war. After I got back from overseas we met each other just one time and we knew that it wasn't going to work. This was going no place. Oh, this is, yes, this is (holding up a photograph) Carl Hamburger. Carl was a corporal, and he was an absolutely fabulous soldier. Now we lost a couple of our officers through either rotation or wounds so I gave him a battlefield commission. Now Carl is one of the general partners today of Stanley Blacker, which makes beautiful sport coats, sweaters, shirts, everything. Well, Carl did his job, but he did it better than he was supposed to do his job. And he had the respect of his people. If you didn't have the respect of your troops, you weren't worth a hoot and a holler as an officer. I knew he would do the job. How many mortars would you have in each platoon?

Four each-a total of eight altogether. I had one platoon that had something I called the million dollar hole, because we never had a casualty in this platoon on the Anzio beachhead. The other platoon was overrun by the Germans one night, and we lost not only the platoon leader, but we also lost the platoon sergeant. Killed. After that we started moving up the Italian boot. We went way up the boot to a place called Caserta. In fact we went past Caserta. Caserta was the rear area, that's where Mark Clark had his headquarters.

What do you think of him (Mark Clark) as an officer and as a leader?
Well, I had no quarrel with him, you know, you've got to realize that people in the lower echelon of command had no idea what was going on. We didn't know what the big picture was or anything. We just knew who was in front of us and we'd take orders and follow them – that's all there was to it.

Did you make the landing at Anzio?
Absolutely. We landed on the 22nd of January at five o'clock in the morning with the 3rd division. When we got to Anzio it was at five o'clock in the morning. Not a shot was fired. There wasn't a German within twenty-five miles of us. Well, we were confused because we never made a landing where somebody didn't shoot at us. But we landed on the beach, got all our troops ashore, got our hospital ashore, and then we sat there. At ten o'clock in the morning the Germans sent their first fighters down. In fact I learned, after we took Rome, that the day that we landed at Anzio they were evacuating the city. We could have gone up there and taken that place I think. But our general wasn't going to move. He just didn't move. And that's one time when I wish that we'd had General Patton leading us because he would have gone right up there.

We didn't move far inland then because the Germans had us literally surrounded on three sides. When they realized we weren't going to move they sent everybody down there because they had to protect their flank. They had troops at the Abbey at Monte Casino, and they protected them by holding us on the beach. We could have gone, I honestly think, we could have gone right up to Rome that day with the 3rd Division. But that was not a happy place. We took an awful beating, we lost a lot of people, lot of people. Colonel Darby's Rangers were decimated and became ineffective as a fighting force. The Rangers were a very special unit. Elite, yes! It's strange, Colonel Darby after Anzio went back to the states. He left as a lieutenant colonel, but the next time I saw him was just before the war in Italy ended and he was a full bird colonel.

Then I was attached to an outfit that was going up to the Po River to keep the Germans from blowing the bridges, a regimental combat team. And on the way up there the regimental commander hit a land mine and was wounded. Darby was there as an observer. Darby was the senior officer. He took over the command and went up to a little town called Garda which was on the north end of the lake.

And they tell me that an airburst came over and killed him. Isn't that fate?

Why do men fight?

You fight to protect each other. That's the whole idea.

Is that a pretty close relationship?

Oh, can't be closer.

Like family?

More than that. It's hard to explain the bond, but you depend on each other. You know. In that little diary you'll read something that I wrote about battles. After we had been shelled, I took a look at my buddy next to me and said, "You know, one second from now we could be dead." That's how precarious your life was. It was just like that – you lived from one second to the next when you were in combat. We were in combat, let's see – it was one hundred and thirty-eight days. Well, in the two years that we were over there we had almost close to five hundred days of combat. They never pulled us out of line. I was wounded once-yes – just above my right eye. It was either shrapnel or pieces of rocket that exploded when the shell hit. I realized that I was alive, I was bleeding, but I was alive. I had my arms, my hands, my eyes, I felt like I was ten feet tall. I never had such an adrenaline rush in all my life. And 1I knew I was going to live through that war. I just knew then that they weren't going to get me.

Did you ever feel that time was running out on you?

Oh, you couldn't have those thoughts – you couldn't do your job if you did. No. I knew that I might not make it, but I still had a job to do and I did it. And my men felt the same way. I mean, they were at risk as I was, but they still did their job.

I had one sergeant who was an absolute warrior. His name was John Matovsky. He was wounded four times. The fourth time he was wounded I said, "John, I'm gonna get you out of here. I don't want you fighting anymore." 'Cause I figured he'd used up every chance he ever had. And he refused to leave us. And I know at the end of the war when I was in the states, I got a letter from the war department wanting to know if I would recommend him for a promotion to officer. Boy, I'd do it in a second. I think he was mad too – he was angry with the Germans. He was Polish, and the first time he was wounded was at Anzio. The Germans had broken through the Third division line, and I think John, single handedly, just stopped – blunted – their attack. Next thing I know John's coming back from the OP with about ten German prisoners and he's all bandaged up. And I didn't find out until later just exactly what he did up there, but he just about wiped that outfit out all by himself. And being stupid, really, I said, "I'm going to put him in for a silver star" – like that was some big deal.

He should have been in for the Congressional Medal of Honor. He actually not only took care of the troops that attacked the infantry, but he also captured all these prisoners and brought them back. And he went back to the hospital, but he wouldn't go any farther back than the hospital. He figured if he went that far back they might send him back to the general hospital down at Naples. He wouldn't leave the outfit. He had a purple heart with three oak leaf clusters on it. Four times he was wounded. He just was a remarkable, remarkable man. I don't know whatever happened to him. I hope he got his commission. I'm pretty sure he did, but he may have stayed in or retired. But he was a war hero.

In June of '44 we started off and were involved in the capture of Rome. This was the first week of June, I don't know the exact date. That's where they pulled us out of the line for the first time since September of '43 and I did all the sight-seeing. I met these people in Rome who were very good to me, but it's like when we spent the summer watching the Germans build fortifications at Florence, Italy. You know, we were on one side of the Arno River and they were on the other side, and we just spent the whole summer looking at them. We waited 'til they got their defenses built properly so they could attack.

Would you comment on these photographs?
This is at our company headquarters in Anzio. It was a place called Campo Morte, the field of death. How appropriate can you name something? That's the name of the place. This is a photo of the original company commander. I was his executive officer. Here's Florence. After we took Florence we were heading this way and hit that German line that was all fortified. I mean, they just fortified everything, but we had to go through this line. We finally got through the German line and we'd gone up here just south of Bologna to a place called Viarregio with the 85th infantry division. While we were there, this is 1944, we got word on Christmas Eve day, the 24th of December, that the Germans had broken through at Leghorne, and they were actually going to capture the city seaport. So I took my company and rushed over to this area, and we got over there and then found out there wasn't anything going

on. We spent seven weeks over there with this outfit. I hate to talk about this outfit, but they were useless and only got shot at one time in the seven weeks. I wasn't used to that. But this outfit had a very poor, poor record, you know. It's too bad.

Well, after we left this place called Viarregio, we went back with the Tenth mountain division – Dole's old outfit isn't it? And we ended the war with them. Then we went up to Lake Garda and there was a tunnel there. The Germans had blown the tunnel and we were waiting for boats to take us up to the north end when the war ended. Well, I couldn't believe it. In fact, the night before I got the message, well, I actually got the message that night but I didn't believe the messenger, I'd gone out and I bought enough Asti Spumante to take care of my division. And we had a party in our headquarters – the troops, everybody – and this young soldier walks in and says, "The war is over." And we literally told him, in a very nice way of course, to get out. And then the next morning we got the word from my colonel that the war is over. And believe it or not, I was on my way home on rotation right after the war ended in May of '45. The day after it ended. But Carl Flamburger stayed.

But, you know, the fun started after the war was over. I mean, lots of things to do and see and we didn't have to worry about getting killed or shot – but I was on my way home. And I was sent back to Washington. That had to be the worst duty I ever had. I wasn't used to it. Maybe it was a post-combat depression, but I just felt awful. In fact the day they dropped the bomb and the Germans, or rather the Japanese, surrendered, I was in a bookstore in northwest Washington, and I remember, they said, "The war's over." The next day I took my papers and I walked them through – my discharge papers. I had all sorts of points and medals and stuff like that and I was out of the service the next day. And I went home long enough to see my parents and then I went to Cornell and met my wife there. Well, I'd been out of school almost six years, but I was gonna go to medical school. I didn't even know if I could still study, so I went back and took some courses in anatomy and embryology and what have you. They were all medical courses. Went there four years. And we came out here in 1950 because they paid interns – they didn't pay interns a family. But we had three children and that's how we got to Dayton. We love this place. 1I was in those days. They gave them room and board, but you weren't supposed to be married and have probably the oldest resident they ever had in Miami Valley.

Would you comment a bit on how World War II changed your life?
Well, you know, I've thought about that many times. I think one thing it
showed me was that I wasn't a bad man – I mean, if I could put up with that
I was doing well. I could stand the rigors of combat without going bonkers.
So I can look anybody in the eye. I learned a lot about myself.

Virginia K. Hess

Interview #9 – J.V. Stone

J.V. Stone was a Centerville councilman for over thirty years, and he was mayor of Centerville for four years. He is married to Elenora (Sis) and they have three children-Sharon Smith, Jeffrey V. Stone and Scott Stone. J.V. was educated at McKeesport, PA, did his undergraduate work at Ohio Wesleyan and took a law degree from the University of Pittsburg. He was drafted into the Army in March of 1943 and served two years in the Pacific Theater.

Where were you born and Raised J. V.?
Well, I was born September 29, 1923 in Delaware, Ohio. My dad was attending Ohio Wesleyan and became married in his junior year. My dad was the son of a Methodist minister. And an interesting part of that was that during the first war he lived in Chillicothe, Ohio where my grandfather was a Methodist minister, and it was the location of Camp Sherman during World War I. As you know, Chillicothe isn't a very big town and it was inundated with about, I don't know how many troops, sixty thousand maybe, in World War I.

But my dad, after graduating from Ohio Wesleyan, had a number of jobs that were related to sales. He sold Super Maid cookware and books. Anything he could get a hold of he'd sell. Then he decided to become a minister and he went to Boston University. He'd also been a school teacher and a principal of the school prior to that. But he went to Boston, up on Beacon Hill is where the theological school is. When my dad was in sales we moved around. I lived in West Virginia and different places in Ohio. This was a door to door thing.

Where did you go to high school?
I lasted about six months in each school because we were always moving. And I've gone to school various places. I went to school in Dayton and Zanesville and when my dad moved up to Massachusetts, I went to a school

up there on Beacon Hill.. I don't remember too much about activities. No sports. I weighed about ninety-eight pounds and all I had was a large mouth which I counted on to scare people. I think I was in student government and I know I was in debate. We won the state championship in debate in the McKeesport High School in Pennsylvania. I thought I was really great. It was the other three people who won the championship. We got the state championship out of it, and our debate coach got a professorship at the University of Pittsburgh in the speech department. It was a great experience. I graduated in June of 1941 and went to work in the mill.

OK, then what happened to you?
As I said, I went to work in the mill for the summer and then went to Ohio Wesleyan in the fall of '41. I stayed at Wesleyan until, you know, things were getting pretty hot. I knew that I was up for the draft, so I talked to the draft board and told them I'd like to finish that semester and that then I'll report in and you can do with me what you will. And that was a disastrous statement too. So they did. And it was very painful. Let me tell you how smart I was. I mean, intelligence really doesn't run in the family, and I was the slowest one of the group. I went down, as I promised my draft board, to Pittsburgh, the old post office, and said, here I am, do with me what you will. And the guy said, what do you want to do? And I said, what do you mean, what do I want to do? I said, I'm here to go into the service. He says, yes, but what do you want-the Army, Navy, or the Marine Corps? And I, here's how I thought. If I go into the Marines, I'm going to get killed with the first wave. Don't do that.

Don't be stupid. I mean, it's such a thing to be patriotic and willing to serve your country, but don't go charging into it head first. The next choice was the Navy. I can't see myself in thirteen-button pants. A man with weak kidneys should not have pants with thirteen buttons on them. I'll never make that. Besides when you're out there in the middle of the water, I don't salute very well. So, the Army's it. He said, you sure you want to go in the Army? I said, I've made my decision and it's an intelligent one. That's where I got on the train in Pittsburgh one miserable night and went to Georgia

This would be in the spring of '43?
Yes, yes. I was ready to go 'cause there was no one else around. I was the only one even in the fraternity house. I about ate myself to death. But

that's how I got to Camp Wheeler, Georgia and into the wonderful heavy weapons, first battalion. That's near Macon, Georgia about seventy-five or eighty miles south of Atlanta? I would say that that was the first big shock I had in my life. I weighed about 108 pounds and guess who was carrying the base plate to the mortar? I was. That base plate is heavy. And all the big guys, six foot three and 240 pounds, they could barely carry a pistol. I think we also carried M-ls. Then after I'd gone in there I got pneumonia which put me back a cycle because I remember those were thirteen week cycles. And then when I got back I was out of cycle. So guess who got to shoot the machine gun, a 30 caliber weapon, over the new recruits? Me! You never saw such stark terror in your life when they saw me with that, with that 30 caliber water cooled machine gun. (interviewer)"! could have been there, 'cause I was at Camp Wheeler in the summer of '43. You might have been shooting over my head." If 'd known that you'd have never made it out of there. What battalion were you in "Oh, god, I can't remember." I was in the first battalion which was heavy weapons. Were you heavy weapons? "No, no. We had, I just lugged around an M-1 all the time." No, I didn't have the honor of terrifying you. I never knew what hot was 'til I got in Camp Wheeler.

Did you ever go down into downtown Macon?
Oh, yes. Oh, yes. Every time you had a chance you went down. That was a beautiful little town. Cherry Street is the name of the main street – it was segregated in those days. We had three battalions of black troops. But they were not integrated with the whites.

No, they were a separate battalion. And the only time I saw those guys was in Macon. And when we go on night marches you could hear them coming, you know. They're coming toward us, we're going toward them. Nobody says anything, both sides are marching along. And their faces are shiny. And never spoke. I never spoke to them, you know, at night, on night maneuvers. 'Course I spoke to them in town. But even then you were pretty much segregated. They went to the black part of town and we stayed on Cherry Street, near the Dempsey Hotel. You know, I was there longer than most men, I was there two cycles because I had been ill.

When did you leave Macon, Georgia and infantry training?
I don't really remember. Probably in the fall. We went to, went by train to San Francisco. I think we went to Fort Ord first, as I think about it.

And then we got the ship there. I went to Fort Ord and then I went up to Camp Stoneman. That's where we actually boarded the ship. Yes. And the big deal was we were going to Hawaii.

I don't know how many men we had on that ship, maybe eight, ten thousand, and that ship was all about what we're gonna do in Hawaii, we're gonna take the town apart and put it back together again. We went about fifty miles from Hawaii and then veered off. And I told my wife I'd never go to Hawaii. They had their opportunity once and I wasn't gonna give them another one. But I went from there to New Caledonia. That's a long trip. You're close to New Zealand. I don't remember doing much of anything. I think I went to a, a camp, you did that 'til you were assigned. And I was assigned to 868th Bomber Squadron. I was completely out of the infantry.

How'd that happen?
Who knows, nothing makes any sense in the service.

I want to show this picture before we go further. Now, tell the viewers about your dad.
He went into the service, too. As I mentioned before, he lived at Chillicothe when the Army camp was down there during the first war. And he was too young to get in. I understand he tried to lie to get in then but he couldn't make it. But anyhow, come the second world war, and I go in. And my mother said he paced the floor from the time I left until he went down and enlisted. Well, I think he moped around there, my mother said, for maybe two months. And he just went down and enlisted. Remember, he was a minister in a Methodist Church and after he got into the service, they sent him to Harvard because that's where the chaplain school at the time was. And then he was assigned to an engineering outfit. And he went to Europe with these engineers. And I went to the Pacific.

And then when the war ended in Europe my Dad's outfit was transferred to the Philippines to prepare for the invasion of Japan. I went down to see him when he was there and he came up to see me once when I was on Okinawa at the time. And we met there and spent maybe a day or so together?

Earlier, he had preached in McKeesport, Pennsylvania and when he got into this outfit, the mess sergeant's parents were Greek and they owned a restaurant in McKeesport. If you didn't think they ate well in that outfit. Anyway, I got down to Manila and couldn't find him. I couldn't find his outfit, you know, there were troops all over the place. Well, I finally found him. He said, let me call Ted.

This was about nine, ten o'clock at night. And Ted whipped up a meal you wouldn't believe. I don't know where he got the food.

What was your dad's rank?
Well, when he went in, I think he went in as a 1st lieutenant and when he was discharged he was a major. Then I had another visit with him on Okinawa, he came to Okinawa? I went down to Manila and saw him and then he came up to Okinawa to see me. And we spent a couple days together.

Now on New Caledonia you're assigned into the 13th Air Force.

Yes. I went into an operations office. All my training had been in the infantry so they put me in an office. That made logical sense. It's called the Operations Office and that office made all the plans for flights. I think it was because I had a year of college or something like that it helped you get an assignment like that? Plus, I could also type. So, what we did was we, in conjunction with the intelligence office, we prepared the plans so that when the crew got up in the airplane, the plans were all in front of them, they knew where they were going and what to look for. They knew exactly what the target would be. These were all for heavy bombers-B24s. Later, I think we went up to Guadalcanal and then we moved up to the islands and finally wound up in Okinawa. And that's when the war ended. We weren't up with infantry. We would be behind, and we would fly over them and pound the target in front of them like Rabaul. I used to go with them, we had our office in the camp, but I used to go with the planes and go up closer before they actually made their bombing runs.

Well, for example, we might be in New Guinea, but we're hitting targets like Jakarta was one of them. We blew that off the map.

What were you doing in the plane?
Well, our base would be way behind. Then when we're ready to make an actual bombing run we would get up closer because the gasoline wouldn't hold enough. Like if you were going from anything way south of the target, you've got to get up closer 'cause you don't have the fuel, you'll run out of fuel. So you get as close as you can. And we had several locations in New Guinea we would stop at. I wouldn't fly all the way. I would go to the last base that was safe for them and then I would stay there. They would go, do the bombing, come back and pick me up and then we'd go back to our main

base. This way you could have more information available to help these pilots on their bombing run? Well, as I said, I prepared the papers we were preparing for them. And there were local people that I dealt with in so far as the planning, plans were concerned. They weren't complicated, they were just typed out on sheets. And they knew the different points they had to go to and when to get the hell out of there and get back.

And then where'd you go from this area of the Solomons and New Guinea?
Well, the last place I remember was Okinawa. Our target there was Japan.

We were preparing for the invasion of Japan then. I remember we'd gone up there for some reason or other, farther from our base, and we tried to get back and the weather got bad. We got into a typhoon and we had no idea where we were. The pilot said, I don't know where we are. And when it cleared up a little bit we found that we were out over China in a place that we shouldn't have been. And we got some fire but, you know, it wasn't even dangerous. You could see the shells exploding and stuff like that. But we finally got back to northern Luzon and we stayed there awhile and tried to get ourselves settled down. Then we went on back to our base.

Did you see any Kamikaze planes while on Okinawa?
Yes. 1 don't remember anything directed against us, our planes were land based planes. B24s. The only thing I remember, we put our camp in a cemetery. You know, they all bury above ground there in big long coffins above ground. And it's kind of eerie going to bed in a foreign cemetery.

And did you have any unforgettable characters that you met in the Army or in the Air Force that you remember? Pilots or ground crew or anybody?
Well, one of the most unforgettable characters I ever met was a guy I worked with there in operations. He was a head of operations guy from Cincinnati, a German guy. And I never did figure him out. What we got into a tangle over was pictures. He detested me and I just thought he was weird. And he couldn't stand pictures of women, particularly naked women. And I had a big picture that I put up just to aggravate him. And he came in one day when I wasn't there and tore down the picture. And we got into a real hassle about that. It didn't mean anything one way or another, but I could get him to the point where he'd almost have a heart attack. But other characters, I don't remember anyone. We were all a little weird.

Looking back on your military career, did you develop any skills while you were in the military, that you've used in your life later on?

Well, you don't use a 30 caliber machine gun on a daily basis. And later I got a Tommy gun. I don't think I ever fired the thing, but that was what they issued me so I carted it around. I said if worse came to worse and they overrun the infantry, I'll shoot them all down with this pop gun.

What did you think about when you heard about the atomic bomb and the surrender of Japan?

I think the main thing that I thought was is I'm going home. That's the way most of us felt. We weren't getting into any high grade thinking, at the time, we were thinking of going home and seeing our girlfriends and our wives and getting a good meal. Just getting out. Getting back to school.

Could you comment on some of these photographs?

Yes, in this one I was on my way to, I think I was on my way to San Francisco, stopped in to see my parents and my future wife.

This one might be interesting to viewers, this is called a lister bag, it was always in the center maybe of the company street. And guys would get a drink, a drink of water here. If you're going to drink water you're gonna get it out of that bag. And it's usually about just under boiling, was the temperature of the water. This one shows a mosquito bar. You slept on army cots under a mosquito bar. If you were going to sleep you had to have a mosquito bar or you'd be carried away.

Did you come home on points?

No, the war was over. I think we flew some place and got on a ship. Everything folded and everyone was getting out. We may have flown down to the Philippines and got the ship at Manila. I think I came back to wherever I left from – San Francisco. May have gone back, excuse me, to Fort Ord.

And were you discharged at Fort Ord?

I don't remember. I don't remember being discharged. "Maybe you're still in" My god, think of the back pay I could collect.

This is V Mail, my wife just stuck them in there. This is free mail. If my wife wrote, or my girlfriend wrote to me, she'd have to put postage on it but when I wrote, we wrote as servicemen, it was free. You know why we don't have anything, I told you, we burned everything. My mother was very, very good at clerical work. Once she was finished with it-gone. And everything was burned at her house. Burned her wedding dress and everything. Burned the place to the ground.

Did you take advantage of the GI Bill?
Oh, yes. I went to finish college, then went to law school. Yes. I went back immediately to Ohio Wesleyan and then to the University of Pittsburgh Law School, always wanted to be a lawyer. There was never any question in my mind I was going to be a lawyer.

Let me mention one interesting thing. My advisor in the political science department at Wesleyan had served with the state department in the Philippines. So when I got back I'd go up and see him in his office which was in the library up on the second floor, and we'd sit there and talk 'til it got dark. When it got dark we left. But he had been in the counselor's service in this one town in northern Philippines and I told him about it and he said, my god, that's where I was stationed. He said, did you know so and so? And I knew those people. And that just excited him to no end because it was probably thirty years or so later. But it was interesting. I believe I graduated from Wesleyan in '48. 1 think I graduated from law school four years later. I think '52.

While I was in law school, I was married and I had a daughter at that time, and I needed more money than the GI Bill was paying. So I went with a retail credit company which is an investigative company primarily for insurance, but for businesses and other things like that. And I could work my own hours and I stayed there until after graduation. Then after that I went with the All State Insurance Company in the claim department. And I was a claim manager for them. And then I went into the regional office in Cleveland before I went into practice here in Dayton. I'd gone to law school with a fellow from Dayton. And he had gone into practice here when I had gone in with All State. And he'd contacted me and asked me to come over here and practice with him. And I stayed with him several years and then went in sole practitioner.

When did you move to the south of Dayton?
Before I came down here I checked the areas that were interesting to me and moved to Centerville in the house we live in now. We've lived here a long time.

Who took over your business?

Scot, my son. Yes, he came in after he graduated from law school and then I had a thought, why should I be working? So I left, being the lazy person I am. Things I learned in the service.

How do you think World War II changed your life?

Well, I think it makes you think about the important things in life, probably a lot sooner than you would have. And you hear a gun go off, that kind of straightens you up a little bit. Kind of gets your attention. And you get into a couple scrapes. I got into one, I don't know where it was, I think it was in Okinawa or some place up north there, bummed a ride on a plane and this guy was an absolute maniac as a pilot. He would be at ten thousand feet and dive. You'd think he's never gonna come out of it. After I regain consciousness I would awaken to this guy laughing. Those are experiences that sharpened you up a little bit. You would think that the Air Force would be closer, that the boys would be closer than they are in the infantry, but that wasn't the case with me. I was closer to the fellows I was in training with than I was... We had more common experiences – yes, I guess that was it. But it was just a short period. It was only a ninety day cycle.

Any last thoughts you want to share with us?

Yes. Now one thing that kind of detached me from my own unit, I got up one morning on Guadalcanal and I had developed an eye infection. And there's a hospital, there was a tent hospital there. And I went over there, and the doctor, the surgeon at the squadron, he said, I don't know what's wrong with you. I was swollen from my hair line down to my chest. And I think it was on this side. You couldn't, you really couldn't see. I mean you had to pry your eye apart with that much blubber before you could find your eye. So I went in there, and there was a young doctor in there, and he looked at me and he said, I'm gonna send you to New Zealand. I said, I can't go to New Zealand. I was trying to get to an advanced unit of our squadron. He said, you can't go? No. I gotta get going. He said, you ain't going anywhere. He said, hey, I got a jackass in here, he yelled to another doctor on the other side. He said, what's his problem? He said, he doesn't want to go to New Zealand. He says, I'll take that eye and I'll go to New Zealand. But he convinced me. He said, you can't get rid of that in the tropics. He says, you been working with it here for a couple months.

You're going. So I went down and got on a hospital ship, a Navy hospital ship. And the doctor who was treating me was from Youngstown. That comes a little later, but I went in and, oh, before we pulled away from Guadalcanal, we couldn't have been three or four miles out, I heard this tremendous explosion. What in the name of god is this? It rocked the ship and it was a Navy hospital ship-pretty good size .. What happened? So the guys, the Navy guys, came back and said there was a Navy hospital ship in front of us and the Japs torpedoed it. And it went to the bottom. My god, how lucky can I get. I'm going to New Zealand to get my eyes fixed and I don't get blown up. It was quite an experience to say the least.

Virginia K. Hess

PART III

THE ARTICLES AND ESSAYS

After the war I wrote and published a number of articles and essays.
You will find a selection of these on various topics which follow.

The Day of the Battle

By A. E. Houseman
(This places the individual's preference against Society's demands.)

Far I hear the bugle blow
To call me where I would not go
And the guns begin the song,
"Soldier, fly or stay for long."

Comrade, if to turn and fly
Made a soldier never die,
Fly I would, for who would not?
Tis sure no pleasure to be shot.

But since the man that runs away
Lives to die another day,
And cowards' funerals, when they come,
Are not wept so well at home

Therefore, though the best is bad,
Stand and do the best, my lad;
Stand and fight and see your slain,
And take the bullet in your brain.

1. From Pearl Harbor to Pulpit

Leader of infamous attack experienced great personal changes after WWII.

With all the recent attention on the Japanese attack on Pearl Harbor, readers may want to know what happened to the man who led the attack, Mitsuo Fuchida.

Two waves of Japanese fighters and bombers attacked Pearl Harbor on Dec. 7, 1941. The naval aviator commanding the first wave of 181 planes, and the man who radioed back to the Japanese task force at 7:53 a.m. the words, "Tora, Tora, Tora" (Tiger, Tiger, Tiger), the code word indicating complete surprise had been realized, was Fuchida.

Six months later during the Battle of Midway, Fuchida was wounded while on board the Akagi, a Japanese aircraft carrier attacked by American dive bombers. He was forced to jump from the gun deck to the flight deck to escape the raging fires caused by the bombing. In doing so, Fuchida broke both of his ankles. He was transferred to the cruiser Nagara, returned to Japan and spent the rest of the war as a staff officer.

In August 1945, shortly after the atomic bombing of Hiroshima and Nagasaki, Fuchida was a member of a group of officers that plotted a coup d'etat in order to prevent Japan's surrender and continue the fight against the Americans to the bitter end. Hirohito's brother pleaded with Fuchida to obey the emperor, and Fuchida acquiesced.

Later, Fuchida was cleared of any war crimes by the Allied War Crimes Commission. After the war, Fuchida wrote a book on the Battle of Midway. In his summation, he said the Battle of Midway was a tragic defeat for Japan caused by the "myth of the almighty battleship, mistaken air policy, technological backwardness and arrogance" (which he called victory disease).

In the unusual meeting with Paul Tibbets, pilot of the Enola Gay, described in Richard Rongstad's obituary on Fuchida, "Fuchida told Tibbets that dropping atomic bombs on Hiroshima and Nagasaki was the correct decision."

In 1949, Fuchida, a Buddhist, converted to Christianity after reading a pamphlet written by Jacob Deshazer, a bombardier who participated in the Doolittle raid on Tokyo in 1942. Deshazer was shot down, captured and tortured by the Japanese, but returned to Japan after the war as a missionary to help in that nation's reconstruction.

Fuchida, too, became a Christian missionary and lectured to Japanese-Americans in San Francisco, Seattle and Los Angeles. He lived in the United States for a few years before retiring in Japan. He died of diabetes in Japan on May 30, 1 976.

Perhaps change is the rule of life.

2. "Wise up Soldier" – 1943

The Gilbert Islands are situated near the point where the international date line crosses the equator. The islands are atolls composed of coral reefs, generally with a lagoon on the eastern side. The first thing we soldiers in the Infantry all noticed as we waded ashore on Butaritari Island (part of the Makin Atoll in the Gilbert Islands) was a huge four-engine Japanese seaplane, her tail assembly destroyed and the tip of her right wing buried in the shallow water. The next thing we saw were the natives – men in cloth sarongs and bare-breasted women in grass skirts – nothing else. We were astonished at the sight but were ordered to keep moving by our officers.

Sgt. Newmann ordered us to "dig in" and prepare for air attacks because we were only 125 miles from Mili, one of the many atolls in the Marshall Islands held by the Japanese. Butaritari was a strategic as well as convenient place for the Japanese to bomb because of its airfield. A friend (John Survill) and I decided to work on a slit trench together. The problem was that the soil was composed largely of coral rock fragments, sand, and tree roots, and it made digging extremely difficult, particularly with an entrenching tool – a small shovel with a hinged blade that converted into a hoe-type instrument. The setting of coconut palms and pandanus trees that grow prolifically on Butaritari was beautiful, but the digging was pure drudgery. We were forced to put all our strength into the effort, and the payoff for straining every nerve was minimal.

We were laboring next to two married men who were more motivated to dig than we were. Survill and I smoked a lot, drank coconut milk, ate our K-rations, talked about the good-looking girls we had seen – and occasionally we even tried to dig a little. But time passed, darkness fell, and we decided to give up any further excavation even thought our two-man "shelter" was only about six inches deep. It was just too much work. The hell with it.

We were asleep when the air-raid siren wailed warning of approaching Japanese planes. Survill and I got up and sat on the edge of our shelter. In a little while a number of our searchlights were turned on and quickly picked up the Japanese bombers – two engine Betty bombers. We could see them easily, so I'd estimate their altitude at about 3,000 or 4,000 feet. No fighter planes (we had P-39s and P-40s at the time) were sent up to intercept the bombers, but some of our 90mm shells seemed close, but the 20mm tracer shells missed the planes by a country mile. We did nothing, just sat and watched, fascinated by the entire spectacle. We heard some bombs land far away and took little notice of this.

We continued sitting on the edge of our shelter with our feet in the hole. At that point our ankles were protected – little else. Then suddenly there was a SWOOSH, followed immediately by a tremendous explosion. Then more SWOOSHS followed by more earsplitting explosions. No one had to explain to us what had happened. We understood immediately. The bombs seemed to be right on top of us. We tried desperately to press our bodies into our long shallow shelter, but to no avail; there was just no place to hide.

So, we leapt into the shelter the married men had dug, right on top of them. They protested vehemently in the GI idiom of the day ("Get the … out of here.") But we ignored them. The need for our physical well-being prevailed over their protests.

The action was over as quickly as it had begun, and when the all-clear sounded we sheepishly left our guest accommodations. All night long you could hear the clink of shovels digging. Ours clinked right along with the rest of them. I don't remember being scared during that first bombing until after the close encounter with the bombs. Frankly, I was just too stupid. But my anxiety fear level was raised very rapidly during the next few days as I began to see and understand the tangible consequences of the bombings. Maybe that might be considered the moral of the story "In life, experience is the best teacher." Wise up soldier.

3. "Shines the Name, Rodger Young"

Born in 1918 in the town of Tiffin in north-western Ohio, the son of Nicholas Young, an automobile mechanic, and Esther Young, a homemaker, Rodger had the nourishing affection of his parents, three brothers – George, Richard and Nicholas – a sister, Betty. His father moved the family to the village of Green Springs, about ten miles north of Tiffin, when Rodger was ten years old, opening a small gas station and service garage.

Certainly, Rodger did not lead a sedentary life as a boy. He enjoyed hunting and fishing with his father. On one day in the field, seeing a cottontail virtually explode when shot, he exclaimed, "Gee, look at the fuzz fly"; thereafter, he was known as "Fuzzy", a nickname that he readily embraced. He was an avid swimmer and ice-skater. Though not physically gifted, he tried his hand in several competitive sports, with unfortunate results in one. He was a fair bowler and played baseball with a pick-up nine in the village. Playing basketball with high school boys – he was a good passer – he fell and struck his head on the floor suffering temporarily double vision and permanent impairment of his hearing.

Rodger set childish things aside, as it were, when he was sixteen years old. His schoolwork falling off, apparently because of his hearing problem, he left high school at the end of his junior year. Years later, one of his teachers, Mattie Steffanni, bristling at reports that he was a poor student, insisted that before his injury "he was a good student".

In January of 1938, Rodger took a step clearly separating him from his adolescent life. Listening to his friend Walter Rigby, who had recently enlisted in Company B, the "Fremont Company," of the 148th regiment of the Ohio National Guard, he followed suit. His oldest brother, George, also joined Company B, as did several other young men from

Green Springs, among them Albert Rigby and Walter's brother. Surely they did not enlist out of a need for money, receiving as they did but one dollar for each weekly meeting. They underwent training in summer encampments at Camp Perry, Ohio, in 1938 and 1939 and participated in military exercises throughout the state in the fall of 1939. The next year they joined thousands of guardsmen from the Midwest for maneuvers out of Camp McCoy in Wisconsin.

At Rodger's enlistment in 1938, war for the nation did not seem imminent. But by the summer of 1939, the European war had begun and in the spring of 1940, German armies swept into France and were threatening to invade Great Britain. Now the alarm bells sounded in Washington, D.C., and the nation started to mobilize resources for war against an expansive enemy, even accepting a peacetime draft. That fall the Department of War federalized the Ohio guard as the Thirty-seventh Division. Commanding the division was Colonel Robert Beightler, an able officer who had severed with the famous Rainbow division in France during the Great War; he would lead the Thirty-seventh throughout the war and, of course, eventually wear a general's stars.

The Thirty-seventh entering into full service in the United States Army, Rodger had to say farewell to his family and his life as a civilian. Since the spring of the year, he had been living with his parents in Clyde, a small town about four miles from Green Springs, his father having taken a position as the chief engineer of the Clyde Porcelain Steel Company, which had a government contract for the production of tank treads. As he had in Green Springs, Rodger soon had many friends there and had come to like the town.

For the next nineteen months, the Thirty-seventh trained at Camp Shelby in Mississippi and the Indiantown Gap Reservation in Pennsylvania. Only a few months before the Japanese attack on Pearl Harbor, it participated in the massive war games in Louisiana and Texas that saw Colonel George Patton emerging as a champion and leading tactician of mechanized warfare. He won praise for his performance and a promotion for it. At the other end of the spectrum in rank, Rodger met the demands of training and despite his poor eyesight became an expert marksman on the rifle range. Receiving plaudits as a "conscientious and dependable" soldier, he rose in the ranks as a corporal and then a sergeant leading a squad.

In May of 1942, the Thirty-seventh shipped out to the South Pacific, one of the first American infantry divisions to enter a war zone. One regiment, the 145th, disembarked in New Zealand, the 145th and 148th in the Fiji Islands. Lying astride the line for communication between the United States and Australia, the islands, were thousands of guardsmen from the Midwest for maneuvers out of Camp McCoy in Wisconsin.

At Rodger's enlistment in 1938, war for the nation did not seem imminent.

The regiments took up defensive positions on Vita Leva, one of the two main islands in the Fiji group. The regiments also prepared for an offensive against the Japanese, taking advanced training in stream-crossings, map reading, scouting and other tactics of combat.

Rodger found Vita Levu rather pleasant despite the rigor of training and the prospect of combat. Writing to Margaret Henry, a first cousin, he noted that the weather was warm and that he and his comrades often swam and played baseball, bingo, monopoly and cards. The natives were "mostly dark," he said, and were "friendly" towards the soldiers. He implied no wish for a miscegenative relationship with any of the women. He struck an amusing note in a letter to his brother-in-law, Charles "Chuck" Young, as he wrote on the day that he knew was the first day of the hunting season in Ohio. "We have bigger game over here," he explained as he referred to the Japanese, "and it don't [sic] cost us anything for the license, [sic] the only thing about this kind of hunting this damn game can shoot back and therefore you become the game."

After spending ten months in the Fiji Islands and New Zealand, the Thirty-seventh was nearly ready to hunt the "bigger game" that might shoot back. In the spring of 1943, it moved to Guadalcanal, where in an epic battle the Marines had finally driven the Japanese off the island. Here the division engaged in more training in preparation of combat against the Japanese in the campaign coed-named Operation Cartwheel. The operation called for a two-pronged advance on Rabaul, the large Japanese base on the eastern peninsula of New Britain. Admiral William "Bull" Halsey, commanding the South Pacific segment of the Pacific Ocean Area, led units of the Navy and the Army up the ladder of the Solomon Islands toward New Georgia, where American seizure of the Japanese airfield at Munda Point would open the door to attacks on Rabaul. Commanding the Southwest Pacific Ares, General Douglas MacArthur had the task of sending American divisions westward along the coast of New Guinea to Lae near the Huon Peninsula, a point that would outflank and permit attacks on Rabaul.

After a painfully slow movement up the Solomons, Halsey was finally ready in July of 1943 for an assault on the Japanese on New Georgia. Like all the islands in the Solomons, New Georgia was the host of various diseases – malaria, scrub typhus, dengue and more; and like many islands in the chain, it was punctuated by thick jungles and an undulating terrain rendering the movement of ground troops difficult.

Earlier in July, Rodger Young had made a fateful decision for himself and his company. Fearing that because of his deficient hearing, he might misunderstand an oral message and thus endanger his squad, he asked his company commander to relieve him of this position and demote him. He explained to the officer that he did not "want to leave the outfit. I want to go – but as a buck private, so I'm only responsible for myself. I don't want anyone to get hurt because of me." A medical examination proving that his hearing was failing, the commander reluctantly acceded to his request.

Rodger learned soon enough that his decision did not spare his company and squad from an agonizing juncture. On the second day at Laiana, after the Japanese had killed four men from Company B on a patrol, the Company found itself wedged into a Japanese ring that it could not possibly break. Then it received an order to disengage from the enemy and withdraw to a new perimeter. Sergeant Walter Rigby, commanding Young's platoon, passed the order to his men; but a Japanese machine gun crew on high ground about seventy yards from the crouching riflemen had them pinned down. Under any condition, a withdrawal could be dangerous and now was more hazardous as the night was drawing near.

Perhaps understanding the precarious position of the company, Rodger called out to Rigby that he could see the machine gun nest and was going for it. As he slowly crept up a slope, he suffered a shoulder wound and then wounds to his chest and right hand. Still he moved forward, with two hand grenades in his blouse. Within throwing distance, he heaved one grenade, crawled some more and finally was within ten yards of the gunners, in a defilade with the Japanese fire skimming over his bleeding body. Then he pulled the pin of his last grenade, rose, leaned back and hurled it as a burst from the Japanese gun struck him in the head, killing him instantly. But the grenade fell into the emplacement, and the Japanese also died.

Now the platoon was able to withdraw safely to a new position.

The next day, after driving the Japanese from positions near the hill, men of the platoon recovered Young's body. Wrapping him in a shelter-half, they buried him where he fell and marked his grave with a crude wooden cross. The regimental chaplain spoke a prayer as the men bowed in reverence and to avoid any Japanese fire. Later, Rodger was interred in a military cemetery on the island.

Soldiers often complained that legitimate heroes did not receive their due and that men not deserving medals somehow received them. But on one had any doubts about Rodger Young's bravery. Certainly Walter Rigby had no reservations about it. "If it had not been for his heroism," he said, "our platoon could not have successfully withdrawn. The machine gun was in such a position that it could well have covered the whole front of our position. We were under rifle fire, and all of a sudden this machine gun opened up. Rodger Young started firing back at it. Then the machine gun picked him up. He fired a couple more rounds, and then he was hit. He kept on going forward, throwing grenades and firing his rifle." Writing to Roger's father about the action, a private recalled that "It happened in a very critical moment, and if that bit of strategy had failed, we would all have been sunk."

4. For Cause or Comrade?

'Saving Private Ryan' says more about war than earlier films.

On Sept. 3 an essay by Arnold Rosenfeld, editor in chief of the Cox Newspapers titled "'Private Ryan' good, but not best," was published in the Dayion Daily News.

Rosenfeld argued that "His second (movie), the finding of Pvt. Ryan, is long and in search of a larger theme." He contended that a "weightier theme" was warranted and that such a theme is present in a 1957 film, Paths of Glory, starring Kirk Douglas.

Since the group I saw Saving Private Ryan with was almost speechless when it ended, I rented the video Paths of Glory to see how the two films might be compared.

In Paths, A French colonel (Douglas) defends three soldiers court-martialed for cowardice after failing to seize a strongpoint. The order for this impossible mission had its origin with an "incompetent and indifferent" general staff officer and was then transmitted to a corrupt field commander -a general concerned with his own promotion and career above all else. The "weightier" theme, Rosenfeld held, is "the responsibility of government and command."

This may be a "weightier" theme, but it has long been a settled issue with professional historians. The incompetent French and British generals, notably Gen. Douglas Haig of the British Army, fought a war of attrition with no new ideas of how to attack. When Haig ordered the British troops forward in the Battle of the Somme River on July 1, 1916, they incurred 57,000 casualties the first day, 19,000 of them dead. He then continued to use the same stupid tactics. Incompetence and/or indifference of commanding officers plagued all the European armies that fought in World War I.

Saving Private Ryan is, as Pulitzer Prize-winning columnist Charles Krauthammer says, a movie about GIs who did their duty. It is a stunning film because:

- It sheds light on what war is really like for the common soldier.
- It bears witness to the daily life of the American infantryman coming under enemy fire from strafing, bombing, artillery and small arms.
- It brings home graphically the lessons one must learn to evolve from a green recruit to a real soldier, as James Jones and E.B. Sledge noted in their books, a combat soldier eventually comes to accept the fact that he won't survive the war.
- It speaks volumes about how profound it is to face sudden, violent death on a daily basis at age 19 – a time when life is supposed to begin, not end.
- It brings to light and helps us understand why soldiers fight -i.e., why soldiers do their duty even when their own lives are put in harm's way.
- It gives testimony to the fact that soldiers see little cowardice and little heroism – rather, what they see is men doing their duty in order to get along with their fellow soldiers. Soldiers take their turn in order to get along with the men in their immediate group.

Paths of Glory and Saving Private Ryan are cinematic polar opposites. Paths of Glory is an 86- minute film (with 12 minutes of combat) about French soldiers in World War 1. It is heavily laden with ideological and patriotic reasons as the cause of why men fight; it shows us the static nature of trench warfare; and it focuses on the wartime role and perspective of upper-echelon officers.

Saving Private Ryan is almost a three-hour film (about half of it showing the most harrowing combat scenes ever filmed) about American infantrymen in World War II. The movie is virtually devoid of the ideological and patriotic reasons of why men fight – instead it is comrade, not cause, that motivates the men in Capt. John Miller's (Tom Hanks) squad in this war of rapid movement. The perspective of warfare in Private Ryan is that of the common man – it is an infantryman's view of a war involving different kinds of combat – seaborne invasion, urban street fighting, countryside ambush and defense in holding an important bridge.

If the two films are compared, as they will be someday in the future in terms of clarity of purpose, craftsmanship and persistence overtime, Steven Spielberg's Saving Private Ryan will surely be judged as an important contribution to knowledge, while Paths of Glory sheds little new light on the nature of war.

5. Documenting the Army Experience

Soldiers have a special obligation, a special imperative, to document their experiences in the Army. The burden of a special obligation is borne not only by those who stood in harm's way because of enemy action, but by all who served in the military. To document means to write the story, get it down in black and white so it's not lost forever.

The form matters not. Consider the contribution to knowledge and understanding of warfare made by the following writers:

- Literature. Read Erich Maria Remarque's *All Quiet on the Western Front* or James Jones's *The Thin Red Line* if you would stand in the shoes of a common infantryman in World War I or World War II.
- Drama. To understand relationships and effective leadership in the military, read Henry the Fifth's speech to his troops just before the battle of Agincourt.
- History. To capture history in the making, Samuel Eliot Morison's 14-volume series on the U.S. Navy in World War II is unmatched. Morison's series may be updated as files are made available to scholars, but it cannot be replaced.
- Speech. For brevity, read the 259 words of exquisite prose that Abraham Lincoln wrote in what may be the greatest words about men at war in history – The Gettysburg Address.
- Journalism. *Here is Your War* by Ernie Pyle captures the life of the soldier. It is a worm's-eye view of soldering in the North African campaign.
- Poetry. British poet A.E. Housman, in his commentary on war, said, "Life, to be sure, is nothing much to lose; but young men think it is, and we were young."

Historical Reasons

Those involved in combat ought to pass the word along from one generation to the next about what actually occurred.

For example, Gordon W. Prange has written three or four books about the Japanese attack on Pearl Harbor on December 7, 1 941. Prange focuses on one fateful day in his definitive work designed to educate and inform readers about what happened.

He delves into congressional hearings, conducts personal interviews, gains access to Japanese documentation, translates the memoirs of Japanese naval officers and leaves nothing to chance- all in an effort to reconstruct the events of "the day of infamy," so that human beings can know the truth of what, where, why, when and how such an event occurred. Prange's sole intellectual goal is to pass the word along.

When World War II started, Samuel Morison went to government officials and persuaded them that there was a need for a history of the Navy to be written while the men who fought it were still alive. Morison's work in these volumes is indispensable to anyone who wants to understand the role of the Navy in World War II.

He participated in naval actions and visited areas of ground combat while the fighting went on. His discussion of the Battle of Midway of the ships, the people and the different phases of that crucial battle, the turning point of the Pacific War, is unparalleled. Much of what we know today of that engagement and many others we owe to Morison and his work.

Soldiers ought to shed light on what war and Army life are really like and how the common soldier experienced them. More needs to be written about the tedium and boredom of daily life; the little-known facts, stories and experiences of men at war; the eyewitness accounts of coming under enemy fire; and the human side of technological struggle.

Two books that do just this, and do it in brilliant fashion are, *Here is Your War* and *Oba: The Last Samurai*, a fascinating memoir by a Japanese officer, Capt. Oba (with Don Jones). Pyle's book is a journalist's effort to document the Allied invasion of North Africa, which began in November 1942 and ended in victory in April 1943. Pyle writes from the bottom up about the daily life of the American infantryman coming under fire from bullets and airplane strafing and of his evolution into a real soldier.

Capt. Oba's book is a fascinating memoir of a Japanese officer and 40 of his men who truly lived the code of Bushido and the Samurai. When U.S.

Marines invaded Saipan in July 1944, the island was declared secure in September 1944. But Capt. Oba and his troops fought on in a guerrilla-style war until December 1945 four months after the peace was signed on the USS Missouri in Tokyo Bay. Capt. Oba simply wouldn't surrender without direct orders from the emperor. Fighting and the struggle for the necessaries of life filled every day. These are the stories, the daily stories, of soldiers at war.

It is important to disclose the feelings and actions of the average soldier the fear, anger, hate, regret, relief, pleasure, hope and anxiety of experiences in the service. Only this facet gives a story the ring of truth, the human interest and the genuine amusement implicit in some tales.

Good examples of such literature include Remarque's *All Quiet on the Western Front* and Jones' *The Thin Red Line*. The writing in Remarque's book is searingly honest and utterly devoted to telling the truth about war as a German infantryman in World War I. Remarque was wounded five times, the last time seriously.

Jones' book has been characterized by some as perhaps the best novel ever written about war from the common soldier's point-of-view. Jones was wounded in action on Guadalcanal, and *The Thin Red Line* describes the emotions and feelings of young men, most of them 19 or 20 years old, men just beginning adult life who must face the distinct possibility of sudden death.

Jones depicts the evolution of a soldier, a real soldier, from the green recruit to the seasoned fighter who has mentally accepted the fact that he will not survive the war.

Soldiers should write to fill the void beyond the mere chronology of significant events as written by professional historians. Whether World War II veterans realize it or not, they were at the center of one of the truly cataclysmic events in human history. The stories and history of the war will command books and chapters for hundreds of years

Social Reasons

Military life teaches young soldiers that life is a profound and passionate thing. It is a profound thing to face sudden death directly at age 19. It is staggering to realize that the enemy's goal is to kill you at 19. Life is supposed to be beginning, not ending suddenly and violently. And this experience is, at times, a daily reality.

Only through the written word or other art form can this reality be made available to a host of people. The significance of life is only clear and lively when one objectively faces its antithesis – death. The fear, anxiety, relief and pleasure that one experiences at 19 is on a passionate level. Few human beings reach so many affective heights so early in life. These affections occur to all human beings, but normally in a rather slow progression as one experiences life over many years. In the military, the number and level may be telescoped into a five-minute experience when all the passions noted above, and more, are realized at a level never again to be attained.

We learn from novels, memoirs, poetry, movies and journalism that human beings in a group can transcend their alienated, isolated and estranged lives as civilians. It is not an everyday occurrence, but it is also not uncommon for soldiers to risk their lives, and give their lives, for their comrades.

Soldiers do their duty in the vast majority of cases, do it when they know their own lives are at peril. How else can one explain the behavior of veterans at "The Wall," the memorial in Washington, DC, dedicated to Vietnam veterans. A military unit (squad, platoon, company) exists; it is a functioning entity.

And it is a marvelous thing to be part of something that goes beyond the individual. The military group can accomplish things no individual can hope to realize.

War is both action and passion, and a soldier shares the action and times of peril with others in his unit. During my first time under enemy fire (a bombing raid), I shared the action and peril with a friend in a pathetic slit trench that night. We were in the trench together (or almost in it as we hadn't dug it deep enough). When the bombs started dropping nearby, we leaped in on top of two other men who had been more diligent and attentive to our sergeant's command to dig in. We shared the experience with others in spite of their protests.

My closest brush with eternity was on Christmas Eve 1943, a night I'll never forget. During the first of five bombing raids that evening, I shared with another soldier on KP the action and passions involved in interacting with an anonymous person. I didn't even know his name, but we went through my most memorable moments of the entire war together. Bombs dropped, flashed and turned us upside down inside our fragile shelter. We cursed, prayed, tried to burrow into the sand, anything to escape the bombs. Our only security, and there was precious little of that, was our proximity to each other. During war, the time of peril is a shared, social experience.

All forms of literature associated with military life during wartime help create conditions that prevent war and at least end to make decision-makers cautious of intervention in war. *The Naked and the Deadly* (Norman Mailer), *Farewell to Arms* by Ernest Hemingway, *The Red Badge of Courage* by Stephen Crane and *The Quiet American* by Graham Greene lucidly tell what it's like to be a fighter in combat.

Ethical Reasons

It is incumbent on those who survive a war to honor those who have fallen in battle. The polished black marble wall in Washington dedicated to the soldiers who gave their lives in the Vietnam War bears poignant evidence of the nation's effort to honor its war dead. The names engraved in the stone are touched by the trembling fingers of friends and relatives. Each visitor, in so doing, seeks to bridge the gap between the living and the dead. The flowers, mementos, letters, poems and other items they carried in battle move many to tears. The bronze monument is a moving sight, but the Wall with its thousands of names is tellingly eloquent in what it says: "Honor the fallen."

Through the written word we are able to express respect for the veterans gathered to hear and to read about events of by-gone days. This respect would be to those with whom we served and yes, to those who served against us. This theme dominates Henry the Fifth's speech on the significance of "St. Crispin's Day" to those who fought with him at Agincourt. Conversely, through writing and speech, we are able to express our scorn for those painless patriots who stood aside in all the wars when the call came for commitment. These painless patriots emerge at every time of war. Oliver Wendell Holmes said it best: "Invisible in war, Invincible in peace."

Only through the written word can we learn about soldiers in combat who did their duty, did it under adverse circumstances. Soldiers see little of cowardice and still less of heroism. What they do see is other soldiers transcending fear and behaving responsibly under stress. The fear doesn't end, but it is manageable. Soldiers do their duty not so much for country, freedom or flag, but to get along with their fellow soldiers. Doing your duty means pulling your own weight, doing what is right, taking your turn.

Personal Reasons

I wrote *Common Warfare: Parallel Memoirs by Two World War II GIs in the Pacific* to tell my family what the war had been like for me. From time to time one of my sons, my grandchildren, my wife or various relatives might ask, "What did you do in the war?" I usually gave a cursory answer, "I was in the Army during World War II stationed in the Pacific." That was usually about the extent of the conversation. With the publication of the book, my family knows me, and I them, somewhat better. Memoirs help a family know and understand each other through the conversations prompted by points made in the book.

I simply wanted to talk about the war and my role in it – in writing. You often hear somebody say, "Oh he never talks about the war. He doesn't like to talk about it." That is nonsense. I argue that soldiers should talk about their experiences and, ultimately, given the right circumstance, they do.

In many ways the exercise of writing *Common Warfare* enabled me to relive the old days to almost, just for a moment, be 19 again. The work itself forced me to relive the old days, to read the 191 letters, to study the diary (my best database) and look again very carefully at the faded photographs. All this helped me to go back in time, to recapture what used to be, to go back to a time when life was just beginning and to a place where it almost ended on a couple of occasions. What a paradox it is to be a young soldier.

Finally, the famous dictum by Socrates, "Know Thyself," was, in part, realized in the writing of the manuscript.

I was able to read a mass of data written by a very young man and then reflect on these youthful musings 50 years later. In doing this, I became aware of areas of change in my life and areas of essentially changeless behavior.

My military experience was a turning point in my life. I still organize my life in terms of my service in the Army before the war, the war and after the war. The war had a monumental impact on me psychologically and socially. This was my personal transition from boy to man.

Army life enabled me to know myself and to understand the meaning and value of equality (when there was little), of privacy (when there was none), of freedom (when all my actions were decided by others) and of justice (when it ofttimes seemed lost). The Army and enemy fire made the aphorism of Socrates a reality.

Additional Reading

Eagle Against the Sun: The American War with Japan by Ronald H. Spector, The Free Press, 1985.

The 37th Infantry Division in World War I by Stanley A. Frankel, Infantry Journal Press, 1948

Touched with Fire: The Land War in the South Pacific by Eric Bergerud, Viking-Penguin, 1996

Weathering the Peace: The Ohio National Guard in the interwar Years, 1919-1940 by Robert L. Daugherty, Wright State University Press, 1991.

Wartime: Understanding and Behavior in the Second World War by Paul Fussell, Oxford University Press, 1989.

6. Some Thoughts on War and Peace

October 2, 2001

Almost twenty years ago, in October of 1982, Harry V. Jaffa, author of ten books and hundreds of essays, and a Professor Emeritus at Claremont McKenna College, wrote a short essay on the duty of military service. As America begins its struggle against terrorism, and as those in the peace movement (called by some our "best citizens") initiate the first of their protests against this war, it might be wise to summarize Jaffa's comments and so lend a reasoned analysis to the debate.

Jaffa argues that those who defy the obligation of military service are often seen as somehow braver and better that those who accept this obligation. He thinks this is "shameful, as well as inconsistent with our interest in survival." But what can we say to the pacifist claim that there is a moral duty, higher than the law, not to engage in military service because of the duty not to kill other human beings? Jaffa contends that most of us believe we have a natural right of self-defense that we may exercise individually (if someone attacks us in our own home at night) or collectively when our nation is attacked (as on December 7, 1941 or September 11, 2001.). " Thou shalt not kill" is not understood by very many to preclude killing those who make an unprovoked attack upon us as individuals or as a nation.

"Military service in a free society is a moral no less than a legal duty" to Jaffa. This moral duty is founded in the Declaration of Independence in the great proposition "that all men are created equal." Abraham Lincoln said that this proposition is "the father of all moral principles among us."

Consider now the Massachusetts Bill of Rights (1780) which says, "the body politic is formed by a voluntary association of individuals; it is a

243

social compact by which the whole people covenants with each citizen and each citizen with the whole people that all shall be governed by certain laws for the common good."

Jaffa then reasons that "those who do not become members of a body politic at its institution, are nonetheless voluntary members by consenting to remain in it." If this is true, then all who reach the age of consent, agree at the same time to obey the laws founded upon that consent.

Now, if we are all endowed by the Declaration of Independence with certain unalienable rights (life, liberty and the pursuit of happiness), then the "common good" surely implies that safety is fundamental. Our national security is the condition for the enjoyment of all the other rights. If a person says he/she will be a good citizen in "everything else except in joining in the common defense, (he/she) is removing the linchpin of citizenship, upon which everything else depends (because) each cannot be defended by all, unless all will defend each."

In addition, if one embraces the notion of human equality, then one "cannot lay claim to an equal right with (one's) fellow citizens, to the protection of the laws, while rejecting the equal obligation, to share the risks without which there can be no protection by the laws. (Finally,) the obligation to respect religious opinion cannot be understood in such a way that the government that guarantees religious freedom may not survive." The goal of military service is the security and safety of the body politic. Of all pacifists in American history, Martin Luther King Jr., a man who was jailed, beaten, stoned and finally assassinated, said there were exceptional times when violence was necessary. Leonard Pitts in his essay of September 29, 2001, quotes King as saying that if he was called to service in WWII, "I believe that I would have temporarily sacrificed my pacifism because Hitler was such an evil force in history."

The events of September 11, 2001 constituted an unprovoked attack on the body politic and resulted in the death of 6500 to 7000 innocent human beings. Peace at any price is no bargain. Remember 1776, 1861, 1941 and 2001.

Robert G. Thobaben is Professor Emeritus of Political Science at Wright State University. He was a soldier in the 111th Infantry in the Pacific during WWII.

7. Artistic License & Cinematic Liberties Taken in The Thin Red Line

The concept of artistic license suggests ideas about the permissible latitude and liberty of one artist performing another's original creative work. For example, American jazz not only encourages improvisation, but it is also a necessary condition of this art form. The performer may change the key, tempo, rhythm or motif (Dixieland, swing, bop), but he or she is bound by a silent pledge of fidelity and good faith to the originating composer and lyricist.

The notion of artistic license in a film based on a novel thus balances midpoint on the dynamic tension between the polar opposites of a film of the book and arrogant self-indulgence. Artistic license can never be mere fabrication. It may not involve contrived devices. The cinematic interpreter must always demonstrate fealty to the basic underlying and essential themes of the original creative activity.

Terrence Malick compromised this fealty in the film version of James Jones' epic novel about combat in Guadalcanal in World War II, The Thin Red Line. Malick misfires, denying us the vital essence of Jones' work in exchange for his pretentious, artsy-craftsy, climactic transformation of the novel. Many film critics have applauded this transformation, and Malick and his picture have been nominated for various awards. Typifying the critics in his language is Tony Williams of Southern Illinois University. Writing for the newsletter of the James Jones Literary Society (Volume 8, Numbers I & 2, Winter 1998-99), Williams declared that Malick "extends Jones's original text into several visually poetic and symbolic directions... Those seeking a straightforward 'film of the book' approach," he acknowledged, "will be disappointed." Disappointed is hardly the word. Malick's film neither parallels nor transcends Jones' book. Malick does not clothe the riflemen of Charlie Company, Jones' collective protagonist, with their genuine vestments. His interpretation reduces the novel's seminal themes to wreckage.

We lament Malick's treatment of the men giving shape to Charlie Company. They carry the narrative along and give it its texture, yet Malick seldom endows them with distinguishing characteristics. He notably fails to define Topkick Sgt. Welsh, a leading figure in the novel. Jones portrayed him as an everlasting cynic, virtually a nihilist who finds war only a struggle for property, a hopeless but perpetual endeavor. Malick has largely drawn him as a passive observer of combat, a man sleepwalking through battle. In the novel, when Welsh risks his life to administer morphine to the mortally wounded Telia, he does so not as an act of compassion as Malick would have us believe – but simply because he is furious with the madness of war.

Similarly, Malick strips Pvt. Witt of his nature. Here is a man fiercely loyal to Charlie Company (though not officially on its roster), extraordinarily brave and proud and sensitive. Malick reduces him to a cipher. Early on, he has him lolling around with native Melanesians in a village and at one with nature. One will not find such native villages in Jones' pages. Not satisfied with emasculating Witt in indolence, Malick has a group of Japanese soldiers shoot him down like a dog. Jones keeps Witt alive because, paradoxically, he must go on to fight and suffer at New Georgia, Bougainville, and so on. Death ends suffering; survival compounds it.

Malick gives short shrift to many other men who flesh out Charlie Company. Storm, Doll, Beck, Keck, Fife, Queens, Dale, Bell and others revealing varying degrees of bravery, cowardice, selflessness and egoism are but sighs and shadows in the film. Less poetic imagery might have given them substance.

To give Malick his due, he limns an accurate description of Charlie Company's commanding officer, a compassionate man who refuses a direct order to send his men into a frontal attack. But what Malick gives with one hand, he takes with the other. Jones' company commander, Capt. Stein, is Jewish and ultimately weak willed. Perhaps concerned about offending Jews, Malick changes Stein's name and ethnicity. At the same time, he invests Lt. Col. Tall, the battalion commander who orders Charlie Company to mount the frontal attack, with an unwarranted centrality in the film. Although Tall is critically important at a crucial point in the novel, before and after this, for 150 pages he plays no significant role in the life of Charlie

Company. Jones, known for his commitment to truth, surely would have decried Malick's Stein and Tall.

In his zeal to humanize the Japanese, Malick distorts the account of Charlie Company's assault on Japanese soldiers in a bivouac. Jones' company literally massacres the Japanese, giving them no quarter, with the Japanese asking none. In the book, a "crazy sort of blood lust" seized the men of Charlie Company. Malick, nearly always forcing the novel to fit his Procrustean bed, has several Japanese soldiers writhing in agony and seeking mercy from the Americans. Unlike Jones, he shrinks from the absolute brutality of combat in the Pacific. His poetic direction endangered, Malick can only imply that an American soldier is preparing to extract the gold fillings from the teeth of a Japanese soldier dead or alive. Malick could have taken instruction from E.B. Sledge, in whose superb memoir of combat in the Pacific, *With the Old Breed*, Americans can lose all restraint in battle.

Though we have said nothing about the casting in The Thin Red Line, we should note Malick's attempt to commercialize his artistry in the use of two stars, George Clooney and John Travolta, in minuscule and meaningless roles. Their appearance degrades the integrity of the film.

As Malick's version of The Thin Red Line will inevitably be compared with Steven Spielberg's Saving Private Ryan, we suggest the latter be declared the victor for a number of reasons:

Civilian life: Malick's fallacious imagery of native life during the vicious fighting on Guadalcanal stands in stark contrast to Spielberg's brutal honesty in the scene showing a French family inadvertently involved in street fighting between American and German infantrymen.

Enemy soldier: Malick's mawkishness is demonstrated vividly in the scene in which the American infantrymen attack a Japanese bivouac area. The viewers' conclusion can only be, "They are just like us." Does Malick really believe that soldiers imbued with a kamikaze mentality as state policy are just like us? Compare this view with Spielberg's depiction of German soldiers surrendering when the only other option is death.

Cinematic maturity: Some reviewers described Malick's film as more mature and more adult when, in fact, it is juvenile and adolescent. This film speaks to the touchy-feely mentality of the 1960s generation. Paradise lost is found again as Malick annihilates Jones' book. In contrast, Spielberg, working with a fragile story line, addresses and answers fundamental themes associated with war – namely, why and how infantrymen fight and the profound, consummate effect on the young men facing sudden violent death.

Creativity; other reviews have commented on the lyrical, imaginative and symbolic dimensions of Malick's interpretation of Jones' epic novel. But authentic symbols must reveal dimensions of an underlying reality, and poetic scenes become prosaic when constructed on a fairy tale. Spielberg understood this fact; Malick did not.

Humanitarian aspects: True, Malick's Japanese enemies are never demonized. But that is how war ought to be fought, not how it is fought. John Dower's War Without Mercy understands the savagery of the American-Japanese struggle in World War II. Both sides employed racism as a tool to vilify the enemy and exalt themselves. In this respect the American and Japanese media and propaganda machines were alike. One might well ask, "What war was Malick portraying in his version of The Thin Red Line?"

Fortunately, Malick's film version of Jones' great novel The Thin Red Line will soon be relegated to the celluloid scrap heap, while Spielberg's Saving Private Ryan is an authentic contribution to knowledge.

8. Japan and the A-Bomb: from 'victim' to 'loser'

There have been many notable anniversaries of WWII recently, but Aug. 6 and 9 will be the bi-centenary – the 50"' anniversary of the atomic bombing of Hiroshima and Nagasaki. The A-bombs shocked the entire world, stupefied Japan's civilians, and stunned its scientists and engineers. Most important, it shattered the mental trance of Japan's political and military leaders regarding its invincibility and enabled them to accept the reality of defeat. Five days after Nagasaki, Japan surrendered unconditionally, WWII ended, and the nuclear age began.

The pros and cons of Truman's decision to drop the A-bombs, the targets selected, and the short- and long-term consequences of that decision have now gone on for 80 years. There is no need to enumerate and discuss again the arguments on both sides. All these are well known.

What is not well known is that Japan was working to develop an atomic bomb of its own before and during WWII. Every nation that might plausibly start a nuclear weapons program did so: The United States, Great Britain, France, Germany, the Soviet Union, and Japan. But knowledge about Japan's endeavor has never been well known.

In 1931, serious research in quantum mechanics and nuclear physics began in Japan under the direction of Dr. Yoshio Nishina. Nishina had spent eight years in Europe studying with Ernest Rutherford at Cambridge and at Copenhagen at the Niels Bohr's Institute of Theoretical Physics. In 1935, Nishina headed a nuclear research laboratory at the Rikken Institute in Tokyo and by 1937 Japan was making significant progress in physics. As war between the U.S. and Japan loomed on the horizon, the Army in its "Nl" program and the Navy in its "F" project ordered A-bomb research and development. Japan's commitment to build an atomic bomb was substantial and backed by the military, political, and scientific communities.

Virginia K. Hess

Would the Japanese have used the bomb had they won the race? Consider the comments of the following:

Derek deSolla Price, professor of the history of Science at Yale said, "The Japanese effort (to build an atomic bomb) existed and reached a maturity in North Korea. No longer can we maintain that a Japanese bomb just couldn't have happened. Obviously, it nearly did." (*Japan's Secret War* by R. Wilcox, 1985)

Did It Not Seem Real?

The following poignant commentary is by a Confederate Soldier, Sergeant Berry Benson. He witnessed the first shot at Fort Sumter as well as Lee's surrender at Appomattox. His adventures in between included combat, capture, and escape. Afterward, he remained active with various postwar activities.

"Who knows, but it may be given to us, after this life, to meet again in the old quarters, to play chess and draughts, to get up soon to answer the morning roll call, to fall in at the tap of the drum for drill and dress parade, and again to hastily don our war gear while the monotonous patter of the long roll summons to battle? Who knows but again the old flags, ragged and torn, snapping in the wind, may face each other and flutter pursuing and pursued, while the cries of victory fill a summer day? And after the battle, then the slain and wounded will arise, and all will meet together under the two flags, all sound and well, and there will be talking and laughter and cheers, and all will say: Did it not seem real? Was it not as in the old days?"

CONCLUSION

The Appendices

The Organization and Weapons of American Infantry Divisions
Important Individuals, Terms, and Battles of WWII

The Appendices

The Organization and Weapons of an American Infantry Division

Unit	Strength	Commander	Parent Unit Platoon-3-4
Squad	12 to 15	Sergeant	squads Company-3
Platoon	36 to 64	Lieutenant	platoon Battalion-3
Rifle Company	180	Captain	companies Regiment-3
Battalion	1200	Lt. Col.	battalions Division-3
Regiment	3,100	Colonel	regiments Corps-3
Division	13,472	Maj. Gen.	divisions

Divisional units included artillery, engineering, medical, signal, reconnaissance, and quartermaster formations.

Weapons
Colt .45 caliber automatic pistol
Model 1903 Springfield. 30 caliber, 5 round magazine. 8.7 pounds
M-I Garand. 30 caliber, semi-automatic, 8 round clip, 9.6 pounds Thompson submachine gun, .45 caliber. 700 rounds per minute, 12 pounds BAR .30 caliber, fully automatic, 20 round magazine, 20 pounds
Machine gun, .30 caliber, air and water cooled
Mortar, 60mm, 2.5 pound bomb, 2,000 yards, 42 pounds
Mortar, 81 mm, 7.5 pound bomb. 3,800 yards. 80+ pounds
Artillery 105mm, 33 pound projectile, 12.000 yards, 3,750 pounds Artillery 155mm, 95 pound projectile, 12,530 yards, 12.750 pounds Artillery 37mm, anti-tank gun

Source: Bradley, Omar N. *A Soldier's Story*. New York: Henry Holt Co., 1951, p. 564.

Important Individuals, Terms, and Battles of WWII

Airborne Forces: The U.S. established its first parachute units in 1940. By 1945 there were four airborne divisions.

Anzio: January of 1944; A part of the Allied invasion of Italy; 30 miles from Rome.

Army Air Corps: It became the U.S. Air Force in 1 947 via the Unification Act of 1 947, and now serves under the Department of Defense.

Arnold, H. H.: Head of Army Air Corps in World War II and member of the Joint Chiefs of Staff.

Atlantic, the Battle of the; This naval battle continued from 1939 to 1945.

Atomic bomb: These were dropped on Hiroshima on August 6, 1 945, and Nagasaki on August 9, 1945; They hastened the Japanese surrender and the end of the war.

Barbarossa, Operation: June of l941; Hitler's invasion of the Soviet Union.

Bataan Death March: Forced 65-mile march by American and Philippine military prisoners that resulted in thousands of deaths due to Japanese cruelty on the march.

Berlin, the Battle of: April 16 to May 2, 1945; the final major battle in Europe in WWII.

Bombers, American (major only): B-17, Flying Fortress-4 engines; B-244 engines; B-25-2 engines; B-29-4 engine long range bomber (called the Superfortress).

Britain, the Battle of: July to October of 1940; Britain freed itself from Nazi occupation.

Bulge, the Battle of: December of 1944 to January of 1945; battle in the Ardennes Forest.

Caroline Islands: Islands held in trust by Japan after World War I and developed into major Army and Navy bases in the years before World War II.

Chiang Kai-shek: Leader of Nationalist Chinese forces during World War II. Later defeated by the Communists, he fled with his troops to Taiwan in 1949.

Churchill, Winston: British prime minister who rallied the British people and led the country from defeat to victory.

Clark, Mark: General and commander of the U.S. Fifth Army in North Africa, and later commander or the 1 5th Army Corps in Italy.

Coral Sea, the Battle of: May 4 to 8, 1942, a draw.

Crete, Battle of: May 20, 1941, a massive airborne invasion by the Germans.

Cruisers: Conventional cruisers of World War II were replaced by guided missile cruisers beginning in 1961.

De Gaulle, Charles: Leader of the Free French forces in the battle for Europe.

Destroyers: World War II destroyers were about 376 feet long and 40 feet wide. There were three classes of destroyers-Fletcher, Sumner and Gearing. The U.S. had 350 destroyers at the end of the war.

Destroyer escorts: A World War II DE was 290 feet long and had a 35 foot beam; 400 DEs were built between 1941 and 1945.

Doolittle, James: Led first raid on Tokyo with B-25s from the carrier Hornet in 1942.

Dunkirk, the Battle of: May 26 to June 4 of 1942; an evacuation of 338,000 Allied troops.

Dyer, Lt. Commander Thomas H: Codebreaker who intercepted Japanese messages at Midway.

Eisenhower, Dwight D.: General of the Army and supreme commander of Allied expeditionary forces in Europe during World War II.

El Alamein, the Battles of: both in the fall of 1942. They prevented further German advances into Egypt and the Middle East.

Enfilading fire: gunfire directed along the length of an enemy battle line.

Envelopment: an attack directed toward the enemy's flanks or rear.

Field of fire: the space covered by the fire of a weapon, particularly a machine gun. Interlocking fields of fire literally created a wall of steel. Terrain and ground cover could obstruct fields of fire.

Fighters (airplanes): Navy-F4F and F6F; Marines-F4U Corsair; Army Air P-38, P-19, P-40, P-47, P-51. These are the principal American fighter planes in World War II.

Flamethrowers: A weapon that projects and ignites a flammable liquid. They are well suited for the destruction of bunkers or caves.

Flanks: the extreme right or left side of an army or fleet or a subdivision.

Fuchida, Mitsuo: Japanese fighter pilot who led the first wave or 180 planes in the attack on Pearl Harbor on December 7. 1941.

Gilbert Islands: Site of two major battles in the central Pacific in November of 1943: Tarawa (Marines) and Makin (Army).

Great Depression: Period between 1929 and 1940 when 25 percent of the American workforce was unemployed.

Guadalcanal: August of 1942; First American Pacific ground attack in World War II by the 1st Marine Division. A six-month campaign and the acquisition of Henderson Field.

Hirohito: Emperor of Japan during the war; deeply involved in all aspects of war planning and execution.

Hiroshima: August 6. 1945; the dropping of an atomic bomb.

Hitler, Adolf: Chancellor of Germany, 1933-1945; committed suicide in 1945 in a bunker in Berlin.

Howitzer: Most common type of artillery; relatively short barrels; 105mm and 1 55 mm are the most common types in American artillery units

Iwo Jima: February 19 to March 26, 1945, a terrible battle with an American victory.

Kamikaze: Member of a Japanese air corps suicide attack force who crashed their planes into American warships; very effective in the Philippines and Okinawa.

Kharkov, Battles of: 1942, German attack in the Ukraine.

Kasserine Pass, Battle of the: February 19 to 24, 1943; first major battle between Allied and Axis forces.

King, Ernest J.: Commander of the U.S. Fleet and member of the Joint Chiefs of Staff.

Kursk, Battle of: 1943, the largest tank battle in history.

Kwajalein Atoll: Seized by the 7th Infantry Division in February of 1944.

Landing craft: LCT (tank), LCVP (vehicle, personnel), LST (tank), LCM (mechanized).

LeMay, Curtis E.: Commander of the 20th Bomber Command on Tinian.

Leningrad, the Siege of: September 8,1941 to January 27, 1944; the Soviets prevailed over Germany.

Leyte Gulf, the Battle of: October 23 to 26, 1944; This crippled the Japanese combined fleet and enabled the Allied invasion of the Philippines.

Lexington: May of 1942; Attack carrier sunk in the Battle of the Coral Sea.

Logistics: All activities related to the supply, support, movement, and evacuation of armed forces. The goal is to provide the armed forces with the correct quantity of material at the right time to do their task.

MacArthur, Douglas: General and commander of the southwest Pacific area.

Marine Corps: Formed in 1775 under the Navy and responsible for amphibious warfare. Marines have their own air support, armor, and artillery units.

Market Garden, September 17 to 25, 1944; Allied Operation to seize key bridges and open the way to a major Allied invasion.

Marshall, George: General and chief of staff of the U.S. Army during the war.

Midway Island: June 4 to 6, 1942; Japan's attempt to seize Midway resulted in their disastrous loss of four major attack carriers and their most experienced pilots. The initiative in the Pacific moved to the United States after this great battle.

Monte Cassino, Battle of: January 17 to May 18, 1 944; a series of battles by the Allies in Italy.

Mortar: A weapon designed to loft a shell (a bomb) in a high trajectory. It is the oldest form of artillery.

Moscow, Battle of: September 30, 1941, to January 7, 1942; a Soviet victory.

New Guinea: A huge island in the southwest Pacific area (1200 miles long), and the site of scores of pitched battles between American and Japanese soldiers, sailors, and marines.

Nagasaki: August 9, 1945; the dropping of an atomic bomb.

Nimitz, Chester W: Admiral and commander of the central Pacific area.

Normandy Invasion: June 6, 1944; D-Day, Operation Overlord, largest invasion force in history, 5 divisions landing on the Normandy beaches.

Okinawa, Invasion of: April 1, 1945; the final island battle before the invasion of Japan.

Palau Islands: Western Caroline Islands group; site of the battle of Peleliu in September of 1944.

Patrol: a detachment of men detailed for reconnaissance.

Patton, George: General; commander of the U.S. IT Corps in Tunisia, the Seventh Army in Sicily, and the Third Army in Western Europe.

Pearl Harbor: December 7, 1941; Naval base on Oahu, Hawaii, and target of a Japanese attack. It brought the US into the war.

Philippine Islands, Invasion of: October 20, 1944; led by MacArthur's forces.

Philippine Sea, Battle of the: 1944; The Japanese lost almost 400 planes in what is called the Great Turkey Shoot, during the battle for Saipan.

Poland, the Invasion of: September 1, 1939; an invasion by Germany and the USSR.

Prisoners of war: American prisoners of war died at the rate of 0.7 percent in German camps and at a rate of 34 percent when held by the Japanese.

Pyle, Ernest: Surely one of the greatest American war correspondents in World War II. Killed in the Pacific in the battle for Okinawa.

Rommel, Erwin: Field Marshall, German commander of the Afrika Korps. Roosevelt, Franklin: President of the United States during almost all of the war. Rundstedt, Karl R. G. von: Field Marshal, German Commander-in-chief in the West.

Saipan, Battle of: June15, 1944 to July 9, 1944; to gain an air base from which to bomb Japan.

Short, Walter C.: Army general at the time of the Pearl Harbor attack; Schofield Barracks.

Sniper: A rifleman particularly trained to kill individuals at long range.

Sonar: Underwater microphones which receive all sounds from the waters around them, particularly useful in locating submarines.

Stalin, Joseph: Dictator of the Soviet Union during the war; died in 1 953.

Stalingrad, the Battle of: July 17,1942 to February 2,1943; a hard-won Soviet victory.

Strategy: the combining and employing of the means of war in planning and directing large military operations.

Tactics: the use and deployment of troops in combat, usually implying small scale engagements.

Tarawa: One of the Gilbert Islands, site of the first offensive in the central Pacific by Marines; the battle there resulted in over 1000 Americans killed and 5000 Japanese killed. Texel: April 5 to May 20, 1945; the last European battle of WWIL

Tiger tank: German tank, probably the best tank of any side in World War II.

Time-on target: the synchronization of artillery fire from several batteries at different points on a selected target.

Tojo, Hideki: Wartime premier of Japan; captured and hanged after the war trials.

Tokyo: March 9 and 10, 1945; fire-bombing with extreme devastation.

Torch, Operation: November 8 to November 16, 1942; Allied operation in North Africa.

Torpex: A high explosive introduced by the Navy in 1943 as a replacement for TNT in torpedo warheads.

Truman, Harry S: Upon the death of Roosevelt, in 1945, he became President of the United States; he made the decision to drop the atomic bomb on Japan to hasten the end of the war.

Turing, Alan: He cracked the Enigma Code of the Germans.

WAAC: Women's Army Auxiliary Corps; became WACs in late 1943.

WAVES: Women Accepted for Volunteer Emergency Service, U.S. Navy.

Yamamoto, Tsouoku: Japanese Admiral, the man who planned the Pearl Harbor attack; killed in an airplane shot down by P-38s in Bougainville.

Zero: Fine Japanese fighter airplane, very maneuverable and fast. Airborne Forces: The U.S. established its first parachute units in 1940. By 1945 there were four airborne divisions.

Final Thoughts

World War II Films   The Navy Hymn
One Last Story   The Famous Kiss

World War II Films

A good way to learn about WWII is through the many fine documentaries and films that have been produced. Every night on TV one can find a selection, particularly on the History Channel, the Military History Channel, and Netflix. Your library is also a good resource.

Here are a few films, films that I personally like, for you to consider, but there are many more.

1. Casablanca
2. From Here to Eternity
3. I'he Great Escape
4. The Guns of Navarone
5. Pearl Harbor
6. Midway
7. Letters From Iwo Jima
8. Hacksaw Ridge
9. Bridge on the River Kwai
10. The Railroad Man
11. The Edge of War
12. Dunkirk
13. The Darkest Hour
14. Band of Brothers
15. Saving Private Ryan
16. A Bridge Too Far
17. Patton
18. Operation Mincemeat
19. Captain Corelli's Mandolin
20. The Imitation Game
21. Defiance
22. Life Is Beautiful
23. The Zookeeper's Wife
24. The Last Days

25. Schindler's List

At the end of the war, one of Oscar Schindler's workers, a master jeweler, made a gold ring for him, a gift from all those he helped.
Written inside the ring is a beautiful Talmudic inscription:
"Whoever saves one life, saves the world entire."

One Last Story

The USS Indianapolis

The USS Indianapolis set out on a highly secret mission. It was delivering the components of the atomic bombs that were later dropped on Hiroshima and Nagasaki. The destination was a U.S. airbase on the island of Tinian.

After completing its mission, it headed into the Philippine Sea where, a few days later, it was hit by two torpedoes from a Japanese submarine. The ship went down in only twelve minutes, but not before three SOS calls were sent out – all of which, for various reasons, were ignored.

About 300 members of the crew went down with the ship, and the rest, about 900, were left floating in the Pacific. They were left there for five days, without food or water, fending off shark attacks. It's estimated that as many as 50 men per day were ripped apart by sharks.

After five days, a Navy pilot spotted them, alerted a PBY, which in turn alerted a nearby destroyer. Of the original 900 in the Pacific, the pilot rescued 56 and the destroyer rescued the others. Of the original 1,195 sailors and marines on board, only 316 survived. A huge loss.

The story of the Indianapolis has been recounted in popular media – both in documentaries and in films, such as Men of Courage and

Jaws, in which the character Quint claims to be a survivor of the USS Indianapolis. As a result of these, many people are aware of the terrible story.

The Navy Hymn

ETERNAL FATHER, STRONG TO SAVE
Eternal Father, strong to save,
Whose arm hath bound the restless wave,
Who bidd'st the mighty ocean deep
Its own appointed limits keep, O hear us when we cry to thee
For those in peril on the sea!

O Christ! Whose voice the waters heard
And hushed their raging at thy word,
Who walkedst on the foaming deep,
And calm amidst its rage did sleep,
O hear us when we cry to thee
For those in peril on the sea!

Most Holy Spirit! Who didst brood
Upon the chaos, dark and rude,
And bid its angry tumult cease,
And give, for wild confusion, peace.
O hear us when we cry to thee
For those in peril on the sea!

Eternal Father, grant, we pray,
To all marines, both night and day,
The courage, honor, strength, and skill
Their land to serve, thy law fulfill;
Be thou the shield forever more
From every peril to the Corps.

Lord, guard and guide the ones who fly
Through the great spaces in the sky
Be with them always in the air,
In darkening storms or sunlight fair

The Navy Hymn was written as a poem in 1860 by English clergyman William Whiting and the melody was published in 1861 by fellow Englishman Rev. John B. Dykes. It is used throughout the British Commonwealth and, with variations in some of the verses, by all branches of the U.S. Military. The hymn was a favorite of Presidents Franklin Delano Roosevelt and John Fitzgerald Kennedy, both of whom were Navy men.

The Famous Kiss

THAT FAMOUS KISS

On V-J Day, August 14, 1945, LIFE photographer Alfred Eisenstaedt captured the world's jubilation in this iconic image, taken in New York City's Times Square. As the picture grew more famous, speculation swirled about who the kissers were. They were eventually identified as Greta Zimmer Friedman, a dental assistant, and sailor George Mendonsa. "It wasn't that much of a kiss," Friedman said years later. "It was just somebody celebrating." Friedman died in 2016 at age 92, and Mendonsa passed away in February 2019, two days short of his 96th birthday.